THE SMART MONEY

The Smart Money

How to Invest in the Stock Market like an Insider

WILLIAM A. KENT

1972

DOUBLEDAY & COMPANY, INC. GARDEN CITY, NEW YORK

Article on "Canny Specialist" used by permission of *Barron's*.

With thanks to Dana Thomas, who suggested that I do this thing in the first place. And thanks to my wife, who pushed me a little when I needed it to go on. And, finally, thanks to Sam Vaughan and Elsa van Bergen who put it all together.

ISBN: 0-385-01934-3
Library of Congress Catalog Card Number 72–76178

Printed in the United States of America
First Edition

CONTENTS

INTRODUCTION

"*They* killed the stock."

"*They* moved it up and caught me!"

"*They're* moving in."

In discussions about the stock market in spartanly decorated barber shops and artistically designed advertising agencies, in crowded department stores and at cocktail parties, investors and their brokers sometimes bemoan their losses in Wall Street.

When asked who *they* are, responses are vague or subdued, depending on the losses the investors incurred, supposedly from the activities of the mysterious "they."

The implication is that stocks are sometimes manipulated—particularly so when the moaner has lost his shirt. When a trade is profitable, little is heard except the proud boastings of the astute trader. That is, until *he* gets it in the neck—and naturally it is *they* who did it to him. At other times, of course, the investor blames his broker or his spouse or an advisory service. But it is *they* who concern us here.

I can imagine my getting letters proclaiming that he or she *knows* of stocks that have been manipulated; nevertheless, let me state categorically that, Virginia, it ain't so. In the sense that some investors mean it to be "rigging," with certain groups buying stocks at certain times of the day or in certain ways with certain types of block trading so as to move stocks in a predetermined path, forget it.

That is not to say that there isn't a *they*, there is. But *they* are individual buyers and sellers of securities who make vast sums of money in the market—millions upon millions, but they do it without manipulation (which is, of course, illegal), for it is just as easy to do it legally.

The latter method avoids the movie-type confrontation of offspring and parent, "Daddy, how could you do it?" or, "So now I know how my father made all that money!"

It also avoids the conscience pangs sometimes afflicting the occupants of sixty-five-foot yachts or six-place Piper Comanches.

It avoids the D.T.'s occurring after too many remorseful glasses of the bubbly; and it avoids the cramped feeling one gets in six-by-six enclosures at Dannemora.

It is not easy or quick, but more often than not it works. How it has worked for many, many singularly well-informed individuals is the subject of this book. It is the story of the "informed minority" and how they made it big on Wall Street, and how you can spot and trace their movements into and out of the market.

Before we begin, there are some things you will need to track their operations, not the least of which is money. You will need the devices of the stock market detective just as the police detective (at least the fictional kind) uses his electronic gear, fingerprint powder, F.B.I. files, and gun.

Besides a fair amount of cash (ten thousand dollars or so will do, though the more the better), you will need some rare qualities of spirit, a respect for the dollar, and a willingness to work. This is not a "quick" course to wealth—and I know of none, though there is a fast course to poverty. The latter is the more popular method, as your friends will tell you.

You will also need a fair amount of skepticism; skepticism about what you read in the financial press and in advisory services, disbelief in "stories" about "hot" issues, "big discoveries," "emerging glamor industries," "dramatic corporate profit increases," "yardsticks" for measuring investments and for judging "aggressive management" and the like; "formulas" for assaying price earnings ratio logic and easy slide-rule measurements of "return on invested capital." You will have to think like "smart money" and act like them, no mean task—for this group, the informed minority, has its own life-style and attitudes toward money and the stock market—one so pervading that it might properly be classed as a subculture in itself. Its values and approaches are so different (and so successful) that the mental transference to their realm is somewhat analogous to visiting Samoa (when it was coming of age) and you were a Margaret Mead, objective and detached.

one

How to Invest with the Informed Minority

"Do you sincerely want to be rich?" That's the title of a book about Bernie Cornfield, who is. But the European buyers of his mutual fund for the most part are a lot less so than when they bought his stuff.

Perhaps you're a widow who has been left a comfortable sum and maybe wants to keep up with inflation. If so, you can take your dough to that imposing-looking bank downtown where the dapper trust man will tell you about the forty-five analysts on his staff who'll make your money grow. If you could get hold of a study of their performance for the past five years you'd see it was about 3 percent, compounded, of course. The furnishings in his office are tasteful though.

Maybe you're the offspring of a guy who made it big in oil and you'd like to swing a little. Just give it to the Hedge Fund in Boston who managed to *lose* 30 percent in the last four years, right?

Perhaps you're the investment manager for a corporation who splits up the money managing between the Wall Street bank, the downtown Chicago bank and two investment counseling firms. Only, half of the group goes for hot stocks and gets burned and the others keep you in bonds and American Can. Is there no middle ground?

If you're the teacher who has a little to invest for a nest egg, there's that persuasive mutual fund salesman who's peddling "professional management." Four of the stocks in *his* portfolio have rocketed into bankruptcy.

Or you're the machinist who's got a piece of a pension fund managed by an investment counselor whose guilt at his underperforming the market for his accounts causes him to get dead drunk every night at five.

Is there any answer? Of course there's also real estate investing. That's what the television commercial calls it for the land developer who bought twenty thousand acres of scrub at twenty-five dollars an acre and who parcels it out to little people in small lots which add up to three thousand per acre.

Can you make money in the market? Well, maybe—if you're *real* careful. There are some people, not many, who do well consistently. Maybe if you do what they do . . .

Stories of "big killings" made in the stock market are as plentiful as tales told at lodge meetings by amateur fishermen. It is not difficult to trade market experiences among friends and neighbors and find someone who made a pile in this or that issue. Usually one accepts many of these tales either out of naïveté or politeness to the teller. Realistically speaking, however, there is a group of people that knows who made how much or lost how much in the market. They are margin clerks (so called even though they handle "cash accounts") at brokerage offices. They record each "buy" and "sale" and compute equity remaining (or observe computers doing it). A poll of these people would probably reveal some amazing statistics. There are no tall tales one can tell margin clerks—they know the *emiss* (truth, in Yiddish). And the *emiss*, sadly, is that most people do not do well in the market. Indeed, many people have come to this writer admitting mournfully that they have lost 50 percent of their capital in a bull market year's time. I don't think too many people are "wiped out," as the title of a popular book warned, but many do quite badly, many who don't have to.

And yet, there is a minority—an *informed minority*—who make money. Methodically, and without fanfare, they rack up the profits that enable them to buy the cooperative apartments on Park Avenue that cost $150,000 and carry a monthly maintenance charge that alone requires more money than 90 percent of the rest of the populace pay for rent. Or take those two-hundred-thousand-dollar-plus houses in New Canaan, Greenwich, and Grosse Pointe. These humble dwellings are not bought with posttax earnings by corporate executives. They are not bought by Mafia "Godfathers," by "successful" horse players, by writers of books—even books on the stock market. Sometimes, of course, they are bought with inherited money—but more often with *made money*—money made in the stock market by the informed minority. Not surprisingly, these persons often have access to "inside information." But it is not the information *itself* that makes these people so fabulously successful in the stock market; *rather it is a combination of factors* among which are:

1. Knowledge of corporate developments not revealed to the investing public.
2. The money to act on this knowledge.
3. The understanding of business practices as they apply to the *business of investing.*
4. The emotional factors that lead to intelligent buying and selling.
5. A real understanding of money—a surprisingly rare talent, but one that can be developed.
6. A cynicism (or wisdom?) born of experience that leads them to be wary of public pronouncements, propaganda, and market oracles.
7. The use of certain corporate and financial tools (perfectly legal, I might add) to facilitate their program of *buying at wholesale and selling at retail* the stocks of the companies in which they are participating.
8. A knowledge of public relations (and I do mean "public") and of "crowd" psychology.

It is my contention that virtually anyone with point No. 2 (money) can *significantly* improve his market performance by considering the other seven; and I will show the reader how once having adopted the other seven, he can even participate (in a pragmatic sense) in point No. 1. There are telltale signs—early warnings or indicators—that isolate and reveal the actions of the informed minority.

What Is "Inside Information"?

Everybody loves a "tip"—on the horses, the fights, a choice vacation spot, and especially in the stock market. It isn't always called a tip; sometimes brokers call it a "story," without using the word disparagingly, as in "I hear XYZ is going to move."

"Uh . . . what's the story?"

Or it's just, "Whaddye hear about ZYX?"

It is common to hear the crowd watching the tape in the back of the board room buzz with excitement about a particular issue that crosses the tape on big blocks.

"What's going on?"

"Well, I heard from soandso that . . ."

The implication behind the word "tip," or whatever name it is called, is that the information is "inside information," that is, it comes from those "in a position to know," and refers to knowledge of some particular event (a merger, tender offer, surprisingly good —or bad—earnings reports, a miraculous scientific discovery or breakthrough, or the gaining of a super-sized contract). The investor can therefore make it big—and fast, by acting "right now."

The Securities and Exchange Commission is constantly on the lookout for such "leaks," which doesn't mean they don't happen. In the Merrill Lynch issue, the SEC charged (on August 28, 1968) that big customers of the firm (but not little ones) knew of an earnings drop and capitalized on it, in some cases going short and making a good profit, and in others selling their stock. But such is one of few isolated examples.

Privileged information isn't passed along all that often. The New York and American Stock Exchanges (and probably the regionals too) have specific rules against Registered Representatives saying or implying that they have "inside information," whether or not they have it. The rationale behind this rule is that usually the salesman (Registered Representative) isn't privy to such dramatic developments—even when he thinks he is.

But let us assume, for purposes of illustration, that an "insider" really did tell someone some "hot" information. Remember the old game "Telephone" that we played as kids? Perhaps your crowd had another name for it. Anyway, imagine fifteen or twenty people sitting cross-legged in a circle. The first person chooses a word or phrase and whispers it to the man on his right who then whispers the same phrase to the woman on *his* right—and so on 'round the circle back to the first person. When the one to the left of the starter announces the word or phrase—followed by the starter telling what he actually said . . . guess what? The two phrases are almost never identical. The garbled nature of what made its way around the circle can be compared to what remains of the true story of three-dollar earnings by the Glubnap Corporation. This emerges from the rumor mill as earnings of eight dollars and sixty cents—not including a nonrecurring gain of a dollar and fifty cents on the sale of a Moroccan subsidiary that manufactures diaper pins and bottles horseradish.

The profusion of rumors surrounding such companies as Fotochrome, National Video, Westec, Memorex, Four Season's Nursing Homes, Parvin Dohrmann, Telex, Mohawk Data Systems, Natomas, and Ling-Temco Vought just before their stocks collapsed leads one to suspect that the people who really started *those* rumors are the same ones who "bagged out"[1] before the truth got out. And what *was* the name of that baking company with the revolutionary television tube? Would you believe the following really happened? Well, it did. I met a fellow who was "touting" a stock just before it became delisted. It seems that the photographic manufacturer had just come up with a cigarette made from lettuce—and he had a sample to prove it. . . . I didn't expect you to believe it!

Who are the "insiders"? Not those whom most people think they are.

They are not Peter, who works as a chemist for that big food company. They are not Jack, your uncle the doctor, among whose patients is the vice president for sales of the Phrazz Division of the

[1] I coined this term some years ago with reference to my old chum Al Myerson, who along with his teaching and singing proclivities used to perform comedy magic shows at parties and gatherings. First off, he would ask a volunteer from among the girls to step forward. When one did, he had her stand on a chair he had placed some distance from the center stage. Next he blew up a paper bag for her to hold while standing on the chair. He then proceeded with the act of cutting handkerchiefs and ropes, making cards disappear, and pulling coins from the air, none of which had anything to do with the girl standing now somewhat foolishly on the chair. After a while, the audience forgot about the girl and became absorbed in Al's patter and act. After completing some twenty minutes of legerdemain, he blithely started to walk off the stage.

"Wait," the crowd would shout, "what about the girl?"

"Oh, yes," Al would reply off-handedly. "That trick is called, 'left holding the bag.' "

The expression on the girl's face at that time was like that worn by the investors who found after the show was over that they too were left out of the action, retaining a piece of paper of another type for a memento.

Ungerlieter Company. And they are not your nephew Arthur, who's a trainee at that brokerage house and who knows some smart margin clerks.

And they are not managers of the big mutual funds who, with few exceptions, don't know what's really going on either.

So who are they, already? The SEC says that they are officers of the corporations, directors, and owners (directly or not) of 10 percent of the stock in the company. *These* are the people who must report their transactions to that government body. *These*, and a few others the SEC includes, can have intelligence about the affairs of the Ungerlieter Company that might affect the price of the stock if the information were released. These "others" include the underwriters of the company's securities and their clients. Sometimes they are the company's lawyers or accountants. But not many, at any rate. And lawyers are not easy people to get information from.

I have dealt with some corporate presidents in helping to arrange merger deals and have occasionally been pleasantly surprised at their honesty and candor. On the other hand, there have been some notable exceptions. As in other sectors of our society, while cleanliness may be next to godliness, truthfulness often isn't.

One day many years ago I called Mr. X, president of a company listed on the New York Stock Exchange, to make a routine inquiry. In the course of our conversations, he asked me if I could find out who was buying his stock, since it was getting quite active. He had determined through which brokerage firms some of the buying had originated—and could I perhaps check it out further. I was understandably flattered and eager to help.

I knew someone at one of the four firms he mentioned quite well and called him. The next day the broker told me that though of course he couldn't obtain the names of the buyers, in the parlance of the street, "There is good buying going on."

To us that means "knowledgeable buying," or in terms applicable to this book, "informed minority" buying.

Dutifully I reported back to the company President, who thanked me. Three months later I was scanning the insider reports (as I am wont to do)—and guess who had been doing that "knowledgeable buying"? The president, for his own account!

The average investor comes into the stock market sometimes with a certain amount of credulous confidence regarding corporation statements—and, indeed, the New York and American Exchanges are concerned about corporate truthfulness and full disclosure—as is the SEC. But sometimes, in spite of their best efforts, that average investor's confidence gets badly mauled.

In the fall of 1967, Mr. Chester Roth, chairman and president of the Kayser-Roth Corporation, was asked by a reporter for the Dow Jones News Service about a sharp rise in the company's stock price. According to the *Wall Street Journal* of November 21, 1968,

"Mr. Roth said he knew no reason for the stock's rise, adding that 'no merger or acquisition is imminent.'" The next day it was announced that negotiations were under way for Kayser-Roth to be acquired by the American Tobacco Company.

"Earlier," continued the *Wall Street Journal*, "in 1965, Mr. Roth denied reports that the company was negotiating with Colonial Corp. of America, another apparel market. A few days later the terms for Kayser-Roth's acquisition of Colonial were announced."

Another example occurred June of 1968. The *Wall Street Journal* reported on wide-spread rumors that American Motors was selling its Kelvinator Appliance Division to White Consolidated Industries, Inc. of Cleveland.

"Asked about the rumors on the morning of the 13th," said the *Journal*, "AMC issued a statement saying that 'we have been badgered by rumors and reports, and we are not commenting on any of them.'"

On noon of the very day of the statement, Frank Hedge, AMC vice president for public relations, was called by a Dow Jones reporter, who asked him about the rumors.

"We have had offers from a number of people to buy Kelvinator," Mr. Hedge told the newsman, "we are not telling anyone right now." Less than two hours later, says the *Wall Street Journal*, "AMC and White Consolidated jointly confirmed that the two companies were in 'final negotiations.'"

Thus the U. S. Court of Appeals, in rendering their decision (guilty), in the Texas Gulf case said, "It does not appear to be unfair to impose on corporate management a duty to ascertain the truth of any statements the corporation releases to its shareholders or to the investing public at large."

The message is: *Forget about "inside information."* You're not likely to hear any, what you do hear is unreliable—and anyway, *you don't need it.* There is a way to help you make considerable money in the stock market—and what is sometimes just as important, keep you from losing much of it. You can participate, to a certain extent, in the vast sums of money made in the market by such multi-millionaires as Tex Thornton and Roy Ash (Litton), Chester Carlson (Xerox), Dr. Edwin Land (Polaroid), Thomas Watson (IBM), Ross Perot (Electronic Data Systems), George Romney (American Motors), the late Charles Englehard (Englehard Minerals), Leon Hess of Amerada Hess, and W. Clement Stone of Combined Insurance.

To a great extent, they made it in the market. And though you may not (indeed, shouldn't) set your sights so high, wouldn't you, that is, if you knew what *they* knew, have done right well for yourself? Yes, but how? Actually, though you may never know what they knew, *you can do what they and others like them did and still do.* You can track their operations just as Sherlock Holmes (with Dr. Watson's help, of course) tracked down Professor Moriarty. What can help you is what I call the "informed minority" method.

It consists basically of five elements:

1. Observing the buying and selling of stock in companies by those who run them—in other words, those presumably in a *position to know what is really going on.*
2. Studying and noting the actions taken by the corporations (publicly) which may be construed as attempting to influence the price action of their stocks, possibly benefiting those same stockholders as in element No. 1.
3. Examining certain published statistics as further clues to the activity of the "informed minority."
4. Understanding the mechanism of public relations as practiced by the "informed minority" to influence investors in ways that may benefit themselves, i.e., cause their stock to go down (so they may buy at lower prices) or go up (to sell at higher prices).
5. Utilizing a certain tool as an investigative technique to determine the important moves of the stock market as a whole. This instrument is used to discover clues to the actions of another segment of the "informed minority."

All are clues to "smart money" buying or selling. All will be elaborated on in this book.

But you will also require (in addition to money) some personal attributes to help you do well in the market:

1. A way of looking at stocks and money quite differently from the manner in which most investors do, but more as the "informed minority" does.
2. A skepticism about corporate and executive pronouncements, annual reports, and other pieces of "information."
3. Patience and guts.
4. A healthy disdain for traditional security analysis.

These methods will be revealed and discussed, and illustrated in actual case studies of popular stocks as they have performed over the past seven years.

Why Nobody Cares About One of the Most Powerful Tools in Investing . . . But You Can!

There is available to the public, for a nominal annual sum ($6.50) a booklet published each month that authoritatively tells what the president and other officers, directors, and principal owners really think about their own company. The information is not based on rumor, "tip," speculation, guesswork, or hope, qualities that promise to decimate the investor's hard-earned shekels; nor is this data exaggerated, falsified, or understated. It is not based on "information" garnered by those who really don't know what business is all about, who do not understand the stock market, or who write "analyses" based primarily on Standard & Poor reports and little else. This information is not based on field trips by impressionable novices.

It is based on fact—and an intimate, informed knowledge of a company's operations. It is the Securities and Exchange Commission's *Official Summary of Security Transactions and Holdings,*[2] and records the actions of "insiders" who put up their *own* dough. Why then, if this data is so vital, is it so rarely used by investors (and analysts)?

[2] Make out your check to and send it to the Superintendent of Documents, U.S. Government Printing Office, Washington, D.C. 20402.

Some are like the economics professor who said that the information arrives too late to do anything about it. What happens is that the monthly "insider" reports (*Official Summary*) are received by subscribers some time *after* the buying and selling transactions are actually effected. Specifically, the December reports are mailed in January and contain purchases and sales of November—and sometimes October. Thus one may ask, "What good are they?" Presumably the stocks *had* run up too much by then. The investor should not be troubled by this sophistry, for:

1. In their tax brackets, it is far more profitable for "insiders" to take the maximum 25 percent tax on capital gains (held six months or more) than the 50 percent tax bite on profits on stocks held for a shorter period.
2. "Insiders" by law are subject to stockholders' suits if they sell their holdings within a six months' holding period, and thus they might be required to return their profits to the corporations. This is both wasteful and embarrassing.
3. It might be said that the insider "knows something" and that news (good or bad) to which he is privy is the reason for his stock market activities. The SEC would be mighty unhappy with an insider who buys a stock in February and sells it in March as the company makes an explosive announcement. Top corporate management plan a company's activities (expansions, financing, sales drives, research and development) on a long-range basis—thus they are aware of a company's fortunes years before these plans result in earnings. So it is easy for them to act on events years before they come to fruition and avoid SEC censure for "acting on privileged information." If President A buys his stock in April 1969 expecting a "turnaround" in earnings by 1972, and sells *then*, who can complain?

Impatience is another reason for misuse—or nonuse—of this important tool.

I know some people who buy stocks in companies because they know of insider buying, and still do not do as well as they might. They do not have the *attitudes* toward money that the informed minority does.

Generally, smart money is quite pleased with a return of 20 percent per year (as they figure it, more often 100 percent in five years). But too often the little guy hungers to get rich quick. Holding a stock for six months and seeing it move little if at all bores him to impatience. How can you look at that lousy stock every day in the paper and see "Monday, up ⅛ . . . Tuesday, down ⅛ . . . Wednesday, up ¼ . . . Thursday, down ⅛ . . . where's the action? Better look for something that's hot."

It is possible with careful (rare) technical analysis to cut the waiting time, as I indicated earlier. But if you want to make a million *overnight*, you'd better start with $999,000.

Therefore it is the average investor's lack of understanding of the actions of the informed minority (of which insiders constitute the major part) and his impatience that cause this valuable tool to be neglected. The average investor's disdain is shared, unbelievable as it may seem, by many so-called professionals—and by the financial press as well.

On July 2, 1968, the New York *Times* reported on a tender offer (later withdrawn) that Howard Hughes made to American Broadcasting Company shareholders as follows:

"As is usual in the case of Mr. Hughes, yesterday's announcement of the tender offer had an air of mystery. The man himself—who makes such a fetish of privacy that *he apparently preferred to lose control of Trans World Airlines, Inc. some time ago rather than make a personal appearance in court*—was unavailable for comment" (emphasis mine).

Crazy like a fox, Mr. Hughes. He only made some 1000 percent on his TWA investment, and the stock (at this writing) is selling for about half the price at which Mr. Hughes was "forced" to sell.

And at the time of the sale, the Dow Jones publication the *National Observer* also shed sympathetic tears for him. But Mr. Hughes is one of the informed minority, wouldn't you say?

Again, on July 7, 1968, the *Times* quoted Chrysler's President Lynn Townsend as being bullish on auto sales. What the paper did not mention (an oversight) was that the New York Stock Exchange had reported about June 19 that Mr. Townsend sold twenty thousand shares of stock in his company and gave away another 3003 shares. Of course, we cannot say that there was any connection.

I believe it is possible to make substantial profits using all of the informed minority clues outlined in this book. Certain people have shown that *following "insider buying" and "insider selling" alone can result in an investment performance significantly better than the market as a whole.*

Fewer people, however, realize that following insider trading can be a powerful defensive weapon. Though I have pointed out that the *patterns* of insider selling in stock after stock in institutional portfolios have given warning signals, mostly I have been met with deaf ears. On one occasion, I indicated no less than ten stocks in a single fund list that had many bearish indications, not the least of which was insider selling in a persistent pattern. This particular fund dropped more than 50 percent from the point that many investors bought it—and it was still, after a prolonged mid-1970–71 bull market, lower than its original issue price. What do you think I got from one of the four money managers I confronted with the news of impending disaster in their stocks?

"Never mind those, just give us a winner," he begged plaintively among the richly paneled walls and plush furnishing in his fifty-dollar-a-square-foot Park Avenue suite. He hadn't learned that it takes a lot of winners to cover one big loser. Thus it is not so much picking winners that counts, it is avoiding losers. Yet among the portfolios of giant insurance companies, bank-managed profit-sharing plans, and mutual funds, not to mention the investment-counseled holdings of high-cost Memorex, National Cash Register, Boise Cascade, and others, I have sometimes found that market know-how decreases as the surroundings become more plush.

Evaluating Insider Trading

At Portland State College, Portland, Oregon, economists have taken certain commonly accepted criteria and tested them for efficacy. One of the tests was part of a study that Professor Shannon P. Pratt and Mr. Charles DeVere, director and assistant director, respectively of the college's investment analysis center, presented to a Chicago seminar on May 16 and 17, 1968 (revised on July 20).

They took fifty-two thousand transactions by "insiders" since 1960, constituting trading in eight hundred companies or about two-thirds of the stocks on the New York Stock Exchange. The study covered the period to June 30, 1966, indicating its thoroughness. Only open market purchases and sales were considered, option buying being excluded. Their work covered only those companies in which three or more "insiders" took part.

Using their own selection criteria (which meant marking a stock "buy" in their calculations after three or more "insiders" bought and the stocks were held by the investor for twelve months), a performance record of 27.1 percent was shown over a twelve-month holding period. The rate of return computation of stocks in which three or more "insiders" *sold* showed only 9.6 percent profit. These are the basic conclusions. The study is too lengthy for complete inclusion here.

Professor Pratt and Mr. DeVere also found that over a period of time, using "insider" trading alone would *double the performance* over that of the market in a comparable period of time. A rundown of this study was published in *Fortune* magazine, July 1968.[3]

A more pragmatic example is that of the former insurance executive who took the proceeds of his company's sale to Greatamerica Corporation and went into the investment analysis business. Armed principally with a mathematical bent and an interest in "insider trading," Perry Wysong (his service is called "Consensus of Insiders")[4] works on a somewhat different principle from that above, one in which he subtracts *the selling from the buying*. He uses only one other of our "informed minority" signals, that of the trading of specialists on the exchange floor, certainly a generally sophisticated group. This device is discussed in Chapter Four.

In a conversation on October 3, 1968 Mr. Wysong said:

"Using December 31, 1962 as a starting point, one hundred thousand dollars invested into revolving model portfolio (based on stocks "insiders" have bought) would now be worth $303,000 (less taxes). Commissions are not figured in, but we would assume that dividends would compensate for them."

"Perry, how has the Dow Jones done for comparison during this period?"

"The Dow was 652. It was 936 at the end of September, and we're using this period also for the model portfolio. That's up 43½ percent."

[3] The complete study as published is titled *How You Can Use the Wall Street Insiders* by Perry Wysong, Box 10247, Fort Lauderdale, Florida 33305 ($4.95).

[4] "Consensus of Insiders" advisory service, Box 10247, Fort Lauderdale, Florida 33305.

What did *Fortune* magazine have to say about Mr. Wysong's approach? It commented as follows:

"*Fortune* also checked Wysong's record against that of the New York Stock Exchange composite index, which has had a better performance than the Dow Jones average in the last couple of years. By this standard, Wysong's record pales slightly—but still looks awfully good. For the thirty years under examination, the Exchange's Index was up, on the average, by 3.8%—in other words, closer to, but still far below Wysong's 18%. In twenty-six of these thirty periods, Wysong's lists beat the index, again usually by a wide margin."

Fortune[5] further tested "insider buying" performance by eliminating option buying, which Mr. Wysong doesn't do. In their study, using the same periods, the group of stocks rose on the average 29 percent, as opposed to 18 percent using options, 3.8 percent on the New York Stock Exchange Index, and the Dow Jones average rise of 0.2 percent.

Our theory was further tested in an M.B.A. thesis on "insider trading" at Ohio State University in 1966. Presenting seventy pages of research and graphs based on an eleven-month holding period after substantial "insider buying" (substantial, that is, in terms of the numbers of "insiders"), its author, Gary Glass, found that his group of stocks almost doubled the performance of the Dow Jones Industrial Index during the period. He found, incidentally, that the optimum holding period, during which his "insider" stock group doubled the results of the Dow, was ten months.

Our research has shown that a better "buy" point is when the "informed minority" *stops buying*—and it is to their advantage to then show better earnings. The "informed minority" somehow finds it easier to *buy* stocks when earnings are poor.

Note that insider buying and selling is a warning tool, not an absolute to follow blindly. More on this in Chapter Eight.

Investors read the financial press presumably to gain insight into corporate affairs that ordinarily may be inaccessible to them. They may also read such publications for investing "ideas." A March 1, 1968 edition of the normally valuable *Forbes* magazine is a case in point in the incomprehension of corporate motivation.

"Inside the Insiders Report" is the title of the piece, and after a

[5] "Personal Investing Ideas from *Fortune*," copyright © 1966, 1967, Time Inc., Chapter Two.

short swing explaining what "the Insiders Report" is (the SEC's monthly *Official Summary*), the *Forbes* writer asks rhetorically, "Do the Insider Reports indeed give a meaningful insight into what the insiders know?"

And he answers, "Perhaps on occasion, but more often than not they simply reflect transactions made by officers, often quite small ones, for purely personal reasons."

His conclusion was based on a series of questions put to these same "insiders" about their motivations for sales of stock in their own companies. Such a method is analogous to asking the inmates of San Quentin Prison if they are guilty of the crimes for which they are imprisoned.

Taking a limited sampling (the *Forbes* writer checked only the two most recent issues of the "Insiders Report") might be unscientific even if one assumes the responses to be "honest"—or, more precisely, "unmotivated."

It may even be that the answers *were* completely honest in this case, since the writer polled those who sold as few as two hundred shares. These sellers might very well have sold for personal reasons. A sampling of only those who sold say, ten thousand or more shares might reveal a different result—assuming, of course, that the correspondent received any cooperation from these executives. *Forbes'* man could hardly conceal his chagrin that many of them appeared disturbed by the "impudence" of a writer asking why they sold. One respondent, a vice president of the New York Central, is reported to have slammed down the telephone.

And there was the Brunswick caper, the American Motors episode, and so on.

The *Forbes* article concluded, "What does all of this prove? Just that executives are people, just like everyone else."

But smarter than most. A conclusion that escaped the *Forbes* chronicler.

How To Think Like the Informed Minority

Just as you can and must get your clues about the movement of smart money directly, depending on no one else's interpretations, you should at least begin to understand the attitudes of the informed minority. Let's look again at those ways of thinking that set smart money apart.

The story of Texas Gulf Sulphur notwithstanding, real "insiders" do not make money because of "inside knowledge" of some dramatic, wild breakthrough. They're much more subtle than that. Generally they buy what they know is a bargain, wait, build up the company, wait some more—and sell when the earnings perk up. Of course, there is more to it than that, as I will demonstrate. But "insiders" normally look ahead some three to five or even more years. Of course, *you* don't have to wait that long, usually—but as a "knowledgeable outsider" you must expect to do *some* waiting.

Take Joe. There aren't many sweeter guys around than Joe—and contrary to Leo Durocher's apocryphal cliché, "nice guys finish last," Joe made money, big money in the market. I'm using the past tense because Joe died last December of a heart attack. The attack was not brought on by the stock market, but by a shock of another sort. The *market never shocked him,* never even disturbed Joe—though it did some of his friends—and there lies my tale.

A good friend of Joe's was an important oil man—so important that his company ranked along with Standard of Indiana, Standard of California, Ashland, Atlantic Richfield, Cities Service, and the like. The oil man (also a nice guy, I'm told) would visit Joe's summer place on the East Coast and stay the weekend. Joe flew out to his friend's daughter's wedding, and so on. Their respective wives were also quite friendly.

Occasionally the oil man would give Joe the names of stocks to buy. They were stocks in companies the oil man knew personally, perhaps had some dealings with—or knew the presidents of—like that. Or he would know the group running the company (which may not always include the president). As a result Joe did quite handsomely in the market. Incidentally, these were not "hot tips" ("hot tip" usually implies that something "big" is about to happen in the company *imminently*); rather these were good, sound, perhaps undervalued stocks.

And Joe, being a "nice guy," would pass along these tidbits to his friend Walter, a neighbor in his posh apartment building on Central Park South. What did Walter do? Usually he bought the stocks. But not always when Joe told him. Sometimes Walter would wait several months, out of fear of a market drop. Sometimes he would wait a week or so to see if the stock would go up. Walter did not have the insider psychology, the fourth of the eight factors I mentioned earlier.

On one occasion, Walter bought the stock right away—and this perhaps led to his later queasiness. Let us say that Walter bought the thing at twenty dollars. In the ensuing months the stock fell to fifteen. Joe couldn't have cared less. But Walter stewed. And fretted. Finally he called Joe.

"What's the matter with that stock?"

"Which one?" the imperturbable Joe asked.

"That lousy twenty-dollar dog you told me about."

"Forget it. The man says it's good." (They both knew who "the man" was.)

"But it's down five points—and I bought a thousand shares!"

"Look, Walter, have we ever gone wrong with him before? Just forget it."

Walter mumbled something and hung up.

But a week or so later, Walter rang Joe's bell and stomped in.

Walter's anguished expression was that of a banker who has just been locked out.

Joe tried to calm him, but as he told me later,

"That's the last one I'll ever give him."

It wasn't to be, however, for after the stock tripled, Joe couldn't keep a good thing to himself and gave Walter other issues. And Walter did quite well, thank you.

The point is that the informed minority doesn't panic. The shaky majority does.

Another true tale is one I can vouch for personally. I was there.

It was at a meeting of a prominent organization that published scholarly treatises on political topics—and holds discussion dinners at which internationally prominent figures hold forth. The food at these events is pedestrian, while the conversation is epicurean.

So there we were, ten at a table, mostly men. We talked about previous discussions, we talked about the evening's speaker, we talked about current political events, we talked about many things, but we never, not ever, talked about the weather.

It was the wife of the president of a quite large department store chain who casually suggested to her spouse, "Steve" (he shall be called here), "isn't our stock down around thirty-four dollars?"

"Yes," replied her tight-lipped husband.

"Why don't you buy a few thousand?"

"Yes, maybe I will."

At that point the husband changed the subject to more pressing matters.

Their stock, you see, had been as high as fifty or so and had been falling of late. Their panic at this prospect could not readily be observed. It could not readily be observed because it didn't exist. Rather than panic, they *bought*—about as casually as you might buy another roll of color film.

The chain-store executive was used to buying at wholesale and selling at retail when it came to men's shorts and badminton racquets, so why not stocks?

The analogy between underwear and securities may seem farfetched. But is it?

Investing in the stock market is a business, just like any other. It involves a sense of profit and loss, a sense of the reduction of inventory, a sense of seeking value. As in any business you sell at the most advantageous price (not the highest price, necessarily, but the one at which the most goods can be sold at the right price). The question the retailer, the manufacturer, the wholesaler, all ask when approaching a business decision is not the one most people ask themselves when "plunging" into the market. It is not the question investors think out after analyzing a year's investing. It is not the question in their minds when they hear a "hot tip."

That question is . . .

"What will my return be on invested capital?"

If investors would ask that question, they might do much better in the market than they do.

The average investor (not the ninety-year-old spinster who is seeking current income) too often thinks of the market as "a place to make it big" or "a place to make it easy."

If the average investor really thought of the stock market as a business like any other [but with some of its own peculiarities], he would be quite satisfied with a return of, say, 10 or 20 percent per year.

He would be like a buyer for Korvette who buys television sets for $160 to sell them for $190 (with overhead and selling expenses cutting out fifteen dollars or so).

He would not give the answer a client of mine gets every time he suggests to a friend,

"I just bought XYZ for fifty bucks."

"Yah, where's it going?"

"I would hope maybe about sixty-five."

"Who needs it?"

He would buy a stock *because* it had fallen from fifty to thirty-four. He would sell a stock *knowing* it was going higher (more on this later).

He would not act like the public . . . which he does . . . and is. He would, in short, act like "smart money." And he would profit.

For the informed minority does make it big—but slowly. They buy on bad news and sell on good. They figure their return on invested capital—"What percentage net profit can I make on my investment?"

For they know that a 20 percent move done five times a year equals 100 percent. Surprised?

They know that the stock bought at two dollars *could* go to four. But more likely it will go to one. And when it does, it is not a loss of one point (as I have often heard said), it is a loss of 50 percent. They know too what kind of pot is really at the other end of the rainbow.

A Dream Stock

Not so very often along comes a company with a product that appears to be revolutionary, or that provides a service or convenience that makes its backers rich beyond their dreams. Such a company is Xerox, another is Polaroid, and a third is IBM. Those who bought these stocks at or near their inception and held them have done quite well in the market. Tales of these fortunate few are legend—but perhaps less Cinderellalike are the tales of investors who bought stocks in the would-be Xeroxes and Polaroids. Though these are many times more numerous than the former, we hear less about these disappointed investors, probably because one does not like to admit being the fool. And those who invest in dreams are generally just that. They do not view the market as if it were a business where one, taking some risks, endeavors to make out somewhat better than at the local bank; a business in which by buying and selling judiciously over a period of time, the investor can increase his capital by moderate degrees. Unfortunately, the stargazer wants to take his five or ten thousand and make it into a million. He may even be willing to wait a year or so to do it.

Fotochrome, Inc. was the object of dreams. A company listed on the American Stock Exchange and principally engaged in the processing of film (like at your corner drugstore). On August 14, 1964, the stock (whose symbol was FTM) was selling at two dollars a share—and attracting as much attention as your maiden aunt's gray scarf. That day, it traded the ho-hum total of twenty-nine hundred shares. A week later it drifted down to 1⅞ on similar volume.

On the twenty-eighth, it sauntered up to $2.25—and the volume rose to eleven thousand shares. By the eleventh of September, Fotochrome was being dealt out at 3⅛. On Monday, the fourteenth, it began to flash, selling at 4⅝. On Tuesday, all hell broke loose—and for some who bought it this day and didn't sell soon enough, hell indeed was where the stock eventually led them. FTM took off to the dizzying heights of seven dollars, trading 171,000 shares. The stock did not trade Wednesday, while many little buyers envisioned a life of ease on tropical isles with their own sloop bought with their profits in the stock moored just offshore. On Thursday FTM exploded to *twelve dollars.* Its run had encompassed 600 percent appreciation in less than one month. They were selling tulips at fifty dollars apiece down there, and there were many takers—and just as many givers, it seemed. But the buyers hardly worried about the givers, for the givers were going to make them rich—just like *that.*

Eventually the stock rose as high as twenty dollars two years later, with many wild gyrations in between. Soon after that, however, like the proverbial grandfather's clock, "it stopped—short—never to go again—when the old man died." But what died with Fotochrome were the wild dreams of the get-rich-quick, the gamblers, the starry-eyed. Many who hardly ever consider *risk,* something successful businessmen always do.

They know that a move in a stock from ten to fifteen is not greater than one from one hundred to 150. That it's *not fifty points, but 50 percent.*

They know that to look for the top (or even near it) is to be a dreamer, a gambler, maybe an astrologer. But not a businessman.

A businessman buys at wholesale and sells at retail. Remember this phrase. It may save you some money in the market. In the market it's buy low and sell later.

The Big Shakeout

There is an advisory service that used to take out full-page advertisements in the New York *Times,* and although its ads are more restrained in tone since the SEC rapped its knuckles, it has pulled in hefty mail responses partly on the basis of such copy as "thirty stocks to split."

One can easily understand how "the public" responds to such blandishments, since it is popularly believed that stock splits (particularly two or three for one) are bullish for the stock's price.

"It brings the price down to a more popular level," say some market observers—and of course this is true. When American Telephone & Telegraph split two for one in 1964, those who wished to purchase a round lot (a hundred shares usually) would have to cough up as much as $140 per share prior to the split. Afterward, the "little guy" only needed seventy dollars. The Question: Is "little guy" buying bullish for this stock? One might observe that "big guy" buying might be more significant. Indeed, for the most part, big splits (two or more for one), with the notable exception of IBM (which is probably too expensive for the little guy, anyway) have proved to be "distribution"—that is, from "strong" to "weak" hands. AT&T still sold twenty points *lower* four years later.

Another notable case is that of Pan American Sulphur. Based on rising prices for the product, the company was showing a fine earnings growth, which appealed to investors as a squiggling, hooked worm to a fish. They showed $.67 per share in 1962, $.75 in 1963, and $1.09 in 1964. In October of 1964, Officer-Director Raymond Devine had sold thirteen hundred shares of his stock and Harold H. Jaquet, another officer, unloaded fifty-one hundred shares. During the same period, the canny president of Pan American disposed of twenty-five hundred. These members of the informed minority sold while the news was *good.* What better time?

On February 18, 1965, the company announced they were going to split their stock two for one. Between then and the time the split actually took place on April 20, 1965, President Harry C. Webb sold another twenty-five hundred (in March, following a thousand in January). February also saw one of the company's directors, Guy I. Warren sell five thousand shares.

So what happened after they sold? I am not saying they *knew what was coming.* I do not know that. But, amazingly and with no apparent warning, Mexico clamped down dramatically on sulphur exports. That government even prevented loaded ships from leaving port with their (then) precious cargo. It started with a halt of loading operations of the company's ship *Surrey Trader* on April 21, and culminated (according to the New York *Times*) with a Mexican presidential decree cutting sulphur exports by foreign (non-Mexican) sulphur mining and exploration companies.

What do you suppose all this did to the stock?

Pan American Sulphur dropped like a pricked balloon, from thirty dollars (post-split) to nineteen dollars on April 28. At that point, said the *Times,* "Uncertainty about the Pan American Sulphur Company's future in Mexico propelled the company's stock to the top of the New York Stock Exchange's active list yesterday. Its shares presently outstanding closed at 37, off 6 points from the closing price on Tuesday, on a turnover of 236,000 shares."

Webb and Warren—clever men—who sold when the news was good, acted just like other intelligent members of the informed minority.

But let us not drop the story there. Few perhaps noticed a paragraph lower down in the *Times* article.

"A single buyer was reliably understood to have accounted for a good part of the opening trades."

"The selling," continued the *Times,* "was said to have come in small lots from many investors." I have no idea who bought—but again, it was "smart money" buying on "bad news." Subsequently, the Mexican Government relented, and a compromise formula was reached. The company (among other producers) was allowed to export tonnages based on their explorations and "finds" of new deposits.

In this as in many instances, "sell on good news" (i.e., good earnings and news of impending splits) was the axiom followed by the informed minority. *Buy* on "bad news" was the complementary axiom followed by another presumably smart group; for even if the latter knew nothing of government-company discussions, it was only reasonable to assume that *some* workable compromise would ensue—and it did.

P.S.: The split stock was then selling at $18.75. It went to over forty dollars just two years later.

two

LTV, for Example

As WE HAVE SEEN, the informed minority perform their operations right out in the open, and their names are known or can be easily obtained by anyone taking the bit of trouble required; in fact, their names are published in the New York *Times* every week, similarly, in the *Wall Street Journal* and in the monthly *Official Summary*. *Why don't millions of investors (or, say, hundreds of thousands) use this information and make as much money in the market as does the informed minority?*

The answer, we've been realizing, is more complex than the question:

1. Hardly anybody pays any attention to it.
2. Hardly anybody knows what to do with the information, because they do not understand the ways of thinking, the patterns of planning, and the emotional attitudes of these "insiders."

Here is one case history that brings together many of the factors we've been discussing. A rags-to-riches case if ever was one, James J. Ling began life as the son of an oil-field laborer, lived in a Catholic school from age twelve when his mother died, and then bounced from an aunt's boarding house in Shreveport, Louisiana to another Catholic school in the area.

"On my own at fourteen," he says, "I got acquainted with life. I hitch-hiked around the country, working in cafes and at other jobs," he told the *Wall Street Journal.*[1] Starting out with a three-thousand-dollar investment in an electrician's shop, Ling became the boss of the 204th largest industrial corporation in the United States and the fastest-growing on *Fortune* magazine's top 500. In 1946 he lived with his wife in the back of the electrical shop. Twenty years later he had built a three-million-dollar French-style chateau in suburban Dallas. He even had a new wife to go with his new home.

As Horatio Alger was fictional, so Jimmy Ling was bigger than life. As Alger did it with hard work alone, the real Ling did it with a mixture of hard work and minimizing of taxes, plus, of course, stock market sophistication.

As for Internal Revenue, in 1955 he earned $192,000, but after paying taxes and other expenses, came home with only $30,000. In 1959, with less income, $150,000, he took home $100,000. What Jimmy had learned was the ins and outs of the tax loophole maze, which eventually shut off some gimmicks in 1970, only to allow others to creep in. In 1959, Ling used the oil depletion allowance ploy, part of the profits from his oil holdings being untaxed on the theory that the oil resource is being depleted as it is taken from the ground. Another gambit was Ling's use of municipal bonds, the dividends from which are tax exempt. Part of Ling's tax reduction also came from capital gains, taxed at a maximum of 25 percent, rather than the 80 percent or so prevalent then at his income level. But Jimmy's big capital gains came from the stock in his own company.

The Record

The clearly recorded evidence on who in Ling-Temco-Vought Corporation profited (Mr. Ling was not the only one, not even the most successful) from the swings in the company's stock can be found in our dependable tool, that little-used monthly booklet *Official Summary of Security Transactions and Holdings,* published by the Securities and Exchange Commission. It can be eye-straining pouring over the six-point type, but it can also be quite rewarding both from an historical and a financial point of view. The publication shows Mr. Ling purchasing on balance seventy-five hundred shares

[1] From *The New Millionaires* by the editors of the *Wall Street Journal* (New York: Macfadden-Bartell, 1960).

in LTV in the name of his jointly owned (with D. H. Byrd) holding company, Alpha Omega Corporation, at around fourteen dollars per share, on October 30, 1962. LTV stock later sold for $165 per share on the New York Stock Exchange, and was sold, incidentally, to some eager buyers. It is also the same stock that subsequently in 1970 sold for fourteen dollars.[2]

In November 1963, Alpha Omega bought 132,000 shares at around $15 per share for a net valuation of $1,980,000. It probably could have been sold five years later for $198 million, and theoretically could have been transferred to buyers at the staggering sum of $326 million! How did the paper value of Ling-Temco-Vought Corporation soar so precipitously? And who got out when the getting was good? Was it all public relations? What part did the media play in the action? Let us see. . . .

On October 7, 1964, Colonel D. H. Byrd, a wealthy oil man who had been an associate in Ling's previous acquisition of the other two-thirds of LTV, Temco and Vought, was persuaded to sell his share of Alpha Omega to Ling when LTV was still selling at around fifteen dollars. It was a good deal for Ling, for buying that quantity of stock in the open market might have raised the price. As for the seller, it was said in the January 1967 issue of *Fortune,* "Byrd needed some cash." In the open market, Ling bothered to purchase eleven hundred shares four months later.

With all the buying, by February of 1965 LTV stock had performed about as excitingly as a bored ostrich watching tumbleweed. Mr. Ling, however, was not bored. Mr. Ling the investor knew that Mr. Ling the conglomerator could pull off the building of a giant whatchamacallit that would command higher prices later. After all, they all laughed at Christopher Columbus, Einstein, and da Vinci. But Ling would conquer new worlds of finance with his own brand of fiscal wizardry, put the whole thing together, and make it fly. And fly it would, no matter that it looked less like a Boeing 707 than a duck-billed platypus.

One interesting (and perfectly legal) gambit along the way was an offer to shareholders (of whom he was one) to exchange the common stock into convertible preferred, with a big dividend sweetener. This did two things: with the same earning power of

[2] All prices have been adjusted for a three-for-two split effected in 1967.

LTV Corporation showing up on fewer shares outstanding, earnings per share rose dramatically. Also, a "thinner" supply made for more volatile movements as demand came in later for the fewer shares outstanding (less supply to accommodate increased demand).

Internally, Ling was "reorganizing," as *Business Week* revealed in its issue of February 13, 1965. LTV's twenty-four divisions were blended into eleven. Management ranks were "thinned from 700 to 166." That is, some people lost their jobs, as the magazine euphemistically put it. Ling described the "tightening up" by saying, "We continually upgrade the herd"—which may or may not give an insight into his attitude toward people.

In the year prior to the article, Ling had been joined in his buying on the open market (just as you and I can) by a director and former president of Temco, Robert McCulloch, who by February 1965 owned 17,376 shares.

Mr. Ling seemed to have been preparing the investment community for the eventual move in the stock he and Mr. McCulloch had been acquiring.

"Since last December [1964], Ling and his top management have been embarked on a 'getting to know you' campaign with press, brokers and city fathers in Dallas designed to overcome hostility and educate the community about LTV and where it is now going," *Business Week* said in its February 13, 1965 issue. Mr. Ling was getting them ready—and he and Mr. McCulloch were getting their stock accounts ready, too. The process continued with Jimmy picking up 21,500 shares from March 22 through March 29 and Robert adding three thousand to his holdings on the sixteenth. This was all revealed in the all-seeing SEC reports, as was Ling's additional purchase of two thousand in early April. All the buying was done in his Alpha Omega Corporation, by the way, as were 10,600 shares also bought in July.

Building the Empire

The story of Jimmy Ling is also the history of a corporate movement, one that was unique in the annals of American business. It was a new type of company, the conglomerate.

It had few of the trappings of the old empires, such as Carnegie's United States Steel or Rockefeller's Standard Oil. These were the result of the garnering of assets and entities with similar or complementary activities. Thus one (by hook or otherwise) bought competitors, enabling the producers, once a monopoly was established, to raise prices at will. The Clayton Anti-Trust Act put a dent into these activities. Another form was the so-called integrated enterprise or lateral form of expansion. Here, suppliers were acquired (backward integration), presumably assuring constant availability of raw materials at reasonable prices. Forward integration is the acquisition of companies that supply the products to customers. All these forms were, whether or not the reader approves, sound business practices, intended to enrich the corporation—or, more directly, the entrepreneurs involved. They did not *necessarily* harm anyone and were considered beneficial in that they made companies more efficient, thus sometimes passing along such efficiencies to eventual consumers.

Now along comes the conglomerate, which gobbles up companies with little or no rhyme and much less reason, if not of benefit in corporate stock price. Of course, it could be construed that the acquiring company could operate the acquired companies in more efficient fashion than heretofore had been the case. Maybe.

There were other conglomerates, earlier ones, like Textron, which got Mr. Royal Little gobs full of applause from the investment community, and Litton, which chronologically fits between Textron and LTV. There were those in parallel times to LTV such as Gulf & Western and a lesser one that began as Barium Steel, changed to Republic Industrial, thence to Vare, and subsequently to Microdot, all hardly affecting Wall Street blood pressure or stock price, to its backers' dismay. There was also Teledyne and Whittaker, and one hardly hears these names now. And, of course, there was Ling-Temco-Vought, our model here.

Thus far, LTV consisted basically of an electronics company and a warplane builder. Ling's idea was to utilize assets that were acquired cheaply to borrow money to acquire more assets (companies) to borrow more money to buy more companies. He was more of a financial builder (some would say, "juggler") than the melder of compatible units.

Kennecott Corporation was a forward-integrating company, having acquired a fabricating company—one that formed copper from the raw metal. And who made the raw material? Kennecott, of course. It seemed quite logical, but the Justice Department felt otherwise and had obtained in 1965 an order from the Supreme Court requiring Kennecott to sell its cablemaker, Okonite. Thus the parent went looking for someone to adopt his court-separated child.

Mr. Ling, you will remember, was in the adoption business, but it was not the child welfare league that put the would-be parents and orphan together. There were at the time some seventy competitors to Ling in the child-rearing business; yet Ling won.

There was plenty of publicity razzle-dazzle in October 1965 when LTV picked up Okonite for $30 million. As so often happens, few pertinent facts emerged from all the clamor. It was some 4½ years later, on April 16, 1970, to be exact, when the chief counsel for the House of Representative's antitrust subcommittee, Kenneth R. Harkins, made some startling charges about the deal.

Harkins made his statements before hearings held to investigate the effect of conglomerate mergers. The House Judiciary Committee, headed by Rep. Emanuel Celler (D., N.Y.), had assigned its subcommittee to look into the activities of such as LTV, ITT, Gulf & Western, and Litton. Conglomerate defenders were heard to object to the hearings, saying they were attempts by "the establishment" to beat down those who threatened the status quo. Whether this was so or not, some of the allegations aired were quite interesting.

Mr. Harkins contended that Paul Dashine, a Kennecott official who had supervision of Okonite while Kennecott was trying to divest itself of the corporation, had given confidential information to Ling without the knowledge of Dashine's superiors at Kennecott. LTV bigwigs disputed the charges. Nonetheless, Mr. Ling admitted that he and Clyde Skeen, LTV president at the time, had met with Mr. Dashine on August 20, 1965 at the Plaza Hotel in New York soon after their negotiations to buy Okonite had begun, as the *Wall Street Journal* reported on April 17, 1970. Ling also admitted that he offered Dashine the job as president of Okonite, if the deal could be made, the *Journal* said. Dashine at the time was getting about forty-two thousand dollars a year with Kennecott, and upon becoming president after LTV's successful bid for the company, was reportedly given almost fifty-nine thousand dollars a year plus a stock option for forty thousand shares.

A Good Deal

Whatever the astute Ling did behind the scenes, the deal proved to be a good one for him. It was apparently also a surprising one to the investment community, for as *Business Week* reported the acquisition in its issue of October 23, 1965, "The unpredictable Ling denied any interest in nonmilitary diversification early this year but admitted things might change."

Let's see how the stock had performed during 1966. LTV began at 49⅞ and rose steadily for the first quarter to 66¾. On January 21, *Value Line*, an advisory service, gave it a boost, with a strong rating at $51.

Ling-Temco stock had begun 1965 at $17 a share and closed it out at $48. On January 21, 1966, *Value Line* attributed the rise "to the acquisition of Okonite, the receipt of a large government contract and several new developments." *Value Line* took part of the credit unto itself for calling the shot on the stock:

"Ling-Temco-Vought has almost tripled in price since it was singled out as an especially recommended stock exactly one year ago," they boasted. If the service was run by a member firm of the New York Stock Exchange, it would have been severely reprimanded for such a statement, since member firm literature may not single out a single "winner" without simultaneously printing a complete record of stock recommendations. In the Exchange's reasoning, presumably, investors might get the impression that *all* the firm's picks turn out as well.

Yet *Value Line* was, and still is, one of the more popular advisory services sold to the public, and its recommendation possibly helped the stock to rise another twenty points by mid-April from the $51 mentioned in the write-up. Perhaps investors were somewhat influenced by the $11 earnings projections made for the 1968 to 1970 period. This judgment would prove to be somewhat optimistic.

One might even ponder on whether Mr. Ling read the piece, for again through his Alpha Omega Corporation he picked up twelve hundred shares of his stock a week after the service's recommendation. He did not have to wait too long for a paper profit, for by December 22, 1966, the *Wall Street Journal* was reporting that LTV was now trying to buy Wilson & Company, the meat packer, through a tender offer at $62.50 a share. Wilson's book value was then around $44, but in those heady days, nobody cared. It was all very exciting, coming as it did on the very day a federal judge in Utica, New York okayed another deal of Ling's, the purchase of Rome Cable from Alcoa, which like Kennecott had been ordered to divest itself of the subsidiary on antitrust grounds. The double-header caused LTV to jump three dollars a share the day the news hit the Dow Jones news tickers in broker board rooms across the country. Apparently the government saw no antitrust problem in LTV's acquisition of two such powerful cable companies, so why should investors ponder the possible overextension of LTV's credit lines, their deepening debt (LTV did not have the cash for the takeovers), or the possible unmanageability of what was fast becoming a colossus? Still, money was being made in the stock (particularly on paper for LTV insiders) as the stock rang out the year at just over $74 a share.

1967–Ling the Man

The year 1967 began with Ling-Temco stock at $75, but not for long. The stock had a lot going for it. Right off, a story in the January 1967 issue of *Fortune* entitled "Jimmy Ling's Wonderful Growth Machine" had just hit the stands and was being digested by that magazine's high-income readership. The article noted:

"The variety of the combinations, the ordering of events, and the consistent making and seizing of opportunities almost before others knew they existed, merit rehabilitation of the over-used and debased terms 'creative' and 'genius.'"

The magazine described Ling's appearance as "reminiscent of a recently retired pro quarterback turned securities salesman," a two-hundred-pound, six-foot-two, soft-spoken type.

It described Ling as contemplative—and well he might be, as he dreamed of the Wall Street coup that later was to result in a single day's gross of $2 million for his own account. For as this story is of Jimmy Ling and the monster machine of a corporation he built with consummate skill in just a few years, his history is an archetypal one, symbolic of what does quite often happen in Wall Street to the benefit of the few.

It seems that Mr. Ling once enlisted in the Navy, where he

studied electrical engineering in his spare hours through a correspondence course. After his discharge in 1946, he sold his house for three thousand dollars and with the proceeds went into the electrical contracting business. It and Jimmy prospered, and he was doing $1.5 million in business by 1955. Still, the really big money comes with public participation, as Jimmy knew, and he "went public" with his company, selling shares himself door to door and giving away prospectuses at the Texas State Fair. Stockbrokers apparently could not get excited about an electrical contracting business, and who could blame them?

His success in selling the stock and subsequent acquisitions tempted Wall Street after all, and a private placement followed in late 1958, giving Ling another $2.2 million to grow with. The allusion to the football player then became more real when the referee in the form of the Securities and Exchange Commission blew the whistle on a roughing penalty. Mr. Ling and some associates who had run a small business-investment company, Electro-Science Investors, Inc., were charged with "gross misconduct" and "gross abuse of trust." The SEC alleged that Mr. Ling had a profit of $485,000 that really belonged to Electro and that he could not have made it "except by virtue of his role as an E.S.I. insider," according to *Fortune*. The case was settled out of court with Ling agreeing to pay Electro $225,000. Chalk up another lesson, as Ling learned that there were easier ways to make money.

In making it big in the market the "informed minority" has the possibly unknowing aid of the financial media plus the naïveté of the investing public—and here we use "public" in the widest possible sense. Yet it is possible for the average investor to participate to some degree with the "smart money" in the stock market by the use of various tracking devices to ascertain the latter's movements, as we shall see in this and later chapters.

1967—Touchdown!

On January 6 the acquisition of Wilson & Company was done by the tender route at sixty-two dollars a share, giving Ling Temco 53 percent of Wilson and putting LTV into the billion-dollar sales club. The juggernaut was moving down the field to the shrieks of the investing multitude. It was now time to put in a new cheering section to accompany the team to victory, and Ling gracefully accepted the aid of the Los Angeles Society of Security Analysts.

Addressing them on January 31, he began (after introducing himself as chief executive officer and Clyde Skeen as president) with a seventeen-minute film. After this, he told how "It is our job in management, as we understand it, to combine science, technology, and people with the working assets of the corporation, further combined with our corporate technology, to produce and maximize values that are meaningful in the public auction market—and to our shareholders." Lest the reader forget, Ling was one of the largest of these.

Ling rhapsodized about his "Project Redeployment," which he described as representing "for us the best of all worlds, the optimum of decentralization. PR provided," said Ling, "a safety feature per (sic) corporate structure, limit risk, provides fuller disclosure, maximum incentive to executives, opportunities for technical and financial breakthroughs." He was using the term "financial breakthroughs" possibly in the broadest sense, as some analysts later charged.

Mr. Skeen also spoke, conservatively estimating 1966's full-year earnings at six dollars per share. In four thousand words of cheer and modesty replete with charts and diagrams, the analysts were sent home with copies of the speeches, a brochure entitled *Introducing LTV*, and a pamphlet describing "Project Redeployment," not to mention memories of the film. This was corporate communications at its nadir. If the crowd were not fired up enough, final results for 1966 showed $6.51 per-share earnings versus only $2.88 for 1965. The annual report announcing these figures was something to behold—for now, by the way, they had understated expected earnings.

"It is our hope that the theme of this Annual Report will be of special interest to today's college students," the report began.

"Few areas of human endeavor offer so much opportunity for constructive innovation as does the modern business scene. Yet business has failed in an important way to get across its story to the young people who will take up tomorrow's leadership," it said, and followed up with the suggestion that the report be forwarded "to a student when you no longer need it."

Was Jimmy Ling prophesying the student rebellion of 1968–70? Could his annual report head it off? What kind of an education would LTV be to the investing public?

The report was certainly on a high plane. Full pages were devoted to paintings or writings of John Locke, Benjamin Franklin, Albert Einstein, Alexander Hamilton, and "The Greeks and their civilization," and half pages to Thomas A. Edison, Nicholas Copernicus, David Sarnoff, George Gershwin, and "The American Housewife." Perhaps if the report were printed today, the Women's Lib movement would demand equal space.

First Down for Ling U.

The crowd was cheering wildly now as Jimmy described his take-over tactics: "If you're blocked, you go around the flank. Once you get a breakthrough, you pour everything you've got into the opening." Joining the ranks of the cheerers was *Business Week*, which headlined in its March 18, 1967 issue, "LTV blitzes its way into ranks of giants." In almost four pages of well-turned-out prose, the magazine possibly added to the furor as the stock went out of sight, having raced downfield to sixty-six dollars by January 17. Around the time the issue broke, LTV was tearing up the pea patch at eighty dollars.

Business Week had described Jimmy Ling as a "rare financial genius. . . . He senses opportunities and knows how to take advantage of them in ways others would be scared of and wouldn't know how to handle." Which was probably true. Combining Fran Tarkenton's flair, Joe Namath's *élan*, Gale Sayers' dash, and Vince Lombardi's toughness, James J. Ling scored a touchdown when in February he sold twenty thousand shares of LTV from his own account with a gross valuation of some two million dollars! And he had done it right in front of the cheering multitude without causing a stir. *Business Week* did not mention it—the New York *Times* did not —the *Wall Street Journal* did not—except that the latter two noted the sales in small type under the heading of insider dealings. Ling had performed virtually a hidden-ball trick, racing over the goal line and in effect ending the game. A strange kind of game; the crowd stayed in their seats and kept buying stock, their eyes on another field, the one up in the stars between the Big Dipper and Orion—the gold at the end of the rainbow.

Jimmy Ling had taken home a tidy sum, but who noticed or cared? After all:

1. Didn't he still have a lot of stock left?
2. He probably needed the money.
3. Weren't the earnings going to go to eleven dollars and possibly more?
4. Wasn't the stock "hot" and why not ride it to glory?

This was said by the few who noticed the sales. Most did not, for they were still watching a phantom game, a game played without any participants. They were still running after a train that had long left the station. They were hooked by the glamor around their star, their champion, their ideal. The idol, meanwhile, was not watching the game; rather he was admiring his bank balance.

Mr. James A. Weldon, an LTV director, also had sold shares—a total of seventy-four hundred the prior month. He had left early in the second half, to escape the crowd perhaps. Maybe he had personal reasons for selling; who could say?

There were a few cynics. The doubters wondered whether:

1. All the publicity lately might be bringing in "public-type" money, putting the stock into "weak hands," as they say on the Street.
2. A virtual tripling in earnings from 1965 to 1966 could be continued at that rate. And if things were so good, why was Ling selling?
3. The hotter the stock, the better the sale.
4. Possibly, as most of the informed minority do, he had bought at wholesale and was selling at retail.

More Good News

Typical of the continuing kudos Ling received from the financial press was the write-up in the April 29, 1967 issue of *Magazine of Wall Street,* which called Ling "master of the corporate chess game." The publication mentioned that he never finished high school (which only shows that making money in the stock market and the big corporate battle does not require a formal education). They began the article entertainingly, stating that for about $130 (including commission) one can buy a share of stock in a company run by a dropout who has offbeat ideas about corporate management. If one should question whether this was a sound investment, "it is one that attracted many professionals—and made them money." Some undoubtedly did make money. But many others lost, as we shall see.

The piece made an impressive case for LTV, at least partly basing its bullishness on Ling's own statements, which they quoted: "'Ling Temco will raise its sales this year to some $1.6 billion from a mere $165 million last year,' Ling predicted recently. 'Net income,' he said, 'should reach $24 to $27 million compared with $13.5 million in 1966. *Profits per share should climb to $10.50 to $13.50 from $6.50 a year ago*'" (emphasis ours). This had to irritate some of the bears, among which was Barton Biggs, who as recently as April 3 had written in *Barron's* that while some of these companies (the conglomerates) have been conjuring up dazzling earnings growth via liberal accounting methods, they couldn't keep making two plus two equal five. Alan Abelson had reiterated Biggs on April 10 in his "Up and Down Wall Street" column, also in *Barron's*. But it wasn't iterated enough. Jimmy was talking to the New York Society of Security Analysts now—and they commanded a lot of financial muscle.

The crowd was still cheering and buying—and who was selling? Only President Clyde Skeen, who cashed in two hundred thousand dollars in convertible bonds on April 26, having followed Colonel Byrd, who had sold one thousand shares in March (when Ling unloaded another thousand), and now Chairman of the Executive Committee Robert McCulloch and Director W. P. Thayer, each having sold two thousand shares. Yet the crowd was asking for more. The colonel sold another 2696 to them on May 17.

The *Magazine of Wall Street* article ended with a quote from President Clyde Skeen: "We desire to grow but as we grow we will always keep our eye on that precious commodity—the shares of our company."

The deeper meaning of Skeen's statement may have escaped many investors.

It has been assumed that the assembling of a conglomerate is done perhaps to provide better management than has previously been the case. The conglomerate, investors reason, provides a pool of talent from which could be drawn the best available to fill needs within the structure. Perhaps financing could be arranged by the larger entity, whereas the smaller independent one might not have as much credit on which to draw. In LTV's case, the pieces were pretty big ones—but other conglomerates gobbled up much smaller bites at a time, such as what was done by U. S. Industries or for a time by Gulf & Western. Litton certainly had some minor acquisitions. In any event, it was generally assumed that an acquisition or series of them would better the whole, bringing more efficient corporations to greater heights, thus benefitting the investors who had put up their hard-earned dough.

Might not an observer question whether companies were grabbed up by larger ones—perish the thought—merely to create excitement in the stock market that might raise the stock's price? Since the thought might appear to be radical in nature, let us just ponder it awhile and move on back to the game.

LTV Flying High

By the end of April 1967, LTV stock was selling for $134 per share, up almost 1000 percent from the time in November 1963 when you or I or Mr. Ling could have paid $14 a share—only he did. Though the record is confused on this, with Ling buying then and selling later and buying back at similarly low prices, the net effect is the same. With money and patience (the latter is as important as the former) investors could make this kind of money. Can they ever again? Possibly not. But who needs 1000 percent? Steady profits satisfy us, and probably you too. Later on in this book, we'll show you how to avoid the big losses that wipe out many a profit.

So there we are, with LTV still going strong. On July 31 LTV took LSD: $203 per share! Whereupon (surprise) Ling announced that he wanted to buy another Dallas-based company, Greatamerica Corporation, in a $500 million deal. Greatamerica was a bank and insurance holding company, owning in addition 81 percent of an airline, Braniff International.

Adding fuel to the summer rise may also have been the one-two punch by LTV in attempting to acquire Allis-Chalmers Company via a tender offer of forty dollars a share the same week as the Greatamerica *putsch.* Allis makes huge generators, such as the one that gives Con Edison some difficulties during New York power troubles. Why a $500 million deal neck-in-neck with another for $250 million? The New York *Times* of August 11, 1967 said, "Some questions were raised in the financial community as to whether the two tenders by L-T-V in rapid succession was an effort to get them in under the wire before Congress passed a bill limiting such offers." The Senate Banking Committee had on August 10 approved a bill putting some roadblocks in front of tender-type deals. Still, the two big deals, combined with a three-for-two stock split on August 1, enticed many investors into the game. As one head raised to the sky in a busy city soon finds many others doing the same thing, yet there may be nothing to look at, so the football game that was over was still being watched and invested in by more and more.

The two-headed drive was all the more unexpected since LTV had just denied any such intention. "On August 2, an L-T-V spokesman denied in replying to a question from the New York *Times* that it was negotiating for Allis-Chalmers," the *Times* said in its August 11 article.

Further, said the paper, "A spokesman also told the *Wall Street Journal* that that day there was 'nothing to' a rumor that L-T-V planned an offer for Allis-Chalmers." It may have been a rather quick decision—or perhaps nobody told him. In any event, such statements to the press are not against the law, right?

Allis-Chalmers stock did not trade until the close of the day, when eighty-three thousand shares changed hands at thirty-five dollars, up from its July 28 price of 25⅞. LTV stock was a hot item too as the fans rose in exaltation at the fancy ball-handling (apparently) of Jimmy Ling and drove the stock to an intraday high of $162 from the previous close of 153½. Perhaps some cooler types wondered what the cheering was all about, for their selling may have driven the stock down to close at $157. Colonel Byrd may have been one of the sellers around this time, as the SEC reports show him unloading another twenty-five hundred shares during the month. If the colonel got only $125 for his shares, they would have come to $312,500 on this bloc alone. If he had sold some three years later he would have grossed only $32,500; but how could he have known?

Profit-taking

Meanwhile, it appeared that the game was being played with all the fury of a John Wayne Western; to some more informed types the fantasy character of the action more often than not corresponded with the good guy-bad man illusions of the screen. Still, the New York *Times* of August 13, 1967 ran a feature article of over fifteen hundred words on Mr. Ling, "Spelling out [his] formula for acquisitions." Would the *Times* spend such valuable space describing an unreal activity? One would think not.

What was holding LTV stock up? One would think that the insider selling would depress the price. But matching the selling was the razzle-dazzle PR job. Just as the football coach reviews the action of the previous day with his players, so Jimmy Ling and Clyde Skeen showed films of their game. It was the same seventeen-minute job they had used for the Los Angeles Society of Security Analysts, only this time, it was the Kansas City Society.

"The philosophy of LTV management is the building and adding of 'lasting values' for the benefits of its shareholders," Ling told the group. And what is more lasting than cash? The cash that Messrs. Ling, McCulloch, Byrd, and Skeen had been extracting from their stock sales is a "value" you can appreciate.

The razzle was really dazzling now: Ling this time illustrated the rest of his talk with slides of the "corporate structure and of the proposed acquisition, Greatamerica." He said he was "Demything the mystique of LTV." After a few thousand well-chosen words, Ling introduced Clyde Skeen, who had his own slides detailing the corporate structure, the sales breakdown among electronics, defense, chemicals, meat, etc., possibly to quiet rumblings about the company's overreliance upon military sales. This was easy to do, since he separated military electronics as having 10 percent of LTV's business, and aerospace as having 18 percent. Separating the two automatically reduced the company's dependence upon war goods from 28 percent to 10 percent with aerospace's 18 percent reclassified.

Mr. Skeen closed with a forecast of LTV doing $2.5 billion to $3 billion in sales by 1970, "*with increases in profits commensurate, if not more so, with the sales increase objective*" (emphasis ours).

There was, you see, still a ball game going on there, a game that could make the crowd rich—rich riding along with the fortunes of a giant company whose growth was just now accelerating into the stratosphere; one whose growth (if one bothered to check), continuing at that feverish pace, would make its assets within ten years greater than the Gross National Product. The stock was selling at $148 a share that day, whereupon a strange thing happened. The day following the meeting the stock fell three points, and then some more, closing ten points lower than at the beginning of the week. Was the Kansas City group smarter than the Los Angeles chaps? Or was there another factor—perhaps some heavy selling pressure coming from another source? Or perhaps a combination of the two? Another look at the SEC's reports reveals a startling fact. Strangely, the very day Mr. Ling and Mr. Skeen were extolling the virtues of the corporation, Mr. McCulloch was selling twenty-eight hundred shares in the open market. Wasn't he impressed with the show being displayed by his fellow company officers? Or perhaps he just needed a bit of cash. If so, the total of some $406,000 might help. Still a bit short? On the next day he sold two thousand shares. On the following day he sold eleven hundred. On September 21 of the following week he eased out of five thousand more. The next day he cleaned up the odds and ends by unloading another nine thousand. All told, McCulloch cashed in stock worth about $2,686,500. If any at the analysts meeting were impressed by the Ling-Skeen presentation, it may have cost them dearly. While the quarterback faked nicely to the halfback, an end-around play saw the end grab the ball and go all the way. Jimmy may not have been Joe Namath's equal with the ladies, but at contract time he could be mighty cool. Of course, I cannot say with a certainty that Ling and Skeen knew that McCulloch was selling—it may have been all coincidence.

One of the analysts at the meeting remarked to an observer that he had cocktails with Ling, Skeen, and McCulloch before the show. Finding them somewhat evasive to his questioning, he sold the stock the following week. The small loss his multimillion-dollar fund endured proved to be one of their better trades.

"The thing didn't smell right," he commented.

While "the thing" was being sold by the more knowledgeable, others were buying, including other mutual funds. Maybe it was the "color" of the cheerleaders at halftime, the bands, and the marchers, all in the form of media-stirred illusion. *Newsweek*, for example, arrived at the desk of Russell Baker, columnist for the New York *Times*, on October 4. The piece heralded "Jim Ling, the Merger King" who had "dazzled Dallas and Wall Street alike by piling merger upon merger." Whereas some of those who got *Newsweek* may have called their brokers to "get in on the action," Mr. Baker only felt his own inadequacy (figuratively speaking) in comparison with the man who took "daily workouts [to] hold his powerful 6-foot 2-inch frame down to a tightly muscled 200 pounds and (who) walks with the spring of an athlete," as the magazine had described him. Mr. Baker had not pulled off any mergers lately, and his frame "had not had a daily workout since 1945. Your thing is praying that the leak in the ceiling will go away. You wouldn't know how to pile one merger on another if life depended on it. You couldn't even assemble a tricycle on Christmas eve," said Mr. Baker of himself.

"Glumness in a capitalistic society is having magazines to remind you that you lack the moxie to join 'the new breed' of merger masters who are busily reshaping the U.S. business structures," he said.

But if Baker's self-deprecation were any indication of what thousands of little investors felt themselves, they could perhaps alleviate the situation. Though they couldn't adopt the methods or mold the personality that *Newsweek* admired so much in Mr. Ling, they could vicariously live the life, economically speaking, of James Ling. On Wall Street there is (or appears to be) a palliative for the "unachieved goal." One cannot be James Ling, but one can buy James Ling's stock. And *Newsweek* could not be blamed if many investors did just that, could they?

LTV made little progress during the last quarter of 1967. It began October at $126 and ended the year at $125, with not a great deal of fluctuation in between. That plateau did afford some opportunity for the insiders to unload more stock. Apollo Corporation, the holding company among whose owners were Jimmy Ling, Clyde Skeen, and two other LTV officers, Dan Burney and George E. Griffin, sold forty-two thousand warrants in December (according to SEC reports). This was the same month that the *National Observer*, a weekly newspaper, told on December 11 of the company's apparently successful plane, the Corsair. It was, the paper said, "a new type of aircraft," and intended to add to "the limited war flexibility" of the American military machine. The football they were kicking around the field on Wall Street was a new type, too. The sight of it may have been elusive to the cheering multitude, but they were "believers." Perhaps some bought the stock because of the story that day as LTV closed at $131. One could hardly fault the *Observer,* since it did not print the article on its financial page. Of course, investors are known to read other parts of newspapers on occasion. Those who paid that price may have rued their decision, for in the succeeding months the stock "found a lower level," or in Street jargon there was "some profit taking." Publicity-generated furor sometimes leads to investors' torpor.

1968–Engine Trouble

January 1968 began with a count of $128 for the stock. Those who had paid $131 may have rested easily. "Still a lot of fun," it was, being a part of the excitement, the glamor of the great game. Look—LTV Aerospace (a division) had just landed a $22,551,000 Navy contract for the A7E attack aircraft. And a few days later, *Barron's* had an ad run by the company about one of its officials, James O. Weldon, the division's chairman of the board. The ad described him as "America's pioneer super-power engineer." Buyers of the stock might also thereby associate themselves with a scientific genius as well as a corporate one. It didn't help. The stock wavered a bit. Perhaps it was just the market as a whole, for though LTV stock fell 5½ points on January 3, Gulf & Western fell 1⅜ to end at 82⅝.

"It was a second-day reaction to President Johnson's program to remedy the worsening balance-of-payments deficit," one broker told the *Wall Street Journal.* There was some other news, however; good news, five days later.

"Ling-Temco Says '67 Profit Rose to $31,000,000," reported the *Wall Street Journal.* James J. Ling, chairman, and Clyde Skeen, president, said that LTV would report that the 1967 profit would come to over $7 a common share. "Sales of the conglomerate last year spurted to over $1.8 billion," the paper said. "Both earnings and sales were slightly higher than various forecasts made during the year." Profits for 1966 had been only $4.34 a share. And if that weren't enough, "Sources that follow Ling-Temco closely assert that the Greatamerica acquisition will bring important changes to Ling-Temco's earnings potential, balance sheet and cash position for further acquisitions," the *Journal* added. The news could hardly be better—so far. But the article concluded,

"Ling-Temco officials are believed to envision several subsidiaries ultimately reaching $1 billion in annual sales each. LTV Aerospace Corporation, one major subsidiary, already has disclosed anticipated sales of more than $500 million in 1968. This could put Ling-Temco's revenue over the $2 billion mark this year even if something were to alter plans for acquiring Greatamerica."

"What a game!" The multitude exalted. "Fantastic!" said the little old ladies in Keokuk. "Go, go, go!" said the fans. Readers, though, if looking closely at their scorecard (the SEC reports) could detect another player idling toward the sidelines. Holding a helmet stuffed with over $125,000 of proceeds from the sale of LTV stock *sold the very day the announcement* made the *Wall Street Journal* (January 8) was W. P. Thayer, a company director. Prudent Mr. Thayer sold his stock for some twenty-six thousand dollars more than he could have done just a month later. Difficult to figure, though, for LTV had by this time sent up more crowd noises by announcing the acquisition of the big air carrier, Braniff. And if that were not all, Mr. Ling had told the *Wall Street Journal* that "Ling-Temco primarily is interested in acquiring companies in these fields: chemicals-drugs, building materials, farm machinery, automotive components-accessories, paper products, food products, construction equipment, electronic components and capital goods."

There was no truth to the rumor that Ling was preparing an offer for Cleveland's Municipal Stadium, where another Jimmy (Brown) had torn through opponents' secondaries, for real.

It may have been an act of extreme self-control that kept the insiders in LTV from buying the stock, considering the company's prospects, viz., a surge in earnings with promise of more to come, and an acquisition plan that rivaled the Roman Empire's. Somehow, they managed to hold back at this time—and their luck held, for the stock was tripped up as though by an unseen hand from the bottom of the pile-up at the line of scrimmage. By February 12, 1968 it had fallen to ninety-nine dollars, or 40 percent below its 1967 high. Of course, it may have merely been "the poor action of the group," as they say in the Street, for Litton was down 39 percent after announcing a fourth-quarter profit drop. But this couldn't happen to LTV—or could it?

A 40 percent drop in price was not one to be sneezed at. The *Wall Street Journal* had an explanation on February 12. It seemed there had been "disappointments involved in recent revisions of (corporate) earnings goals." Further, the paper said, "some analysts are harboring a suspicion of a less-than-vigorous revival of the business boom."

The analysts cited were of course wrong about business conditions (not the first time). As for LTV, management had not thus far "overstated" earnings. Yet the stock was weak. Perhaps some of the crowd noticed that the emperor had no clothes on—or in our football analogy, that the game was over and the winning team had taken home the ball (and the house receipts, the goal posts, and the stadium chairs).

One such doubter was Mr. John Wall in *Barron's;* he really gave it to the conglomerates on February 5:

"Dear Jack: Thanks for your letter telling me that you've decided to become a conglomerate," it began. "It's about time you wised up and resolved as they say to flourish and make megabucks instead of knocking yourself out trying to keep the earnings of your crummy foundry from going down.

"You ask how to do it. Brains, guts, funny money, a smile and a shoeshine ought to be a sufficiency. It's really not much harder or very different from promoting one of those chain-letter games we used to play when we were kids. And don't kid yourself, it may end the same way. But you make a lot more money."

The article went on to detail how to glamorize your company by euphemizing businesses you've bought such as calling ship-building "marine systems," a steel company "materials technology," etc. Perhaps some people sold LTV when they read the piece. But others bought—they were the believers. It was the believers, too, who bought computer-leasing stocks in 1968, or nursing home stocks in 1969.

Game Over

By February 12 the same *Newsweek* that had admired Jimmy Ling when the stock was "hot" was headlining an article, "THE LOW STATE OF THE HIGH-FLYERS," among which was LTV, of course. Gustave Levy, chairman of the Board of Governors of the New York Stock Exchange, deplored the "herd instinct" he saw among many institutional investors, the magazine reported. Many had taken positions in LTV, which presumably was one of the manifestations Mr. Levy had referred to.

With the conglomerates apparently past their peak, the "news" about them got a little less bullish. Of course, LTV, Litton, and the like still had their boosters. A roundup of first-quarter 1968 holdings showed that twenty-four fund managers still had Ling-Temco stock in their portfolios. Indeed, four mutual funds made *new* commitments in LTV during the period. What they did not see (along with many small investors) was the over-all pattern of smart-money practices in the stock market—indeed, the very dynamics of stock patterns going back to the Middle Ages. It often goes like this:

1. The informed minority purchases stock in a company. Corporate news is nonexistent or bad. Newspapers are not featuring stories about "geniuses" building "money machines" or empire builders buying and selling the Empire State Building (à la Zeckendorf). The company president is not being featured in "man in the news" columns in daily papers around the country, and *Time* is not illustrating its cover with his portrait. Earnings are down or flat. Sometimes the company is actually incurring a deficit. Dividends have been cut or omitted. Advisory services are not taking ads in financial pages telling about their writeups featuring the stock. And annual reports are dull two-color jobs.
2. A bit of good news comes out—a merger, a change of corporate name,[3] or possibly new management. Unprofitable operations are sold off. Maybe earnings improve somewhat. The stock starts to rise gradually at first. This is the preseason warmup phase.
3. The boom phase. Earnings are jumping radically—doubling, for example. Management (unlike previously) is talking to all analysts who will listen—and telling them wonderful things. Perhaps it is being hinted that profits will rise even more rapidly in the future. The stock rises dramatically—and many of the chartists jump in. Of course, the smarter ones got in at Phase 2. The insiders are selling.
4. Madness. The stock splits, dividends are raised and then raised again. The stock really goes—up. Stop orders are banned on the exchange, and short interest rises dramatically as some knowledgeable traders sell short. Market observers and hedge fund managers buy the stock "because the shorts are being squeezed." Who really is being squeezed can be seen later. The

[3] More recently, names have been changed after the stock passes from "strong" to "weak" hands—that is, after the game is over. Darn clever, these insiders.

stock is split again. The annual report fattens, comes replete with die-cuts, and is printed in four colors. It is a joy to behold, an example of the "blending of the arts of the artists, the lithographers, and the writers," as the public relations man would say. It is also an example of another type of art, the art of con.

5. The piper arrives on the scene, awaiting payment. The stock drops as fast as it rose—maybe faster. *Then* the bad earnings come out. Stop orders are banned on the downside. More bad earnings come out; the bad news is widely and soulfully discussed among the analysts who liked it higher. The news media is stunned by the "unexpected turnabout." The process can now start all over again, over a period of years. The informed minority has the patience that the masses do not.

Of course, different stocks have their patterns within the "master plan." Styles differ. Sometimes, as in the case of Ling-Temco, the company takes out ads in financial periodicals, extolling its virtues. The stockholders, of course, pay for these ads out of company expenses.

Questions, Now

After a brief sojourn in the rarefied atmosphere of over $106 per share in mid-February, Ling-Temco stock again drifted lazily downward. The league office (that Department of Justice) was beginning to make noises like maybe a penalty should have been called. "Where the hell does LTV get the gall to pick up so many other companies?" they seemed to be saying. There were some grumblings from Congress. "If Gulf & Western, Litton, LTV, Automatic Sprinkler,[4] Teledyne, and Whittaker keep at it, they'll own America," was heard in the halls on the Hill.

So President Johnson appointed a panel of experts to look over the legalities of the conglomerate acquisition caper. The president of the American Bankers Association was telling his confreres to hold back the money-lending open-handedness that had been abetting the conglomes. Even the American Institute of Certified Public Accountants was uneasily eyeing some of the practices that may have aided the earnings statements of the LTV, et al. group. But

[4] These are also conglomerates with roughly similar stock histories, except that Charlie Bluhdorn of Gulf & Western stayed in the game.

there was an even more fundamental problem related to the acquisition: mania.

"These guys are bidding up prices so high, I'll take it easy for a while," a corporation buyer told me. "I'll come back when it's a buyer's market again. I've got time." At which point he sped off to his Mexican villa (not the Long Island estate, the Spanish cottage or the Mayfair flat, this time).

There had been 2975 mergers in 1967 throughout the country. The acquisitions chief of a diversified chemical company was quoted by *Business Week* on March 2, 1968 as feeling that more than 80 percent of them were "financial" in nature, that is, unrelated to the normal business reason for mergers, that of increasing the earnings of both. Others felt that the conglomerates were using "Chinese money" to acquire companies, that is, the payment being with stock selling at inflated values. What they were all saying, in effect, was that the game was over. Very few investors knew what the game was, strangely. The game was not conglomerating, as so many thought. *It was making money for yourself by buying stock low and selling it high.* It had happened before and would happen again. But by this time, the smart money would have to change the *name* of the game, not the action.

The Dow Jones average, in the meantime, was having its own seasonal injuries. On March 4, with the average at 840, down from over 900 in January, the *Wall Street Journal* implied that institutions had been selling the high flyers. "Recent selling pressures have been heaviest in stock issues with big fund ownerships. For instance, investment companies at the end of 1967 held 25% of Burroughs stock, 23% of Sperry Rand, 25% of Control Data, 39% of Raytheon, 32% of Ling-Temco-Vought, 29% of Northwest Airlines and 21% of Polaroid." Which points to another lesson, dear reader. Buying a stock that has substantial institutional ownership can have its dangers. They do sell, you know.

Ling Fights Back (with guess who's money)

LTV had been getting a bad press recently (unusual for them), and Jimmy Ling was not going to take it lying down. So the corporation anted up for an expensive two-page ad in *Fortune* magazine's April edition (it came out in March) that patently was an attempt to combat it. The ad began, "Much has been said and written recently by various business observers about highly diversified companies (commonly called conglomerates) relative to their financial soundness, structure, motives and profitability," and it went on in refutation. It apparently worked for a time, for in April the stock rose back over $100 to close out the month at $122. The magazine is especially good in its editorial effect on the stock market, I have observed, well worth its $1.50 price per issue. But those who bought the stock on the basis of such ads might have found it costing them thousands.

The May issue helped too, for in it Ling-Temco ran another two-page ad, also financed by the crowd (excuse me, stockholders).

"Progress profit '68: LTV shirtsleeve summit formulates policies and develops potentials," the ad began. "Strategic planning in symposium with the patent company management is a central element in LTV's approach to *corporate technology*" (emphasis theirs). Also, such phrases as "beneficial symbiosis" and "optimum decentralization" were sprinkled in the ad. Shades of John Wall, who might have prophesied these very words in his *Barron's* piece on February 5 when he wrote, "Never use a little, simply understandable word when you can use a big complex one. Talk about market matrixes, core technology fulcrums, modular building blocks and the 'nucleus theory of growth.' No one from Wall Street may know what you mean but everyone gets that nice warm feeling of being in on the mainstream of the thrust of technology."

Ling-Temco ran another ad in the same *Fortune*, this time only one full page, on LTV Aerospace Corporation, the subsidiary. "Man was not meant to fly," it began, and it told of the efforts of LTV Aero in promoting the advancement of the state of the flying art vis-à-vis "jumbo jets, the SST, new generation military aircraft and the advanced designs of the future." It might have been construed as promoting the sale of the company's services, rather than its stock, a refreshing change. Then again, it could hardly hurt the stock, either, particularly in those hawkish times.

The big gun LTV fired off, however, was a piece of written material used by many corporations to enhance their image with present and potential stockholders, the annual report. Received around this time of the year (March–April), it probably contributed to the stocks' spring rise. Whereas the 1966 report (issued in 1967) was a forty-page public relations job one could admire, the 1967 summary (released in 1968) outdid itself. While the previous year's front cover was in good-quality heavy stock, the current one was coated (more costly). The contents also jumped over 25 percent, to fifty-one pages, including a foldout. The current year's job dropped one irrelevancy (drawings of Copernicus, et al.) for another. This annual talked about "The 1975 Man and His World," with colored charts illustrating population growth (and how LTV would serve the masses), increases in disposable income, new family formations, and capital and government spending (a $260 billion increase was predicted in government payout alone), and contained twenty colored photos as against the previous year's five (taking the place of those drawings of Edison, Einstein, etc. in the prior issue). All in all, an impressive job. And you know who paid for it, though it should be mentioned that Messrs. Ling, Skeen, McCulloch, and Byrd were also stockholders.

LTV was helped out, too, by a stock market recovery that saw the Dow rise from a low of 817 to a high of 935 the first week of May (spurred by President Johnson's announcement that he would not seek re-election). Ling-Temco stock enjoyed a brief respite in the sun again, rising to a high of 135 during the trading on May 8, though closing the day at $132, a leap of 30 percent from its March closing. One more factor in LTV's stock rise may have been still another ad, this one in *Barron's* May 6 issue. The advertisement, for LTV Electrosystems, closed out with an illuminating revelation, "We welcome the continuing interest shown in our company by the financial and business communities. For our 1967 Annual Report, please write . . . ." The company's target was being identified in no uncertain terms, wouldn't you say?

That price rise was about it. Although the Dow Jones average would later come back to a high of 994 a few weeks before Christmas, gift-giving time for LTV shareholders would have to wait a far longer time, perhaps forever. That is, except for some of the insiders in LTV. Colonel Byrd, for example, added to his larder to the tune of some five hundred thousand dollars grossed in June by selling some more goodies to the populace. But what about Jimmy? Did he sell any more of his stock? If not, why not? Perhaps we can guess the answer. But first, let us briefly review some of the events that accompanied the stock's massive fall from grace that would take it as low as eleven dollars a share in mid-1970. "Return to sanity" was the way it was dubbed in some Street quarters.

On May 9, 1968, LTV announced plans to sell some subsidiaries of its Greatamerica. Some analysts viewed this development as bullish, and not, as later turned out, the beginning of a deconglomerating spiral, spurred on by government antitrust action and later by a bone-crushing cash squeeze, every bit as painful as a Jerry Kramer block. How Colonel Byrd viewed the action, however, was his own affair. He undoubtedly had his reasons, but whatever they were, his selling was duly noted in the SEC reports for all to see, though few saw. He sold, incidentally, despite a May 10 announcement that LTV was again in the corporate gobbling business, this time with the giant steel-maker, Jones & Laughlin. This announcement didn't help the stock much, surprisingly. Why? Because the game was really over, and the realization of this fact was beginning to permeate the investment community. By June's end, LTV was back again selling for $106 a share.

The Whistle Blew

On July 8 the Federal Trade Commission announced that a broad study was being made of the accelerating trend toward conglomerate mergers. Two days later the New York *Times* featured an article in its financial section, "Conglomerate Mergers Get Spotlight," replete with a chart of LTV's divisions and a photo of the prime progenitor of the breed. An advisory service, *Indicator Digest,* said on July 23 that the conglomerates were "Down, But Not Out." LTV by this time was selling for $90 a share. It may have looked "cheap" to some—that is, if there really were a game going on. Yet as the stock descended slowly into the West, it had its boosters. Another *Times* piece (on July 28) wondered whether the interest in steel acquisitions (there were others, such as Penn-Dixie Cement and Continental Steel) was that "the acquiring companies believe the price is right." The paper pointed out that steel companies were generally selling for ten times their estimated 1968 earnings and that "many [steel] industry experts believe that within the next three years, improved conditions in the national economy and the steel industry will enable some of the stronger steel companies to reach new heights in sales and earnings." Then there was the substantial cash flow that most had. The piece may have contributed to a brief flurry in the stock to $102 a share by July 26, but the next week the stock plummeted twenty points. There were still more drops to come after the government's order to LTV to divest itself of Braniff, accompanied by questions, such as those posed by the *Wall Street Journal,* in its article of July 25, "Anti-trusters, Investors Eye Combines Warily," and, on August 5, "Even Accountants Find Some Financial Reports [of Conglomerates] Baffling." LTV had, the paper pointed out, announced 1967 per share net for LTV of $7.69. Yet on the same page was listed also $7.11, $5.96, and $5.56. The paper seemed to ask what the true earnings were.

At this juncture there were more detractors than admirers. But there were admirers. One of the latter was a brokerage-firm analyst who said of conglomerates, "There are the good ones and the rotten ones and you've got to be selective." An example of his selectivity was illustrated when he listed "the good ones": Ling-Temco, Houdaille Industries, City Investing, Textron, and Walter Kidde.

The S&P is to investment analysis what the A&P is to grocery stores. That even Standard & Poor's can be wrong can be shown by their September 9, 1968 issue, which featured LTV. It was rated by the popular service as a "Speculative Buy." Speculative was the proper word, it would seem, for as the service pointed out, LTV was selling for $87, or almost 50 percent below its August 1967 high. Seven months later the stock had dropped more than 50 percent from *that* level. Still to come was a net loss of $38 million for 1969's business, revealed in an annual report shorn of color charts and pictures, devoid even of usual full-page photos of James Ling and his associate, Clyde Skeen. Down to twenty-nine pages, forgotten now was Copernicus, the American housewife, and the booming growth visualized the prior year.[5] Now the 1969 report (released in the spring of 1970) detailed problem after problem—J & L steel had experienced two strikes, Braniff had startup costs, Okonite was hit by high copper prices, LTV Electrosystems' costs on government fixed-price contracts were higher than anticipated. Even Einstein could not help them now.

But what about James Ling, who later was relegated to the rela-

[5] The earning drop was announced in the financial pages on February 19 and showed a net loss of $8.3 million. What the loss actually was, was academic to the investors who had suffered 50 to 70 percent drops in stock values.

tively inactive position of "vice chairman of the board"? What about all the stock Jimmy had left and hadn't sold when the selling was easier? What about the fact that Skeen, Byrd, and McCulloch had unloaded a greater portion of their holdings than Ling? What's it all about, Jimmy? Well, who can say what went on in James Ling's high-I.Q. mind? Perhaps it was, as some observers said, that "Jimmy got caught up in his own image." Or perhaps, as others opined, "He really believed all that stuff." Whatever the reason, it appears that Jimmy forgot to kick the extra point. But the point for investors to remember when they are thinking of selling stock because of insider activity, and their friends caution, "How much have the insiders left?" is that it doesn't really matter. When the game is over, it's over, even if the shrill ghosts of former players and plays and days of glory haunt the memory of some of the informed minority. Ling-Temco-Vought stock eventually sold as low as eleven dollars a share in 1970 and a bit lower in 1971, the price area from where it all began.

LING-TEMCO-VOUGHT, INC.

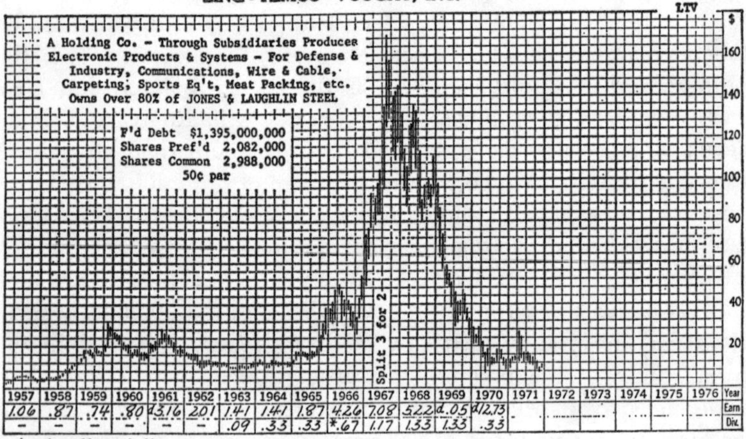

* and small stock div.

Chart courtesy M. C. Horsey & Co., Inc., Salisbury, Maryland 21801

three

The Experts

DRIVING down the East River Drive a few years ago one could see a building on the right with a sign emblazoned on it proclaiming that *The Outlook*, Standard & Poor's weekly advisory letter, is "illuminating." Perhaps. But possibly we can illuminate some of the market recommendations of this and other advisory services.

The subhead on the first page of *The Outlook* reads, "Analyzes and Projects Business and Market Trends." An examination of just how the service does this might prove interesting, if not rewarding. One first might substitute the word "reacts to" for the word "analyzes," since Webster's New World Dictionary defines analysis as "a separating or breaking up of any whole into its parts so as to find out their nature, proportion, function, relationship, etc." Anyhow, let us analyze *The Outlook* and its value to investors.

We could start anywhere—and not arbitrarily. I noticed similar patterns during the four years I did a market commentary for a radio station in New York. Let us begin with a rather exciting time for the market—November 11, 1968. Things were bubbling on the upside, and S&P said, "Near Term Strength Possible," a bullish but lukewarm opinion. Using the service's own index to measure its performance, the S&P 425 Industrials then stood at 112.65.

The following week, with the market going up to 114.43, "Selective Shopping Should Be Rewarding" was their opinion, a little more bullish than the previous week, and "The market's action last week left little doubt that stocks had broken away from their trading ranges of the preceding five or six weeks."

When the S&P Industrials average reached 115.43, *Outlook* said that the "Market Climate [Is] Still Favorable." Although there is a basic attitude the service maintains against speculation and for conservative or hedged opinions, the crew at Standard & Poor's seemed to be getting more bullish with "Subject to normal reactions from time to time the market is expected to work its way higher."

When their own average reached the 118.03 mark and they said, "Purchases Still Recommended," their bullish bias seemed to heighten. "Good news," they said, "on three fronts was largely responsible for the buoyancy." Whereas we have learned that the informed minority would be selling under such a barrage of "good news," this more public-thinking service intensified its optimistic leanings. They cited the apparent resolution of a European monetary crisis, as well as important steps toward peace, with the South Vietnamese Government's agreement to send a delegation to the Paris peace talks. "There was also an array of reassuring business news suggesting that expansionary pressures remain so strong that any thought of overkill because of the tax surcharge is out the window." The service blithely expounded in the face of all the statistical evidence to the contrary that "mutual fund managements, probably motivated by the same or similar considerations as the share buyers cut back their cash positions [bought significantly] for the first time in three months," as a *bullish* phenomenon. Actually the reverse is true: The greater the cash position of funds, the more bullish the market; the less the cash position, the more bearish.

In the chart, note that mutual fund cash rose to a point of 7 percent in the middle of 1958. Their cash had increased with their selling of stocks, and culminated at a "buy" point in the Dow Jones average around 450. As the market rose to just under 600 at the end of 1958, the funds bought back in to return to their "normal" 4½ percent cash position. The Dow continued higher, to the 675 area at the end of 1959. The market declined to just under 600 toward the end of 1960. This proved another "buy" point, as the Dow shot up to the 735 area at the end of 1961. The funds had been selling and had to reverse themselves, buying on the way up. The peak found the institutions "bought up." They sold through the early 1962 decline but continued doing so to a crescendo (around 7 percent cash piling up) just past the middle of 1962. They should have been buying, as the Dow set off in a tear that took it close to

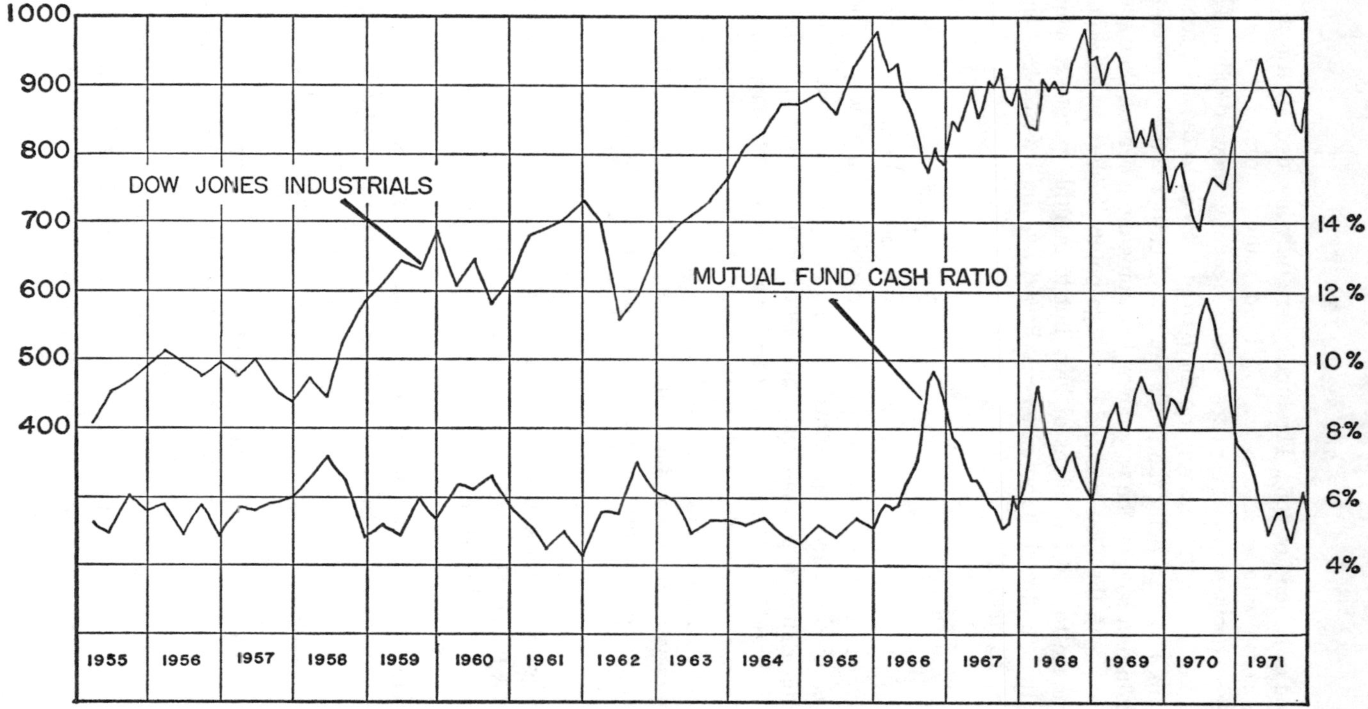

1000
900
800
700
600
500
400
DOW JONES INDUSTRIALS
MUTUAL FUND CASH RATIO
14 %
12 %
10%
8%
6%
4%
1955
1956
1957
1958
1959
1960
1961
1962
1963
1964
1965
1966
1967
1968
1969
1970
1971

1000 at the end of 1965. The funds were fully invested (in a historical sense with 4 percent cash). Their selling through the subsequent decline saw their bearishness reaching new depths. The market sawtoothed its way up then, from just 800 to the 1000 sector again, at which point the funds ran out of cash, relatively speaking. Again they sold on the way down, becoming more bearish than ever, whereupon the Dow zoomed some 250 points. [Chart prices do not conform to absolute highs or lows but to monthly points at which mutual fund cash information is released by The Investment Company Institute.]

Another Chance

Of course, one could say that we are being unfair with Standard & Poor's. After all, they do have many people working away in their research department, presumably doing analysis. So, though I have better things to do than read their *Outlook* week after week, let us be fair and investigate their record for a more recent time, 1971.

It was much easier tracking their work that year, since S&P's Industrials Price Index is located on the same page as their market summary. This index starts out the year measuring the market at 100.90 accompanied by cheerful hope, "Prospects Favor Further Rise."

"Monetary and business factors continue to provide a background for favorable stock market performance in the period ahead," Standard & Poor's said. The recent rise had taken the market to rather high ground (an "overbought condition"), but any drop "would be temporary."

The next week the service led off proclaiming that the "Rise Had Further to Go," as the week had ended with little change, at 100.79.

On January 18, the modest drop that had earlier been predicted did not happen as their index closed at 101.55, and they said the advance was "more orderly."

On January 25, with the index at 103.75, investors were advised, "Accumulation [is] still in order." So, if you had not bought as much as you might, you should buy more (always with the caveat of "selectivity"). The following week the service could be proud of itself, as the market rose to 105.12 (as measured by its index) and their bullishness continued unabated. Indeed, "Notwithstanding the length and extent of the advance, the market shows few signs of tiring," they said.

On February 8, with the index up to 106.38, Standard & Poor's felt that "a pause would be healthy." That pause did not materialize (give it time) as the market rose to 107.52 by their February 15 letter. "The market's action is impressive," they said, but the possibility of a "brief respite" was increasing, which when it happens "should not worry investors." These investors, presumably, were still buying (if they had any money left), for [The] "Major Trend Remains Bullish."

When their average fell to 106.17, Standard & Poor's could be justifiably proud of itself, for they had been forecasting a minor drop. "An expected correction," they called it. Their March 1 letter, following another drop, this time to 105.37, said that one should now "look for buying opportunities."

The service's abilities to forecast the market had seemingly improved since 1968, with an advance taking place the following week to 108.86, reaching 111.13 by the edition of March 22. The market should continue to move upward, they said, though by a more restrained pace. "A constructive approach remains warranted," they said, meaning buy—or at least don't sell (yet).

By the April 12 issue their index had zoomed to 112.49, with "further upside progress likely," and one could be getting real confidence in S&P's research by now.

The next two weeks saw another advance (to 114.94) and investors could rest assured, knowing they were in good hands. All one had to do was follow the premier investment advisory service on timing while using their stock recommendations for specific buys. Don't worry, they seemed to be saying. But as you know, when people tell you not to worry, start worrying.

If investors were lulled into complacency by Standard & Poor's, they had a rude awakening in the following weeks as the market dropped sharply to close at 111.71 by their May 24 letter. At this point, "further correction [would occur] before [the] advance resumes." This short-term bearishness saw the market rise to 112.13 by June 7, and they were beginning to zig when they should have been zagging.

The rise convinced the seers at 80 Hudson Street that the "market's underpinnings [are] healthy." Of course, there may be some "backing and filling in for a while," and you should seize the opportunity to buy "sound commitments."

Those who follow the meanderings of the service might have said, "Here we go again," as a drop the following week to 111.91 caused S&P to say that the "market pause could be extended." "But you just said. . . ." might have been the investors' cry.

When the market fell again, to land at 108.19 by June 28, the service said that the "market [is] digesting recent developments," which may have caused the investor to reach for his Tums, particularly when he read that more time may be required to absorb "recent developments." Eventually, however, his stocks would come around.

Outlook, after preparing their readers for more weakness for a while, took on a collective dumfounded appearance when the following week saw the market go up to 110.02. "Market action [is] encouraging," they said. "To whom?" John J. Investor asked.

A further rise to 111.01 by the July 12 letter caused Standard & Poor's to say that the "market prognosis [is] favorable." After this statement the market only fell again, to the tune of 109.14. This shook up the "white shoe" crowd at S&P, and they reacted by claiming that the "market [is] still in [a] testing phase." Another drop saw their countenance move in concert, for now (on July 26) they said that the "restrained mood may persist."

The more the market moved down, the more restrained S&P got. The more restrained they got, some cynics would say, the more likely a market advance. This came with the President's new economic policy announcement, which sparked a market rally back up to 108.49 by the letter of August 23, whereupon they turned bullish again. And so it went. It seemed much like the old days at Hollywood's Republic Studios, where as many as five cowboy movies were being shot simultaneously, each looking much like the other. The outcomes were all preordained; only the scriptwriters changed the names of the characters. On Wall Street, it is ever thus.

Why Services?

What are the functions of market advisory services, and who runs them? The ostensible objective of services is to make money for their subscribers (and keep them from losing too much). Their more practical purpose is to enrich themselves through the sale of their services. There are the statistical types, such as Standard & Poor's in their *Daily Dividend Record* bound volumes found at many brokerage offices; likewise S&P's *Corporation Records*. The service's *Stock Guide* also is a handy capsule record of earnings, financial positions, dividend payments, and price records. These, as with the five-by-seven-inch loose-leaf sheets analyzing companies, have their function. When Standard & Poor's tries to evaluate, that's another story. Evaluation involves more than statistical observation. It involves, for one thing, the art (rather than the science) of judging security values, and—in our view—judging the stage stocks are in (being picked up or accumulated by the informed minority, or being sold by them—or somewhere in between).

But there are other advisory services, many of them not as good as *The Outlook* and costing far more. Many cost the entrepreneur but a few cents an issue to print—though that fact alone should not cause them to be ruled out, if the information were valuable to the investor. But is it valuable? One could, of course, take all the recommendations made by all the services and see how they worked out over a given period of time. If one were going to spend the three or four years necessary to do this, one would first, of course, have to obtain all back issues. However, many would rather not open that can of worms. If the services did not keep them as records, some would rather burn the evidence. We know of one popular technical service that has a record of something like minus 200 percent, though it would have taken the reader three years to lose that much. We know of another that printed his record in one edition—and then stopped out of embarrassment. It would help if all services were required to do this, say once a year. We know of an additional fellow who did do this—only he neglected to list his short sales. And so it goes . . . .

There is one way the investor can gauge the efficacy of the advisers as a group—and the record is available. Investors Intelligence service of Larchmont, New York prints twice a month—and gives the subscriber an evaluation of what the sixty-two services they monitor are saying about the market.

Investors Intelligence provided us with the record of how the sixty-two advisory services have performed since 1965. Beginning with August 13, 1965, the number of bullish observers was 35 percent of the total. This is a rather low figure, as you will see. The market then rose to 960 over the next month and a half, whereupon the number of bullish services rose in stages to 60 percent. Just as the uninformed majority does (these services help to mold majority opinion), they became more bullish as the market rose. At this lofty point, when almost two-thirds of these "experts" were optimistic, the market was close to a peak that would take it two years to top. The advisers' bullishness waned to the 51 percent area a month later when the Dow Jones average rose to 988, at which point it and the market nose-dived. In the middle of the week of March 1966, optimistic advisers numbered only 28 percent of the group, with the Dow Jones Industrials around 922. With so few expecting a resumption of the advance, the move up was almost sure to follow; thus the market rose about twenty-five points in the ensuing month, *after* which the number of services that became bullish hit a new high in their enthusiasm; 64 percent of them now foresaw new highs in the averages, but the new highs subsequently accomplished were the new highs only in their own excitement quotients.

This feverishness may have sucked in some investors who became infected with the advisers' enthusiasm; if so, their ecstasy of bullishness was to lead to dismay and dejection, for the Dow did an almost immediate somersault, falling a full seventy-five points in only three weeks.

In studying the workings of the services, one is amazed to find them so wrong so often. It appears to be an interesting phenomenon, that is, the service used as market indicator—in reverse! When an overwhelming proportion of investment advisory services become bullish, *sell.* When they become bearish in the same degree, *buy.* One would not like to base one's entire investment program on so slender a thread, but this indicator, along with others found to be helpful in the past, certainly merits attention.

The Record

Then again, the reader may say, "Sure, it worked out in 1965 and 1966, but do you think your research into the subject is complete? Do you think it is fair to them by observing only two years?"

Good point—perhaps we were too hasty. Let us go on into 1967. At the outset of the year only 29 percent of the sixty-two services followed by Investors Intelligence were bullish, and the Dow Jones was just over 800. This leads us to the bull market rise of '67, with a 130-point rise during the year. Of course, once this move up had been accomplished, over 50 percent of the services had turned bullish again.

Why So Wrong?

An examination of the news background (propaganda-developed) opinion at the beginning of 1967 could, the scientifically inclined observer might reason, yield clues as to the reasons for the bearishness apparent among advisory services at the time. Further, it might yield clues to the direction of other markets and their possible predictability.

So let us go back to that time and see what the writers (analysts) for the services were reading in the press, for they, like the rest of us, are consciously or not affected by the cultural rainfall that hits us all in the form of media seedings.

The now defunct New York *World Journal Tribune* published at the time (January 8, 1967) a "World Economic Survey" featuring a set of predictions for the year. Though the paper no longer exists, its financial editor now serves in the same capacity for the New York *Daily News*, and his and the paper's observations were the standard ones among the financial press. And this overwhelming majority viewpoint, fed to the public in large doses, affected their investment decisions no less than it did those of the investment advisers who read the same papers. What is rare among the services, as it is among other segments of middle-stage opinion molders, is the cynicism and steel guts to snicker at all the pap being fed to it. Rare, that is, except among the informed minority.

With the standard hedging clauses, here is a sample of what the reader found out about world affairs by reading this and other newspapers: "STOCK MARKET: Viet Nam will hold the key to the market, but assuming present level of conflict holds, experts foresee a declining market, especially at [the] start of year. . . . Most of any expected decline in business now discounted by stock prices, but testing of October, 1966 lows probable."

What happened: Vietnam did hold that level of conflict, yet the market took off. Correctly, the paper said that the "expected decline" had been discounted, except that there was *no* decline. There was no "testing" of the October lows, as the experts expected there would be.

The prediction: "The boom has lost much of its buoyancy and in some key lines, like motor cars and housing, there is a definite turn down. If business capital spending does more than level off, after several years of record-breaking expansion the economy can be in trouble for the fifth time since World War II. However, present intentions for business spending still show some gain over 1966, but the growth rate has definitely slowed and the year is yet young.

What happened: The paper was expecting either a leveling off or a decline, yet neither happened.

Where did the opinions the paper discussed come from? The popular economists of the nation. There are the "experts" who influence so much of public thinking on economic and stock market matters—and the public includes the advisory services. All predicted a recession, a year of "adjustment" rather than growth, and they were wrong as it turned out.

And they were not alone. The *Wall Street Journal* reported in early 1968 that the President's Council of Economic Advisers "is less than a wizard at predicting how important segments [of the economy] will fare." The paper reported that the council was off in its prediction of the Gross National Product by $5.2 billion.

On the whole, the bearishness of the economists was countered by the *results* for 1967 as reported in the New York *Times* on February 18, 1968: "The United States economy is clearly booming." So much so that the Secretary of the Treasury, Henry H. Fowler, viewing 1967's results, said, "The economy is in grave danger of overheating."

Poor predictions by Establishment economists are not rare. For just one more example (a student could cite thousands), another chairman of the President's council, Raymond J. Saulnier (who held the post under President Eisenhower and now teaches at Barnard), said in late December 1968 that a "credit crunch" was unlikely—after which 1969 saw that very thing happen. The *Times* reported Professor Saulnier's views of the money pressures—and further, that he was not concerned, in the longer-term sense, about inflation. He may yet be right, but through the first six months of

1969, prices rose quite dramatically—in *one month* they went up as much as 1 percent.

They are also not new. Victor Zarnowitz, professor of economics at the University of Chicago, studied the Gross National Product forecasts of "economists and others in business, government and academic institutions" for the National Bureau of Economic Research (in the January–February 1966 issue of *Challenge* magazine). He found very little correlation between the predicted changes in the GNP and the subsequent actual changes. However, as one economic expert said, "One of the most satisfying aspects of being a forecaster is that few people take the trouble to look back and see if the forecaster was right."

Thus one can see that the Establishment economic voices influenced observers in the wrong direction—which in part may also explain the advisory services' frailties.

They're Not All Wrong

Back to their record. In early 1968, one might have gotten bullish prematurely by following the advisory services (on a reverse basis), for only 22 percent were bullish in late January, with the Dow around 880. Yet the market fell farther, to 840 and below. This fall turned them even more bearish, as can be expected, with only 10 percent remaining optimistic. Thus the Dow again rallied, going as high as 994. It may be said to the services' credit that as a group they were not as bullish as they had been at prior "tops," with only 44 percent confident.

In 1969 the buoyant group numbered 28 percent when the Dow was at 951 in February, and dropped to 13 percent when the market fell to 905. This predictably saw the averages rise again, this time for almost sixty points—as the services followed, sheeplike. What happened then? Right—the market fell apart, sinking to well below 900. This drop, like most others, saw many market observers panic. Panic affords the informed minority the "bargains" they so often sop up at wholesale to sell later at retail—to an eagerly buying public. Why eager? The Establishment press, many services, analysts, and the like help heat up the buying fever—to the delight of the sellers, and the process begins again.

What You Need Is a Good Analyst

Mutual fund managements are in an unenviable position. Since the fund buyer is paying for "professional management" of his portfolio, he naturally wants to see that "professional advice" pay off in terms of profits. But fund managements continually face the limelight of publicly announced results, which may not help the fund salesman trying to sell to the prospective buyer. Thus, slowly but inexorably, fund purchasers of the 1950s and 1960s have been sellers of the 1970s, as redemptions catch up with purchases. By 1971–and continuing into '72–more people were cashing in than buying. You can fool some of the people some of the time.

But you can't fool the computers at the Wharton School of Finance and Commerce (a graduate branch of the University of Pennsylvania). Thus it was that in August 1970, Professors Irwin Friend and Marshall E. Blume, after consulting their printouts, concluded:

"Mutual funds showed neither superior nor inferior ability to direct capital into those areas of economic investment which subsequently turned out to be most profitable."[1]

The visibility of fund performance has proved a handicap, so much so that John C. Bogle, president of the $1.3 billion Wellington Fund, sadly admitted,

"[Our] performance on the upside has been inferior, and on the downside hasn't been much better."[2]

To indicate how the thinking of some of the "professional managers" goes, let us peek into the SEC's complaint in the notorious Parvin-Dohrmann case (another bag job).

Remember Jerry Tsai, the boy genius at Manhattan Fund? There is no truth to the rumor that the fund is moving to The Bronx. He was not so dumb, having sold out to CNA Insurance for millions. His shareholders may not have done so well. As the Washington *Post* of November 2, 1969, reported on the SEC's complaint,

"William Scott, Parvin's president, phoned an analyst at Tsai's shop and told him that, while Parvin would be writing off a lot of money for 1968, it would report the resulting loss concurrently with

[1] *Wall Street Journal*, August 14, 1970.
[2] *Forbes*, March 1, 1972.

earnings for the first quarter of 1969, which would be 'very substantially higher.'"[3] Tsai Management then bought more than 49,000 shares of Parvin for the accounts of three funds it manages.

"On April 7, the complaint says, Tsai Management sold 3,000 shares of Parvin for one of its funds. The next day, Scott called the analyst and told him the earlier information 'still held.' Between then and April 18, Tsai turned in its tracks and bought an additional 11,000 of Parvin, according to Capital Gains Research Bureau, which keeps track of fund holdings."[3]

It should be noted that the SEC was not making any charge against the funds. They were merely showing how, in their view, the stock was manipulated. The funds were not doing the manipulating; rather, it would appear that they were the manipulated. The stock did not do well.

It all shows up in fund performance, of course. To compound the error, fund managers sometimes shoot off their mouths to the press, a fact that again puts their judgment in the spotlight.

If Not the Funds, Maybe the Insurance Companies or Banks

When the Philadelphia Phillies changed their name some twenty-five years ago after finishing last in the National League, columnist Tom Meany remarked, "Come out, fellows, we know you."

Those inquisitive Wharton School professors removed the cloak of secrecy[4] surrounding the performance of banks, insurance companies, and investment advisers on February 16, 1972. As the New York *Times* reported that day on their findings, "There are no sizable differences among the investment performances of various institutional groups between their results and the general market."

More specifically, James Sharkey, who works for a computer consulting firm in Denville, New Jersey, did a study of the way six major banks handle individual accounts. As reported in the *Times* of September 30, 1969, he found that "the so-called portfolio reviewer who manages 'Aunt Elizabeth's' money ordinarily oversees perhaps 300 to 400 similar but widely varying accounts totaling $70 million to $80 million."

[3] Washington *Post*, November 2, 1969.

[4] Not so secret to some of the "little old ladies" who have seen their stock values stagnate in bank trust accounts.

The function of a portfolio manager, therefore, is usually that of a clerk, for which he is paid generally about eight thousand dollars a year according to Sharkey.[5] The bank has no way of checking up on him to see if its recommendations are followed nor to monitor his performance.

Mr. Sharkey noted that beneficiaries are "locked into a trust setup by persons now dead. They have great difficulty getting through to the bank and getting results," he told *Times* man Robert Metz.

In one instance, one twenty-five-year-old fellow had inherited a trust and, "He didn't hear a word for over two years—no statements, nothing. When he investigated he found 40% of the money was invested in municipal bonds." These are usually bought for high-income people who wish to escape taxes.

"But he was in the 20% tax bracket—or thereabout—so the yield on this bond was around 4%. He would have been better off if the money was in the bank's savings department."

Mr. Sharkey told the reporter of other such inanities. But the reason Mr. Sharkey was talking at all was that his firm was setting up a system for banks to monitor their trust accounts, presumably so that their investment research people and portfolio managers could more directly effect changes in stock portfolios. Judging by the Wharton School study and other stories I've heard about bank stock market activities, maybe the investor would be better off left alone.

And I know of another gentleman whose mother-in-law had received $100,000 in 1941 from her late husband's estate. After thirty years the bank had run the portfolio value "up" to $90,000 in toto.

The billion-dollar Fiduciary Trust Company of New York has advertised in the *Wall Street Journal* saying, "We don't publish anything." I can understand that.

In a study by the actuarial firm of A. S. Hansen, bank-run pension funds averaged a return on only 1.5 percent during the 1966–70 period. Insurance companies averaged 1.2 percent, while mutual funds did only somewhat better at 2.5 percent, as reported by *Forbes*, May 1, 1972. Thus you can understand why some banks are spinning off their investment advisory sections to operate independently—they would be less recognizable as bank trust departments.

Yet the media still refer to the practices of these money managers

[5] It has since been raised a few thousand.

as though their expertise were manifest, viz., the following quote from the Newark *Star-Ledger* of October 28, 1971: "Bank trust managers don't follow fads in buying or selling stock. Their method is stringent selectivity based on careful analysis of industry and company prospect."

The question rises from the ashes of trust accounts, "Why don't they do better?" Some possible answers were presented by an ex-trust analyst turned investment counselor in the September 1968 issue of *Institutional Investor* magazine. "The major problem that a bank has in managing money is simply size," he said. The holdings in particular issues are so immense they present a problem when the bank decides to unload.

When a *sell* is ordered on such an issue, "everybody runs for the [telephone] at once and the last customer gets mauled." And of course if you are that customer, too bad.

Naturally realizing this, assuming they care, that is, the bank might not sell when it should do so, much like the effect upon a jury that contemplates sending the defendant to the death house, whereupon their reluctance to do so affects their judgment of his guilt.

Another problem, according to an ex-trust man, is that "Banks are structured to prevent a capable man from doing a good job. There are a number of coaches; the head of research, the head of trust investment, and the man who, as I did, runs the advisory operation. What the manager tells the coach is this: 'OK, coach, go to it. Here are the restrictions and, of course, I have veto power. But I'll fire you if you don't do a good job.'"

This former bank man also rails against the committee system. Many good analysts told me they were frustrated when their recommendations were turned down, only to find the trust committees reversing themselves later, at higher prices. And the continued refusals by the committee, particularly in view of the stock selections having worked out favorably, eventually turn the analysts to some other form of endeavor. And then there is the long waiting period before the trust committee, which generally oversees all investments, can meet and agree to buy the stock. Very often that waiting period results in the trust department paying too much for stocks.

Another problem voiced by the former bank hand is that accounts are bounced from manager to manager. Furthermore, administrative detail takes too much time away from portfolio managing, and so on.

Here's what the managing editor of *Barron's,* Alan Abelson, said about bank portfolio managers on May 29, 1972:

"Little Orphan Annie. We must confess we don't follow with the anxious assiduity we once did the adventures of that ageless moppet, but one thing we've never forgotten about the kid—she always wore the same dress. Actually, we're convinced, in real life Little Orphan Annie has grown up and is now a senior portfolio manager for one of the larger bank trust departments. For that singular single-mindedness in choice of clothing suggests the kind of approach to stock selection which characterizes the breed. Not only do they buy the same stuff day after day, week after week, but they also do so in virtual concert. To paraphrase our Vice President, if you've seen one trust portfolio, you've seen them all. Not that we're implying collusion on the part of these institutional investors. Nothing conscious about it, we're convinced (any more than there typically is about their process of investing)."

The basic situation is that there isn't that much analytical talent to go around. The analyst profession is not like that of the medical, law, or engineering, all of whom have their problems. Indeed, if engineers had as much ability as the average bank (or investment counselor), it would be a risky thing to drive your car across a bridge.

It Pays Off, Anyway

Charisma, it seems, does pay off. One economist[6] reportedly gets a four-thousand-dollar minimum for his speeches before business groups and investor mockups, not to mention a hefty fifty-thousand-dollar fee for the privilege of talking to one of his analysts and listening to "Mission: Impossible"-like tapes that self-destruct after delivering their magisterial messages from on high. This, plus the honor of meeting the master occasionally, makes up the package.[7] I have even heard that his speeches were quite entertaining.

[6] As Shaw said of the breed, "If all the economists were laid end to end, they wouldn't come to a conclusion."

[7] *Forbes,* March 15, 1972.

But entertainment was not what investors got who bought the Rinfret Fund in 1970 or early 1971.

Pierre had apparently made the mistake of exposing his stock selection record to public scrutiny when he launched the fund a few years previously.

"In 1971 with the Dow up 6.1%, the S&P 500 [Standard & Poor's] up 10.7% and Arthur Lipper Corp.'s mutual fund industry average up 18%, Rinfret's two-year-old Rinfret Fund grew a meager 4.2%," besting only the very ten worst performing funds in the nation, *Forbes* noted in its March 15 article.

"I'm totally dissatisfied with our performance in 1971," said Rinfret.

Economists, when they stick to their lasts, make predictions as much as five years ahead, which has the added protection of reader memory problems. "At least spell my name right," as the saying goes.

Adviser's Adviser

"Let me make one thing clear. I am not in the market guessing game. Nor am I a market technician," a famous economist told New York *Times* man Vartanig G. Vartan on November 1, 1971.

"Then how do you regard your role?" the writer queried.

"My role is to be an adviser's adviser."

The interviewer noted that the "adviser's adviser" had advised "some forecast misses."

This did not deter the economist, Eliot Janeway, from saying subsequently, "I see the Dow getting down to 500 in 1972 as a test level." To some market observers, Mr. Janeway's bearishness has been chronic and therefore suspect. Their cynicism is perhaps overdone, since it did take four weeks for the Dow to actually reach its bottom for the then recent period, after which it soared some hundred points in the following three months from the point at which the prognostication was made. Still, Mr. Janeway remains a popular speaker at businessmen's and broker's affairs. He is apparently forgiven—and, after all, 1972 isn't over, yet. Since I know of no records being kept of Mr. Janeway's other predictions, he should be given the benefit of the doubt.

Others did not give him that benefit, and Mr. Janeway became the butt of market observers' wisecracks as the market rose after his statement. Heinz H. Biel, for example, writing in *Forbes* of May 1, 1972, said,

"It goes without saying that a bull market is a most enjoyable period for all investors, except for the small minority of speculators who took premature short positions, or the would-be stock buyers who were left out in the cold because they listened to perpetual bears like Mr. Janeway."

That came out, of course, after the market had gone to 975 on the Dow. But immediately on the heels of the "Adviser's adviser's" prediction, letters flew from the angry pens of *Times* readers. Peter K. Dunk wrote to the paper's financial editor, "Your question and answer interview with Eliot Janeway [Nov. 1] borders on irresponsible journalism.

"You have included an opinion from a security industry 'Cassandra' which is just that—opinion not facts on the financial page.

"What right have you," he asked, "as a paper to editorialize opinion about the stock market in a section of the paper supposedly devoted to the presentation of financial facts?"

To which I might add, "Oh, *that's* the section devoted to facts! I always thought it was the obituary section." Actually, I applaud the *Times* piece—and others devoted to examining Wall Street ideas. They need all the exposure they can get.

M. D. Kornfield wrote, ". . . Mr. Janeway is a chronic bear, often not right, and also often takes credit where credit is not due. During the previous bear market when the D.J. reached 650, he predicted it would go to 500, whereas in fact it turned and rose to about 950. . . .

Mr. Paul E. Deutsch also disputed Mr. Janeway's claim to have called the market in 1970—and Mr. Reuben Rosenberg slammed the whole "fraternity" when he wrote, "The trouble with the market these days is that there are too many so-called analysts and advisers who hurt the investor, rather than help him."

But all the preceding goes to show that Mr. Janeway is only human . . . a point that he underscored when he *also* wrote a letter to the financial editor,

"I want to reply to the stock-market followers who have recently set themselves up as authorities on some of my past judgments. . . .

"First," he said, "I did not predict 500 on the Dow as a magic number which would immutably mark the bottom of the bear market that came out of Lyndon Johnson's Vietnam escalation.

"I projected 500 as an eventual test level—and not necessarily as bottom—because I anticipated that better-grade industrial equities would offer a 6 per cent yield basis by the time the bear market had run its course."

Though the vaunted "adviser's adviser" did not mention specific stocks when interviewed over the airwaves, more than once I heard him counsel his listeners to buy real estate. Perhaps Mr. Janeway was being somewhat subjective, for he had made a substantial commitment, probably his largest investment, in a company listed on the American Stock Exchange that dealt in the field. Mr. Janeway is an "insider" in this company, Realty Equities, but apparently his inside position did not qualify him to be one of the informed minority. Mr. Janeway had acquired 46,213 shares in his own name, in partnerships, and in his own company by December 1968. At that time, the stock sold as high as $37 a share, with a total market value of over $1.7 million.

What happened since? In an attempt to certify Realty Equities' financial statements, the company has gone through four accounting firms in three years. In fiscal 1971, Realty showed a loss of $4.5 million, and for the nine months ending in December 1971, it lost $3.2 million. The stock has acted accordingly, falling to a $2.50 bid on the over-the-counter market by March 1972, the stock having been delisted. Mr. Janeway's stock thus would be worth only $115,000 (vs. $1.7 million) except that he bought more in March 1970 and in May 1971, all according to SEC reports.

What better person to be the author of the book, *What Should I Do with My Money?*, issued in 1971.

four

Your Own Early-Warning System, or When the Action Is

Buying Bargains

The informed minority, as we have said, generally buys at wholesale and sells at retail. But how are they able to do so in a market that at first appearances allows an opportunity for all to participate on equal terms? First, the informed minority can buy stocks *when earnings are severely depressed*—when they foresee a turnaround. The investor normally views "good" earnings as being bullish and "bad" as being bearish. Since one would expect good earnings to accompany higher prices and poor earnings to mean lower prices, the informed minority may buy when the lower earnings lead to lower prices (wholesale) and sell when a "turnaround" in earnings is effected, leading to higher prices (retail). The investment analyst sometimes aids and abets this practice, particularly in the case of the institutional investor, who is sucked into the game at, shall we say, inexpedient times.

Another device the informed minority may seize to effect his wholesale buying and retail selling is the totally independent action of governments that serve to depress prices. A case in point was the seizure by the Mexican Government of sulphur shipments, depressing stock prices of the producers in 1966. Other types of opportunity occur when, for example, an agricultural crop is afflicted by disease or poor weather, a government action lowers or raises taxes particularly affecting a certain industry, or a realignment of currencies aids or hampers exports.

And there is the effect of *a change in dividends.* Actions by corporations can depress stock prices, such as the cutting or omitting of dividends, which will be detailed later in this chapter. Conversely, stock prices are often boomed by the addition or increase in dividends, particularly when the action or actions are effected frequently in short time spans and/or when the raise is violent. The accompanying stock price advance (which may occur over a period of time) may aid in the obtaining of a "retail" price for informed minority shareholders. This may shock investors who are under the impression that corporations are run for their benefit even if they would disdain the notion that politicians exist to better the public welfare, rather than their egos or pocketbooks.

Splits

Another device to affect "retail" prices is *the split.* In the more common type, shares are increased in number, with each resulting share retaining the same relative stockholder ownership of the company. Thus, when American Telephone & Telegraph was split in 1964 on a two-for-one basis, common share owners then owned two for the one they had before. But since there were twice as many shares outstanding as before the split, the relative ownership in the company represented by the shares remained the same. Thus, in terms of equity in the corporation, splits do absolutely nothing. They do, however, tend to attract investors—and one may say that this is their principal *raison d'être.*

The converse of the conventional split we have found to be especially bullish over the long term, even though it too does nothing to enhance stockholder equity. It is a rarely used device, however. It is the *reverse split,* which device may, assuming it is a voluntary action,[1] enable the informed minority to buy stocks at wholesale levels, for it apparently often frightens or dismays the average stockholder. Whereas the investor seems to think he had more because he had twice as many shares, the reverse split gives him fewer shares than he had before. Whereas he may have owned

[1] On occasion the American Stock Exchange forces companies to reverse split possibly to counter the impression that it is a low-priced stock exchange.

a hundred shares of XYZ[2] Corporation, after a reverse split he then, let's say, holds only fifty; or one for four gives him only twenty-five. So there the guy finds himself an odd-lotter.

"Me—an odd-lotter! Are you calling me a 'little guy'? I can afford to buy round lots—I don't have to fool around with little pieces," is the typical investor's reaction to a reverse split. Indeed, much of past mutual fund growth can be attributed to the abandonment of the investors' odd-lots for fund shares.

Irrational as odd-lot psychology is vis-à-vis round lots, it is also destructive to his equity values. We put the twenty-one (reverse splits are not common) split reverses found in the over seventeen-hundred-stock chart book of Horsey & Co. into a computer, and it spewed out the following data:

1. Eleven of them (53 percent) rose during the eighteen-month period following the reverse split.
2. If all the stocks had been held for more than eighteen months, eighteen (86 percent) would have shown rises following the reverse splits.
3. The actual price rise of the entire group in the eighteen-month period was 97 percent.
4. The actual price rise for the period over eighteen months was 178 percent.
5. On a yearly basis, the longer-term holding averaged a 55 percent gain.

Please note that points 4. and 5. have excluded Monogram Industries, whose 2600 percent gain would have distorted the figures.

Following is a chart that shows how many stocks advanced to what degree for the *stocks held longer than eighteen months:*

[2] XYZ Corporation has had a sparkling record of adapting to change. In 1900 it made horseshoes; it switched to tires in 1930, to airplane loading gears in 1949, to computer processing in 1963, to operating nursing homes in 1966, and to "soft" lenses in 1971. The stock is not available in this country, being traded on the Casbah Exchange by a small man with beady eyes and a German accent who appeared as a double for Peter Lorre in an old Bogart movie.

Stocks gaining:	*No. of Stocks*
over 500%	1
250%–499%	5
100%–249%	10
50%–99%	2
less than 50%	3
TOTAL	21

NOTE: Most companies that were observed in this study reverse split their stock from 1962 through 1965, so that we now have succeeding time to measure performance.

And if these figures are not enough, we have come up with additional data to help the investor:

1. If a stock that reverse splits shows *no* price rise within eighteen months after the split, it is likely to show an ultimate *below-average* price rise after the eighteen months. Stocks that show some price rise (greater than 20 percent) within the first eighteen months will tend to show an *above-average* price rise after the eighteen-month period. Thus one could improve performance by waiting eighteen months after the reverse split—or by buying stocks that split, say, two years earlier, if they showed more than a 20 percent total rise since the split.
2. Another phenomenon the computer discovered was that 75 percent of those stocks observed *dropped* in the succeeding few months after the reverse split. Thus waiting out the two months after the split will give you a significant increase over the 178 percent and 55 percent gains shown in points 4. and 5. above.

The Dividend Game

Div′-i-dend. A sum or quantity, usually of money, to be divided among stockholders, creditors, members of a cooperative, etc. (Webster's New World Dictionary).

The informed minority doesn't always operate out in the open. You can't always find their trading in the SEC reports—for they aren't always insiders. On the other hand, the public, when they *do* move, often move into and out of stocks for rather obvious reasons and in rather obvious ways. Few people today buy stocks *purely* for the purpose of collecting dividends, though many do take this facet into account when deciding on a purchase. It appears that the informed minority does too, our studies indicate, but in surprising ways.

A statistically sound "informed minority" indicator has evolved in our search for the "footprints" of the group that has yielded startling results over a period of time. This indicator is based on dividend action by corporations and is based on a study of companies listed on the New York Stock Exchange during 1967. Where there was a specific dividend action, we followed the stock's performance for twenty-two months, to be careful of avoiding "fluke" happenstances.

What are dividends? Corporations pay them, apparently sharing out their earnings. Corporations (on occasion) make profits as a result of sales of products or services. Part of this money is plowed back into the company to pay for expansion, modernization, or the like. Part of it is paid back to the stockholders in the form of dividends. This is the standard explanation you can find in textbooks and popular reading on the stock market. You will also read elsewhere that stockholders can hold onto stocks, watch their dividends increase over the years, and so eventually gain a handsome return on their money. This is true, in part. But it does *not* explain how *the uses of dividends can play a part in the accumulation and distribution of stocks by the informed minority.*

To utilize this tool in your profit-making (as a clue to the operations of the informed minority), we must delve somewhat deeper than is usually done in textbook discussions of the subject.

If dividends were what they seem to be, according to the popular understanding, then the prices of stocks should rise when their dividends do—*and fall when their dividends fall, right?*

Wrong! A little detective work on the subject reveals that, for example, in 1967, seventeen stocks we studied[3] had their dividends cut or omitted. Horrors! Better sell—for this means that the company is not doing too well. Look—they can't even pay dividends to their stockholders; or they have to resort to reducing them to make ends meet. This, again, is the "popular" or textbook version.

[3] Names of the seventeen and the dividend action dates were provided by Harry Lankford ("Quote N.Y." chart service) P.O. Box 213, Wichita, Kansas 67201.

Examination reveals, however, that of the seventeen stocks, *seventeen rose during the period following the cut or omission.* That's no misprint—it was seventeen out of seventeen! And yet, presumably cutting (or omitting) dividends is a bad sign. Our studies also reveal that of the seventeen, four rose 100 percent or more, five rose between 50 percent and 99 percent, and seven rose 10 percent to 50 percent.

The average price rise was 78 percent. One (American Zinc) rose 24 percent in only two weeks. The range of increases was 10 percent to 350 percent.

How long did it take on the average? Well, here's the breakdown.[4] The average waiting time from the dividend action to the maximum price rise was fifty-two weeks. Five stocks rose to their maximum price level within ten weeks after the dividend cut or omission. One rose to its maximum within twenty-two weeks. Four did it in forty-eight to fifty-five weeks. Seven took the eighty to ninety weeks' observation period and were still climbing at the end of it. How much did they rise? Seven of the stocks rose between 10 and 50 percent, and five jumped a whopping 50 to 90 percent. Four flew to 100 percent after the "damaging" action of having their dividends cut or omitted.

We also studied the difference between cutting and omitting, to see which yielded better results. One would expect that eliminating a dividend would be more bearish than cutting it (according to standard or textbook versions). Our analysis showed that it was more bullish. Stocks that had their dividends cut averaged less gain than those that had their dividends dropped entirely. Cuts averaged 48 percent gain; omissions, 100 percent.

If you were to use only this indicator, you would typically wait one year to gain an over-all average of 78 percent on your money. The hitch is that you cannot buy all of them. However, this informed minority indicator has certainly proved its merit—and is added to the other indicators mentioned so far.

Incidentally, for comparison, the New York *Times* index rose 12 percent during the period and the Standard & Poor average rose 23 percent.

[4] The period of observation was January 2, 1967 to November 1, 1968.

Short Sellers–the Real Pros

"Brokers also attributed some of the early strength yesterday to short covering or buying to replace borrowed shares that had been sold earlier."[5]

Perhaps in the spring a young man's fancy turns to thoughts of love–but it is probable that such musings are not limited by the calendar. There is one phenomenon that *is* virtually limited by the dateline, and that is the crowding around the Dow Jones news ticker in boardrooms around the country, particularly in bull markets, when the "short interest" appears, generally about the eighteenth or nineteenth of the month.

The pushing and shoving to get a look at how his stock stands in the short-interest derby is almost as hectic as the scene at a ladies' bargain basement sale. The cries of "Who took Fairchild off the list?" is almost like the plaintive cry of a man who's been robbed, and the analogy is real to some–for in the mythology of the Street, the short interest in a stock is sometimes considered as vital as its balance sheet.

Again from the *Wall Street Journal* (this time on April 22, 1966): "Brokers said the market again was helped by the high mid-April short-interest position," and,

"Some brokers regard short interest as potential demand for stock. 'The market took heart from the high short position,' commented one broker."

Many advisory services also view a high short position as bullish; note the following from the *Dines Letter* of September 22, 1967: "The fewer the outstanding shares, the harder it is for shorts to find stock with which to 'cover'–adding upside potential. *Avoid shorting those issues closest to the top of the list, and especially those of rising* [increasing short position total] *rank.*"

What is this "business" of short position, believed (by the majority of market observers) to be so bullish?

The short seller sells stock he does not own and replaces it at some future time, hopefully at a profit. A broker, upon receiving an order from a customer, "borrows" the stock from another customer (or another brokerage firm's customer).

[5] *Wall Street Journal,* April 11, 1968.

One "sells short" if he expects the stock to go down. The conventional buyer expects his stock to go up, and so "buys" the stock—or in Wall Street terminology, "goes long." *The short seller profits when his stock falls, loses when it goes up.* For most people, this is quite confusing—yet the practice (without the terminology) is common in business. The magazine publisher sells what he does not own when he sells you a subscription. He takes the money and returns it to the buyer, say, in two years (minus profit) in the form of the magazine every month. When borrowing money from a bank, the bank is not giving you its money, but the money of its depositors.

Who sells short? Largely professionals. Most short selling is done by either specialists on the floor of the exchanges or member firms for their own account. "The public" sometimes tries short selling but to an amazingly small degree. Indeed, I suspect the individual who does so rarely makes a profit, principally because he panics and "covers" (buys) at a higher price.

A mythology persists; the popular belief is that high short interest is bullish. The rationale is that the short sellers are potential buyers—and that their buying will "support" the stock if it should fall. Also, when the short position rises dramatically, this creates a "squeeze" position wherein all the little shorts will run for the exits—only there won't be any. This naturally will drive the stock up—and we'll all make a lot of money selling the stock at a higher price.

Unfortunately, however, there is no Santa Claus on Wall Street. We took sixty-five stocks that showed a hundred thousand shares short or more at any time during the year of 1967, and carried the figures through the end of the year. We noted the price each month of the year at around the time the short figures were released. Then we gave the data to a client-statistician.

He ran all the data through a computer to determine just what happened. He found:

"*A sudden increase in the short interest of a stock will not usually lead to a price increase in the stock, but in fact will tend to lead to a price decrease.* Data on sixty-five stocks yielding fifty-four observations tend to support this theory."

Specifically, let us see what the computer-based studies showed.

1. A 25–50 percent *increase* in the short interest will cause a 20–30 percent *decrease* in the price of the stock.

2. Lag time, or the time between the sudden rise (up from one hundred thousand shares) in the short interest and the price rise of the stock, averages about four months, but ranges from as short as one month to over twelve months.

3. Our results do not appear to work on lower-priced stocks. We don't really know why, but it might be that the "smart money" does not short low-priced issues.

4. The method appears to work best on stocks that have little fluctuation in the short interest *before* the sudden rise in the short interest—and it appears best to wait for about two to three months to make certain you have little change in short interest first. Then when the steep rise occurs, you may have something.

5. Also, contrary to the mythology of the Street, sudden drops in reported short interest are particularly bullish. Possibly the "smart money" knows something, since this leads to a rise in the price of the stock, averaging 25 percent in about four months.

6. A stock that fluctuates widely has not been considered in this analysis; it appears that widely fluctuating securities do not follow any particular pattern in their price movements. The reason for this is unclear; however, I ought to point out that this interpretation of our data might be simply because I have been unable to clearly see a correlation that in fact may be present. Frankly, it is very hard to get a handle on stocks that fluctuate widely. Too many factors become important in the analysis of these stocks.

Table A. Breakdown of Analysis between Short-Interest Volume and Subsequent Stock Price Movements

Part 1: The short-interest volume suddenly *increased*

73%	27%	100%
Price down	Price up	

Part 2: The short-interest volume suddenly *decreased*

72%	28%	100%
Price up	Price down	

Table B. Stocks Selling under $25

80%	20%	100%
Did not work	Worked	

Theory & Corollary of short interest

Now that we know what short interest signifies, you may follow it (published monthly in most newspaper financial sections and certainly in the New York *Times, Wall Street Journal,* and *Barron's.*

The data is there. But it doesn't fit into the Establishment philosophy of investing, as I explained once in an open letter to money managers:

Dear Mr. Young Tiger:

Your institution's Board will never accept your explanation of why you sold out in November of 1968, or May of 1969, or November of 1969, or September of '71. Never matter if your performance might double. When next you meet the board or your trustcommittee and are asked why you sold their favorite stock, your answer would get a reception not unlike the one that "my astrological chart told me to sell," or the attitude your overseers would adopt if you told them you sold because "I was in a selling mood." No, it will never do. You cannot tell them the truth, "I sold because the specialists on the floor of the New York Stock Exchange and the other members of the exchange were selling short in their own accounts." This method, obviously, is "technical,"–it has nothing to do with the earnings prospects (i.e., the propaganda) of the company, the price–earnings ratio (which is really technical but now widely accepted), or the return on equity. You cannot even tell them that you had a tip from a broker, because this isn't true, though they are more likely to approve this rationale. It would do no good to tell your inquisitors that judging major market moves correctly is as important as picking stocks, even though that appears to be the case.

No, it is better to play the game. Perhaps doing so has hurt your personal achievement standards, but it also keeps you employed at twice the pay you could make if you took a real job. There aren't many engineers or industrial designers or advertising copywriters who make what you do or have your prestige in the neighborhood. Bucking the system would mean leaving it—and the rewards and comforts are too great. And there is always the hope that if you're a good boy, you'll end up managing private money and make megabucks. Still, couldn't an outstanding record do that? No, too risky in the meantime. However, just for an academic exercise, let us see if a method can be devised to judge the important market moves, based on historical precedent and a little-used device of *studying the actions of specialists and members trading for themselves.* After all, it does sound plausible that they should know what's going on down there amid the tumult and the shouting at Broad and Wall. Perhaps they have no "inside information," but it is possible that these people are better able to judge the supply and demand relationships of stocks which, after all, is a prime reason why stocks go up or down anyway (but let's not tell anybody). The only problem in this experiment is that possibly they can only judge (if at all) the *short*-term moves, which would be of little use to an institution of your size. If it could call the immediate or long-term action, that *would* be something.

Putting aside the charge that specialists on the floor of the New York Stock Exchange "manipulate" stock prices (anyone even remotely familiar with the goings on at Broad and Wall can tell you otherwise), how do they do at making money for themselves, and better still, can we follow them to make money for ourselves? The function of the specialist, according to the NYSE constitution, "in addition to the effective execution of commission orders entrusted to him, is the maintenance, in so far as is reasonably practicable, of a fair and orderly market on the Exchange in the stocks in which he is so acting."

Nevertheless, in some instances they have been known to be concerned with the profit motive. How good are they at it? Individual specialists have been known to suffer under the blows of wild selling bombardments and buying panics. To accommodate a substantial buyer (an institution, for example), a specialist will have to supply stock when there are no sellers within a reasonable markup from the last price. He will at some point "short" stock to the buyer at prices (1) that he feels can be justified under the "orderly market" doctrine, and (2) where he is likely to make a profit. For example, say fund XYZ wants to buy twenty-five thousand shares of Cockamaymie Industries (formerly Decalamania Corporation). The stock last sold at fifty dollars. Assuming that the fund's broker comes back with an indication from the floor that he would have to pay up to fifty-two dollars on a sliding scale, this might work out at five thousand shares at fifty dollars, five thousand at fifty-one dollars, and five thousand at fifty-two dollars. The last five thousand might be the specialist shorting five thousand shares for his own account, with the others coming from other sellers. The specialist feels that he can make a profit at that price by covering his short on the way down, as the stock has "exhausted itself" by running up so fast and is likely to attract sellers at the high price. He may, since he doesn't pay a commission, make a profit on only a quarter of a point, or he may hold out for more and end up wealthier. It is his judgment that decides these things, and obviously he is taking the risk that other buyers will come in and drive the stock up more. His judgment on such trades is put to the test many times a day, depending on the stock's volume, and the results show themselves in the fact that few specialists ever go under—and some have been around for fifty or more years, passing on to their offspring the awful responsibility.

That their business is profitable can thus be taken for granted, although at certain points of time they can, possibly temporarily, take quite a beating. I heard of one fellow, an old-timer, who lost a cool million a day for two weeks when he "absorbed" a secondary in a blue-chip issue. He recovered eventually (it happened a few years ago) and is still in business.

The question of the moment is: Can we observe specialist dealings and use this information to call the market's shots? The answer is yes, to a certain extent. We can do it by noting specialist dealings on *Barron's* Market Laboratory page or by subscribing to the SEC's *Statistical Series,* which, by the way, is free by mail.

What is the indicator? It is the number of shares sold short by specialists on the floor of the exchange, as a percentage of the total shares sold short, on a weekly basis. Thus if the specialists sell 1.5 million shares short in a particular week during which three million shares are shorted, the figure is 50 percent. We have found that a typical figure is 55 percent, which is to be considered normal and therefore not significant. When the figure drops below 50 percent, the result is quite bullish, and when it rises to 67 percent, it is bearish for the market. With some exceptions this has been a handy guide to *major* moves in the Dow, which may surprise some who regard it as a trading tool. It would, for example, have gotten you out of the market in November of 1968, again in May of 1969, and in November of 1969, and in September of 1971, after which substantial market drop occurred. This indicator, like some others you have known, is no magic button to riches, however. There are times when it doesn't work, and thus we have had to develop other parameters utilizing other member firm *buying* and *selling* for their own account, their short sell-

Table C. Significant Buy (B) and Sell (S) Points, 1966–70

1966		*1967*		*1968*		*1969*		*1970*	
Mo. and Day		*Mo. and Day*		*Mo. and Day*		*Mo. and Day*		*Mo. and Day*	
2–18	67% S	2–10	67% S	3–1	44% B	5–2	68% S	1–2	68% S
3–4	69% S	3–10	67.5% S	3–8	43% B	5–9	68% S	4–10	43% B
4–15	68% S	6–16	68% S	5–10	67% S	7–18	44.5% B	4–17	40% B
6–26	44.5% B	6–30	67% S	5–17	67% S	7–25	40.5% B	4–24	38.5% B
9–30	44% B	7–7	71% S	5–31	68% S	10–17	68.5% S	5–8	43% B
10–7	38% B	7–14	73% S	6–7	68% S			5–15	37.5% B
10–14	40% B	8–4	67% S	6–14	71.5% S			5–22	35% B
10–28	44.5% B			6–21	68% S			5–29	41% B
				7–12	71.5% S			6–12	41.5% B
				9–27	68% S			6–26	38.5% B
				10–22	68% S			7–3	35% B
								7–10	38.5% B
								7–24	42.5% B
								7–31	39% B
								8–7	40% B
								8–14	32.5% B
								8–21	40% B
								10–23	44% B
								11–20	38% B

ing, and so on. However, let us for the purpose of discussion assume that you are using this indicator alone and see how it has worked.

Taking relatively recent market action, we shall observe first the action in the September–October period in 1966. We divided the 1.5 million shares sold short by the 4 million shares shorted overall in a particular week. This yields a 38 percent figure, which is a "buy" signal. The Dow advanced from about 750 to 880, at which point the figures changed. Note the preceding table.

In early 1966, the Dow Jones Industrial Average had just reached the golden total of 1000; market observers were predicting a rise to 1200, at the very least. During the week ending February 18, specialists on the floor were selling short 67 percent of the total shorting done that week. The institutions were, of course, buying—and the specialists were accommodating them. The specialists continued their apparently bearish ways, and by the week ending March 4, they were shorting 69 percent of the total. The Dow had slipped to 932, and in the words of the financial press at the time, there was "some profit-taking." This euphemism for decline is often used to explain market drops during bull markets, though no one can say for sure that such is the case. Nor is it often observed that those who "took profits" really knew what they were doing and would not come back into the market until prices dropped precipitously lower.

The market continued to fall, and yet the specialists possibly were more bearish than the analysts, who saw the drop as a "technical correction." The specialists were selling short some 68 percent of the total sold short the week ending April 15. The Dow was at 947. By June 26 the market, as measured by the senior average, was at 780. Specialists were shorting only 44.5 percent of the total, and possibly they thought selling by the public was overdone.

The summer rally of 1966 proved to be somewhat elusive, and at the end of the first week in October the Dow had slipped to 744. The specialists again reduced their short selling to only 38 percent of the total, and it would appear that they remained bullish (judging by this indicator) through the month. For the week ending October 14 they were shorting 40 percent, and for the week ending October 28, still to a low degree, at 44.5 percent. It was a period when money was tight and business slow, and one broker was heard to lament, "The market is oversold and my customers are overbought!"

The October 1966 period was one in which the specialists' figures remained at that low point for the longest time since 1962, another buying time for more sophisticated investors. Similarly, the Dow took off during December and January of the ensuing year (1967), to turn in a sparkling 100-point rise. As the move became more frenzied, specialists were forced to supply more stock to the eager buyers, and their short selling increased to the significant figure of 67 percent during the week ending February 10, 1967. Specialist shorting made a saw-tooth pattern, duplicating the 67 percent figure in the week ending March 10 (well, almost duplicating it—actually they surpassed it by .5%). The Dow stood then at 848. After some fiddling around, the market rose again to 885, which found the specialists coming in again with a 68 percent total on June 16 and shorting 67 percent by June 30, with the Dow at 860. Specialists made available stock they did not own (legal—and helpful to maintenance of orderly markets, naturally!) by shorting a whopping 71 percent on July 7, with the Dow hovering at 869.

The following week they upped it to 73 percent. That summer rally *was* a summer rally, and the Dow stood at 923 the week ending August 4. It was a time that college endowment funds were heeding Mr. Bundy's admonition to invest more aggressively rather than hold onto their seedy bond portfolios. They were zigging when they should have been zagging; not the first nor the last time they would do so. Specialists were shorting 67 percent, still a respectably high figure.

The summer headiness of the Dow led to the fall's headachiness of the analysts as the Dow dropped from a high of 951 in mid-September to a low of 839 by mid-November, a drop of some 12 percent. The market looked cheap to some at that point, and nimble traders did fairly well. Watchers of the specialist indicator cooled it, though, and a rise to 920 in early January 1968 was not too helpful to long-termers (insiders of public corporations, one may note, were selling long). The Dow fell with a bang that winter, until it drifted slowly to the 840 area by March. March 1 saw specialists shorting down to only 44 percent, the lowest total since the 1966 bottom. The following week they sold short 43 percent, which may have proved fortuitous for them and their watchers, for the Dow took off on the Johnson abdication announcement on an almost 100-point tear within the space of one month.

Early May saw the market reach a high of 931 and the specialists' totals a high of 67 percent. That's the way it went for the rest of the month and the next, with figures of 68 percent, 71.5 percent, 68 percent, and 71.5 percent as the market rocked in a relatively narrow range. The range was widened somewhat with a neat drop of 70-odd points by August 9. Thereupon, with the specialists shorting 52 percent, the Dow took off again on a 110-point binge as mutual funds, pension funds, bank trust departments, and investment counselors poured on the coal. Meanwhile, back inside the furnace, the specialists threw some coal back, shorting heavily again to supply the increasing demand. The amount reached an interesting 68 percent the last week of September and another 68 percent three weeks later. During this period the Dow averaged around 960, so specialist-watchers did not catch the top. The market reached a pinnacle of 994 on November 29 as the cries of 1200 for the Dow were heard from Wall to Franklin to La Salle to the Avenue of the Stars. Board rooms were crowded again, financial magazines hailed the new era, brokers cheered and often left at three-thirty to play golf or follow other esoteric pursuits. It was easy. The go-go boys were in full bloom, praised by *Time* and gazette.

The Reckoning

The market had a bit of a fall, a hundred points or so, as mutual funds' cash position reached a low point at year end (they were bought up). Specialists' figures did not excite their observers till early March of 1969's 46 percent. And—the Dow subsequently rose to the 970s (974.92, to be exact). Around the time of that peak, you guessed it, the fellows down there did 68 percent of the short selling during the first two weeks of May. Institutions were buying heavily during the period, which is usually the other half of the equation. The more frantic the institutional buying, the more pronounced the specialist shorting to provide them the stock for their ravenous appetites. It may be noted that some of the more aware financial institutions are making attempts to improve their timing, unlike the foundation analyst who told me,

"We never pay attention to the market. We just buy good stocks." In any event, it was a fortuitous time for the watchers of this indicator, for as we all know, a somewhat precipitous drop developed.

On July 18, 1969 at 44.5 percent and on July 25 at 40.5 percent, the aggregate registered a "buy signal." This preceded a 60-point rally until the red flag was hoisted when the number rose to 68.5 percent on October 17, followed by persistent warning indications through the month, with the averages in the 860–67 area. A 100-point drop followed, after which a 50-point recovery occurred. This takes us to the week ending January 2, 1970, when the specialists again stepped up their shorting to the ominous 68 percent level. The subsequent decline from 815 to a bottom of 627 wiped out many a bull market gain, including some investments of a prominent health and accident insurance company's mutual fund, which had been "trading" a mobile home builder. Their last trade stung a bit.

Yet even the specialist figures showed prematurely bullish in April 1970. From then through the May debacle, however, they were shorting lightly: 43 percent, 37.5 percent, 35 percent, 41 percent, and so on. During the week ending June 3, specialist figures were again 35 percent, attesting to the power of the bullish activity. It was a period in which institutional selling reached a crescendo of anguish. To their credit, they came in strongly on the buy side in October and remained bullish, as did specialist short selling right through the rise of 1970–71. Astute financial institutions, able to disdain the popular prejudice against "technical" indicators, could possibly have doubled their long-term performance by investigation of this indicator.

Nothing Always Works

One should note the indicator's "failure" in April to perform in its customary manner. In working out the statistical validity of various parameters using the SEC figures that are released weekly, certain "probabilities" were discovered. This business of judging market moves is really just that—an evaluation of probabilities. This particular facet, specialist shorting, had a 70 percent reliability factor for major moves since 1961. This would, of course, allow for a number of failures—against which one should develop additional parameters to improve performance (the latter again an acceptable word, though also being prostituted to mean chasing after junk). This is especially important, since the likelihood is that as this indicator becomes more popular, it will go the way of others that proved fallible, e.g., *Barron's* Confidence Index, odd-lot activity, and even the venerable Dow theory (which has proved, if not quite wrong, at least woefully late). Another caveat we would suggest is that the efficacy of the specialist in making orderly markets is weakened by third-market block trading. Institutions sometimes take this alternative in an attempt to better their executions. But the more often they do so, the more the specialists' ability to narrow price swings is impaired. Aside from the self-defeating (though defensible) third-market activity, the indicator utilizing specialist short selling may weaken. One can visualize scores of technicians running studies of specialist activity and committing funds to the apparent "signal." Those who wish to utilize this helpful tool should develop parameters on the relationship between buying and selling by specialists, buying and selling by member firms for their own accounts, total member shorting as a percentage of total market short selling, public shorting, etc. The back figures are all published by the SEC to aid in your work. It shouldn't cost you more than $125,000 or so in computer time. Have fun!

This Dynamic Market

The above piece appeared (in somewhat different form) in the March 23, 1971 edition of *Barron's*. The reader will note all the places I warned about overreliance on singling out this method to determine the future course of the market. It didn't help. The three advisory services that I know about, and probably many others that I didn't, seized on it as a market forecaster. Two fellows working in research departments at Chicago banks called me to get the back data on specialist shorting to check it out themselves. Three mutual fund research men added it to their bag of tricks. And I got over a hundred letters from individual investors who wrote that the way *Barron's* listed the data each week confused them, and they asked whether I could explain how to make the calculation so they could do it regularly (and presumably use it to determine buy and sell points in the market). One might guess that this sampling indicates that many hundreds of individual investors took to it, with possibly ten or twenty institutional investors. Actually, their eagerness to do so, while indicative of possibly slipshod research, also indicates the welcome observation that many are willing to investigate new approaches apart from the conventional in improving their performance. Indeed, several large insurance companies, a few medium-size banks and a handful of fund managements have started utilizing the trading done by specialists and other members for their own accounts in *more complete form* (with guidelines of the fourteen component sell signals and twelve component buy signals which, combined, now comprise the method).

The point is that if one used the one indication mentioned in the article (that of the 67 percentage figure of specialist shorting as a percentage of total shorting), one would be just as guilty of shoot-from-the-hip investing as is the conventional approach that has been found so wanting. Specifically, if one were waiting for the 67 percent figure to sell, he would not have gotten the sell signal of October 8, 1971, when the specialists were shorting only 61.7 percent. This preceded a market drop of over 100 points in the Dow Jones average.

And hanging onto any *mechanical* point is, I am afraid, going to lead to poor investor performance because of the dynamic nature of the market. When my statistician, his programmer, his former professor of mathematical statistics, and myself started out with the hypothesis that the specialists and other members of the Exchange were better at calling the market than most others, we did not expect what a Pandora's box of data we would have to sort out to come up with something. After a full year of work, we had come up with only six statistically validated signal components (for example: What is the level of buying to selling by specialists that constitutes a buy or sell signal? What influence does the volume of trading have? Can the level of short *covering* by specialists be measured and utilized? What does the amount of short selling by members other than specialists reveal?, and so on). Only two years later did we come up with twenty-six ingredients to the method to achieve satisfactory predictability.

The problem is that investors too often seize on "magic" formulas. Too often do they assume that making money in the market is easier than their present occupation allows. Anybody for a quick course on brain surgery?

five

"Please Adjust the Color Control, Dear"

In 1964, the popularity of color television was still around the corner. Sets were expensive ($800, $1200, $1500) and less reliable than they are today. Colors were not as "true" as they would later become, with flesh tones particularly bad. Repair costs were high (though they haven't gone down too much), and repairs and adjustments were more frequent. Further, when your set was working, there wasn't much to see. Of the three major networks—NBC, CBS, and ABC—only the first was showing programs in color with any frequency. Of course, NBC had double motivation since its parent, Radio Corporation of America (RCA), also made sets.

So why was Zenith (ZE) one of the "super growth" stocks? It had risen from a 1962 low of $44 to a high of $84 in the fall of 1963. Earnings, on the other hand, only rose from $2.20 per share to $2.30 at 1964's end. It was a classic case of "anticipation." Stocks often go up on the *expectation* of good news, e.g., earnings rises, to a point that they eventually overdiscount favorable happenings.

Zenith would later (in 1968) show earnings of $5.00 a share (unadjusted for a split) and the market, realizing the potential of color TV was beginning to reflect its future growth. Insiders in the companies involved tend to look ahead too, but usually farther ahead than the investing public. The story of the color TV boom has its lessons for readers in "tuning in" on informed minority thinking, which is more often than not a highly profitable way of operating.

Thus it was in the $80 per share area that some of the officers of Zenith took the opportunity to sell some stock. In January, Messrs.

Ferren, Franczak, Kaplan, and Kuhajck got out of some shares as the stock market "realized" Zenith's potential in the color field—and, some would say, overacted in overevaluating. Certainly, the stock's popularity gave the informed minority the opportunity to get higher prices than would be the case when (or if) it would be less so.

As for the other companies in the industry, their stocks were not so "hot," and so there was less reason for insiders to sell. Their time would come later. The financial publications were not eagerly plugging the potential of color yet, though Zenith would seem to have been a forerunner of the setmakers' stocks action to come.

Early Backers

On August 8, 1964, the *Magazine of Wall Street* featured a story on the color TV group, with special emphasis on RCA and Zenith.

"Soaring demand for color TV is the brightest spot in the industry," they reported. They also said that Motorola (MOT) was in production "via National Video" with a twenty-three-inch color tube.[1] NVD had switched its production from black-and-white to color tubes and garnered some fancy contracts from the TV setmakers. NVD's stock averaged around twenty dollars a share for the first quarter of 1964 and appeared headed higher. Generally, however, during this period (except for brief flurries, such as the one of February 12, when it ran up to twenty-three dollars on over fifty thousand shares), NVD was a fairly quiet number. The public had not yet caught on, it appeared. Not yet!

The newspapers were chary about stories of color TV, which may in some measure account for the public's apathy (except, as noted, that Zenith had been a "hot" item before the rest of the industry caught fire). Magnavox was still to have its place in the spectrum in 1965, flashing on the screen from thirty dollars in 1964 to over one hundred twenty dollars in the ensuing two years.

On May 14, 1964, while things were generally muted, the New York *Times* reported that RCA had cut its color television set prices by over 10 percent. The company said it had done so "in an attempt to broaden the market," and this was probably true. Besides price, the sets had been too bulky, and RCA announced that its new tube would be slimmer, allowing for smaller sets.

[1] National Video Corporation (NVD) was making tubes for Motorola.

"Also shown were new 19-inch and 23-inch portable TV sets with new tubes that require no safety glass. These are lighter in weight and less costly," the paper reported. There were, to be sure, technical innovations to improve performance. It was quite apparent—or was it?—that a long-lasting boom would take place that would yield tremendous profits for companies taking advantage of the trend. And certainly RCA, Zenith, and Magnavox were hardly slouches at turning products into sales dollars.

And yet why were insiders in Zenith selling? Why were insiders in RCA and Magnavox not buying? Didn't they know that color TV was here to stay and would get better and cheaper? Could it be that the Zenith brass were selling on strength—that is, *selling at retail prices the stock they had bought at wholesale?* Here again is a mighty important clue the investor should check out before buying stock. He should ask the question, "If it's so good, why doesn't the 'smart money' buy?" Who should know better?

As a matter of fact, some insiders were buying, as any investor could have found out by studying his SEC material. One lonely insider at Zenith bought a bit on the open market on June 26, 1964. More importantly, President Frank Friemann of Magnavox bought six thousand shares of his stock in May and June, with the stock hanging around thirty dollars. In the year and a half following this purchase, the value of his stock *more than doubled.* Was he lucky? An investor buying at the same time as Mr. Friemann (observing the SEC reports) would certainly have considered himself fortunate as opposed to typical investor performance. His buying was a clue that it was still early in the game.

Other insiders were buying stock in their companies through the option route, a less reliable avenue for the investor to follow. Executives are given the perquisite of buying stock in their companies at below-market prices. They expect to sell eventually, and the resultant profit can be seen as a "sweetener" to their salary. This device was originated to entice talent to firms, but its effect has been blunted with its popularity. Obviously if every corporation does it, its value as a competitive tool in drawing wanted executives lessens. There is another rationale: the personal stake the option-buying executive has in the fortunes of his firm, since presumably the better he performs, the more profit the company makes and the higher the stock price, *meaning the more he gets when he sells.*

Observing stock option purchases (they are so identified in SEC reports) have, I believe, less validity than open market purchases for two reasons:

1. Stock option purchases are exercised at less than market prices, so they may be considered "relative bargains" by the executive using them regardless of their potential value.
2. Stock option purchases are generally utilized by lower-echelon people, who presumably are in a lesser position to judge over-all company results than the president or board chairman.

Still, stock option purchases should not be discarded entirely as an investment tool, but merely rated lower on the scale than open market purchases in judging them as clues to informed minority activity.

Admiral versus RCA

An interesting sidelight to the color television story is what appeared to be a tiff between Admiral Corporation and RCA. Up to this time RCA made most of the industries' tubes not produced by National Video. Now, Admiral was one of RCA's customers; but RCA, having close to a monopoly on tube production, was getting some fancy prices. RCA possibly admitted this when it said:[2]

> The sale of color tubes and color sets has been contributing materially to RCA profits in the past two years, but in the light of the substantial investment RCA has made in pioneering color television, we do not feel these profits are unreasonable.

The Admiral president, Ross D. Siragusa, did not agree with this. In announcing his company's decision to produce its own tubes, he said, "RCA had an abnormal profit margin for color tubes it sells to other television manufacturers."

A spokesman for RCA replied, "RCA charges essentially the same for tubes today as it charged ten years ago," rather an oblique answer.

In announcing Admiral's impending tube production, Siragusa

[2] *Times.*

said, "Our target figures indicate the tubes will cost substantially less than what we're paying today."[3]

Aside from the verbal brickbats produced, that last statement was a big red caution light for owners (or future buyers) of stock in National Video. NVD derived virtually all of its profit from the sale of tubes to set manufacturers who did not at that time have color tube facilities of their own. Motorola, as I recall, was their biggest customer at the time. Would MOT, and certainly General Electric (GE), not eventually produce their own? And where would that leave NVD?

A Sharp Picture

Stocks of television setmakers really took off in 1965. Zenith went from a low of $13 in January to $121 in December! Magnavox, as indicated, showed its colors from $32 to $84; staid old RCA reached heights not achieved since the pre-1929 crash days; Motorola tripled; and that little old tubemaker, National Video, began the year at $17 and zoomed as high as $61 on May 11. *Why?*

By March of 1965, purchasers of color sets could watch a somewhat varied color fare on NBC, with 70 percent of their programs spectrumed. Now the company announced that shows in color would be increased to 95 percent by the following season. Of the twenty-nine NBC shows only two were to be in black-and-white—and one of these, "Convoy," was largely made up of footage taken during World War II originally shot in black-and-white. ABC was making plans to show about 6½ hours of color programming each week for the fall. CBS had remained somewhat in the background in this area thus far.

Nostalgia fans might like to recall the names of some of the leading shows of the time—and others may be impressed by the transitory nature of TV programming, noting that none remain today, except as reruns. Here's a sample: "I Dream of Jeannie," "The Wackiest Ship in the Army," "My Mother the Car," "The Virginian," "Daniel Boone," "Hullabaloo," "Run for Your Life," "Please Don't Eat the Daisies," and "The Fugitive." Did I leave out your favorite?

On March 12, 1965, Val Adams wrote on the TV listing page of the New York *Times* that CBS-owned stations would begin showing

[3] Ibid.

films in color in the fall. Now that the "big three" of network broadcasting were going to offer the viewer the variety necessary to entice him to buy a color set, it would seem that the result would be big profits for the setmakers as their market opened up. Indeed, if one factor could be said to most influence the growth of color television in this country, it could be the expansion of color programming. Yet little insider buying showed up in SEC reports.

Why weren't the informed minority in set manufacturing still buying their own stock? They weren't buying because they had already bought. Frank Friemann had bought stock as early as October 1962, when he grabbed up five thousand shares long before the public realized color television's potential, and a month later, Messrs. Kaplan, Robertson, Schroeder, and Truesdell had picked up options in Zenith. In January of 1963, insiders Lynch, Smith, Watts, and Werner of RCA acted similarly toward their corporation's stock. Zenith executive Joseph S. Wright picked up forty-five hundred shares by the option route the same month. In May of 1963, more Zenith executives bought the same way, including Donald MacGregor, Hugh Robertson, and Mr. Wright again. Eight insiders in ZE bought that month, and only one, Leonard Truesdell, sold any. There were also RCA men Douglas Ewing in August and Walter G. Bain in September (the latter at open-market prices). Delbert L. Mills and Theodore A. Smith, also of RCA management, added to their holdings in October, as did Melvin Karns, who bought nineteen hundred shares in the open market in February of 1964. This was the same month that another RCA bigwig, Robert L. Werner, continued his option buying, with eight thousand shares. In April 1964 the RCA men continued their accumulation the same way, this time represented by Arthur L. Malcarney's pickup of three thousand shares.

And so it went. The insiders in the color TV firms were not buying *after* the news was out about color programming expansion, but *before* it. Not that they knew precisely when it would happen. The event might very well have been inevitable. Provided investors could have mustered the patience that most insiders have (though less was required in this market move than most), they could have picked up valuable clues to future profits by scanning the SEC reports for buying indications one, two, or three years back. Checking further, particularly in this case, would probably have yielded the reasons.

National Video got a boost on May 1, 1965 when the New York *Times*, on the first page of its financial section, ran a story that began:

"Sales of color television sets are so strong that a critical shortage of picture tubes has developed." The paper was interpreting a statement by RCA that "called on other set makers to look for other tube manufacturers for their needs," meaning that RCA might ration sales among their set-making customers.

The reader-investor might logically inquire what companies might benefit if setmakers had to turn from RCA to other sources. Farther down in the story the *Times* mentioned that in addition to RCA and Sylvania (a subsidiary of General Telephone) "the other color picture tube makers are the National Video Corporation of Chicago and the Zenith Radio Corporation and its subsidiary, the Rauland Corporation."

The *Times* did not tell investors to rush into their broker's offices to buy NVD, but many quite possibly did just that. Additionally, the Street was made more aware of this relatively unknown company and its "growth potential."

Still Early

Investors could still have bought RCA at around sixty-eight dollars and Magnavox for forty dollars when a story broke in the New York *Times* Sunday business section on May 9: "1965: This is the Year That Was for the Arrival of Color Television in the U.S."

RCA had just announced two days prior that it was running into a tube shortage. And Fred J. Borch, president of General Electric, had already told those at his company's annual meeting, "Color television is the most rapidly growing segment of the consumer goods market." The *Times* also reported in the May 9 article that "Industry statistics have placed color picture tube production for this year at about 2.2 million units," with RCA making about 1.5 million of these and National Video most of the balance.

It was still not too late for investors. For one, stories about the industry were just beginning to invade the press. This was a clue that the cycle of stock price advance and decline was still early in the advance period. For another, prices of stocks in the group had not (except for Zenith) gone up too much. Most were yet to double. Magnavox, for example, had basically traded between thirty and forty-eight dollars in the prior four years. Brokerage firms for the most part had not been hot on the group as yet. Advisory services were still quiet on color TV. Check these factors out when you are thinking of investing next time.

The Ratings System

That television shows stay on the air or are dropped is determined by the number of viewers they attract (enabling network salesmen to sell time to advertisers) is no secret to the viewing public. That stocks go up and stay up or go higher according to the ability of the press and sometimes corporate officials to excite the public's greed responses is less well understood. It is even harder to prove.

I can only say that TV setmakers did seem to make a lot of bullish statements as 1965 rolled on. One can observe that National Video's President Asher J. Cole was reported in the May 15 issue of *Business Week* as saying, "There will be a shortage of color tubes this year and next." And who made these hot items? NVD, of course.

And Joseph S. Wright, president of Zenith (and coincidently a stock buyer) was quoted in the same issue: "There is a good possibility that there will be a shortage of color picture tubes this year if sales demand is in the 2.4 million range." This was apparently because of RCA's decision to cut back production of certain types of tubes, plus the increasing public demand. As for RCA, it was forecasting sales of 2.6 million sets, according to *Business Week* in the same May 15 issue. The magazine described color TV sets as being "this year's most spectacular growth product."

The volume of "good news" was increasing, which should have been a warning to investors. With the middle of June came an RCA announcement that it planned to double tube production, preceding by one week a statement by Sylvania that it too would double output by expanding facilities at its Seneca Falls, New York, factory. The carrot was there—and the public leaped after it. And this carrot was not a pleasing orange but a bright green.

On July 1, Zenith was selling for seventy-four dollars; on September 30 it was at ninety-nine dollars, having topped one hundred dollars four days earlier.

The meteoric rise of the group did not go unnoticed by the financial press. Vartanig G. Vartan, who later wrote a Wall Street novel of passion and death, wrote up the TV group on September 5, which appeared prominently on page 2 of the *Times*' Sunday business section. "Boom Is on for Color TV," it was headlined. "Retail sales of color TV sets have been phenomenal in 1965," Vartan wrote, "and merchants are looking beyond Labor Day for more records to topple. In the stock market, color TV stocks have advanced this summer along with retail sales." Good things were said about RCA, Zenith, Motorola, and Magnavox.

Had Street analysts noticed the stocks? There apparently was nary a bad word said there about the group, and Zenith was especially favored.

"Wall Street analysts note that Zenith has concentrated on consumer electronics while some competitors were busily diversifying into other fields," Mr. Vartan noted. "As a result, the company has become a highly efficient specialist and its growth rate has been much swifter than that of the general industry," he reported Wall Street as saying.

On September 11, *Business Week* weighed in with a story of over three pages on the industry, featuring Zenith. President Wright even made the cover. "Zenith aims at the top in color TV," the story was headlined.

The article ticked off recent happenings, which also provided investors with a handy guide to the profusion of publicity surrounding the leading setmakers at the time. The head of Admiral, readers were reminded, had earlier called the color set business, "the real glamour product of the electronics industry today," and RCA within recent weeks had "cut off sales of color tubes to competing set makers who have other resources, and put other competitors on allocation."

This week [September 11] Motorola, Inc. announced a stepped-up production schedule of 21-inch color tubes in its own plant to be ready for volume production next March." Admiral was also mentioned as promising a 21-inch console with tubes made by National Video.

RCA, said group Executive Vice President W. Walter Watts, was still No. 1 in television, "without a doubt." In the color field, Zenith was quoted as targeting 25 percent of the market in 1965, to which Watts countered, "We'll get much more than that." And *Business Week* said it had a scoop in that Zenith Sales Division President Leonard C. Truesdell would be announcing record orders for both black-and-white and color sets on September 19. Mr. Truesdell had possibly set another record for himself, which was not mentioned. He had grossed some $220,000 in a single day in August on his own Zenith stock sales.

Magnavox's Friemann also sold 14,000 shares. It was easy at the time.

Mr. Truesdell had been quoted in the same issue by *Business Week* as saying about Zenith, "We are stronger, and more consistent, and do a more professional job of managing our inventory than anyone." And who could doubt him? He had effectively reduced his own inventory of stock holdings, selling twenty-five hundred shares of Zenith on August 17.

As all the publicity coming out was (and is) a warning to investors to beware of (or sell) their own stock in the companies mentioned, so did it enable insiders in the color TV group to sell their stock at good prices. Mr. Friemann garnered another (roughly) $700,000 on his stock sales in September.

On September 30, National Video stock zoomed to over $75 a share, completing a 400 percent move in just nine months. It was being mentioned in the same financial breath as RCA, Magnavox, and Zenith, but still being a young company, it would, some investors thought, be another Xerox—a giant in the making. On October 14 it closed at $111, trading 107,000 shares. NVD's public popularity could have been measured by that volume and should have been another warning to investors. Yet it kept climbing for a while, losing sight of itself on the twenty-first at $137 a share, with trading turnover reaching 132,000. Another indicator the investor can use is the short interest, for we have seen that when this rises precipitously, stocks usually fall just as fast. Certainly this was the case in National Video when the huge short position of 165,000 showed up in September. *Note the combination:* a plethora of "bullish" articles on the color TV group, wild price rises on big volume, large short interest in some issues, and insider selling in a distinct pattern.

On October 20 the *Wall Street Journal* front-paged a story about retail prices being raised by Magnavox, a company that had earlier not gone along with previous RCA price cuts.

"The move," said the *Journal*, "was symptomatic of the growing seller's market for color-TV receivers." It was also pointed out that production was not keeping up with demand.

Does P.R. Sell Stocks?

Business Week turned to the color TV group again on October 30 in an article that pulled out all the stops.

"Color TV rides high, selling all it can make," the article said, and it used such phrases as "the hottest product to grace appliance dealers' shelves in years."

A vice president at Westinghouse was quoted in the same piece, "You'd have to be the world's worst salesman, and have bad breath besides, in order not to sell color today." The financial press was using all the copy the industry would provide, as its corollary, insider selling, continued to show up, with three different insiders selling stock in September, followed by four others in October. Mr. Truesdell continued ecstatic about Zenith's business, describing it as "fantastic" in the same *BW* article. It should be noted that he sold only 280 shares this month, and three others in the company sold minor amounts. It was Magnavox's Friemann who really cashed in on all the excitement, but of course he had more stock to sell. Friemann sold some twenty-three thousand shares in a sixteen-day period in October, grossing over a million and a half dollars.

The *Magazine of Wall Street* had some good things to say in its October 27 issue about National Video, some very good things, in fact. The tubes NVD had developed along with Motorola "are in amazing demand," the financial publication said.

"Production is expected to be about one million [tubes] a year by summer 1966." Further, their new rectangular design resulted "in a narrow cabinet, which takes up less space in the living room."

Though qualifying their kudos with a warning that the shares were "highly speculative at current prices," the magazine also predicted a more than doubling of sales for the following year.

National Video's stock had recently been split two-for-one, with the new stock going for sixty-one dollars a share. NVD's split was the harbinger of other splits within the color group, a bearish factor to add to the previously mentioned caveats. Another *Magazine of Wall Street* article on November 27 was headlined, "Demand for Color TV Gaining Momentum." National Video's largest shareholder, Ralph Stolkin,[4] may have noticed the demand for stocks in the group, so his selling picked up noticeably, with 175,000 of his holdings going out on November 15. A month later he eased out of another two thousand shares.

With all the money National Video, Zenith, and Magnavox men were getting out of the color TV boom, perhaps RCA people felt left out. This was not for long, however, as the pattern of big insider selling combined with a good press perked up there, with an RCA corporate official, Kenneth W. Bilby, selling twelve thousand shares in November.

By December of 1965, Zenith was selling for $100 and National Video for $83 ($166 on a pre-split basis). It was time for another write-up by *Business Week*, which came up with "Color TV Makers Dial a Sharp Profit Picture" on December 25, which had more truth than they may have realized.

"The big set makers—and hordes of their suppliers—are racking up record earnings. The sellers market on color TV will help keep them rich for months to come," the magazine said. Translating that to stock sales, particularly in the case of Mr. Friemann, it would keep him rich for years. The sellers' market for stock shares was every bit as good for the informed minority as it was for their sets.

One dissenter was noted on Wall Street by *BW* as saying that "the transition from abnormal to normal conditions would bring an uninspiring earnings trend, even with large increases in volume and reasonable margins." And, we may add in a clichéing vein, seeing the cloud despite the silver lining often brings the pot of gold at the end of the rainbow nearer. Whatever Frank Sleeter, another RCA official, saw, he sold twenty-one hundred shares on December 17.

1966—Year of the Climax

The year 1966 came in as gracefully as Marilyn Monroe and went out as daintily as Ed Sullivan. To some degree, the tone was set at

[4] In SEC reports, all shareholders owning or controlling 10 percent or more of the outstanding shares are so listed. They may or may not be officers or directors, but they are classified as part of the informed minority in our work.

the outset with a January 17 story on the first page of the financial section of the New York *Times*, "Price of TV Sets Expected to Rise." They were talking about black-and-white sets, but also mentioned was that NVD said its tube prices would join the rise. More "good news" for the new glamor stock.

Fortune magazine, in its January 1966 issue, said that "all-day eruption of color on the nation's television screens has produced a red-hot market in color TV receivers." And what would the color boom mean to the set manufacturers? RCA's General Sarnoff said that without color TV, "they'd be out on a corner eating a ham sandwich."

The article told of the battle shaping up for the consumer dollar among the set manufacturers. But perhaps there also was a battle for investor dollars. For some who bought then, and didn't later observe the clues to informed minority stock distribution, their own color sets might have to wait a while (that is, if they expected their profits to buy them one). Yet, at the time, things looked rosy for investors. *Fortune* concluded its story with "One thing is certain: the battle for the glamourous color-television market is going to get a lot hotter. And within four or five years, much of the glamour will be gone." Perhaps some investors thought they would get a nice fat capital gain if they held on that long. It wasn't to be.

On January 20 National Video raised its per-share dividend from six to fifteen cents. It was still pretty low, but the percentage rise was impressive, particularly to the impressionable. One of the informed minority at NVD, Secretary-Treasurer Joseph Grossman, sold ten thousand shares by the tenth of the month—he just didn't wait for the dividend. Mr. Grossman grossed about $780,000, something more than he could get by the dividend route. Had he waited too much longer, he would have gotten considerably less, though the dividend checks would have been larger. Most insiders are in the market for the large capital gains they can get, and poof at the dividends, another lesson for investors.

Another pointer for investors: Mr. Grossman was not selling at the top, but on the way up—as do most of the informed minority. With NVD's short interest still high in January at 137,000, the aforementioned NVD officer-director, Harold Cole, cashed in a few the following month: one thousand shares on the seventh, two thousand on the ninth, and another two thousand on the tenth. Did the split make it easier to sell his stock? Possibly it was a combination of factors—the split lowering the price (but not the equity position of shareholders), the publicity feeding the stock price bonfire, the earnings jump providing the explosive charge, and the noise of it all, making it easier to slip away with a few honest dollars.

Meanwhile, the *Times* performed something of a service—to investors, that is, those who were not so caught up in the euphoria of the activity. On January 16 the paper reported on the helter-skelter increase in productive capacity in tube manufacture then being engaged in by the industry.

Writer Gene Smith questioned whether there might be a risk in overproduction, since this was what had happened before, with black-and-white sets. But RCA group Executive Vice President W. Walter Watts told Smith that he "feels that the industry has learned its lesson and that the use of computers these days helps guide production so exactly that oversupplies are highly unlikely."

If the color TV industry had learned its lesson, it would have been a unique event in corporate practice. The aluminum industry had already overbuilt capacity to the point that it undercut profits, possibly permanently. DuPont had extended capacity and promotion without accurately gauging demand for its Corfam, resulting in a ten-million-dollar write-off in 1971. Ford had its Edsel. The steel industry, by and large, had not modernized into continuous casting processes that European producers pioneered. Eastman Kodak, with all its vast resources, experimented for years with a wet process photo copy system that was doomed to commercial failure (Xerox's process is dry). Borden bungled its way into and out of the ice cream business, and only by 1971 did it cut back on its somewhat ill-fated chemical operations. Two decades of observing corporate activities have led this writer to observe that insiders are much better at managing their stock operations than the companies they run.

Back to RCA, while Mr. Watts appeared hopeful on industry prospects, Mr. Sleeter, another official, had sold his two thousand shares in December, and Delbert L. Mills unloaded sixty-six hundred in February 1966. We cannot say there was any connection; at least during that period of time, Watts himself did not sell.

Another Indicator

Monday, March 7, 1966 began a wild week for the group and showed up another item for the investor's notebook. Admiral fell that day by $7; Zenith fell over $12, traded at 130⅞ Tuesday, and finished at 137¾, up 6⅝ for the day. Magnavox dropped 4½ Monday, fell to 92, and ended half a point over 98, up 1½ on the day. This kind of wild trading is also indicative of near-top action, and should be regarded (at least so it goes in my experience) as another *sell* indication. Also, most of the group made the most-active list.

Another big day was March 28. Motorola jumped 10¼, no doubt helped by the news that it expected to manufacture a full line of semiconductor devices in France. Zenith moved up 4½ the same day. It was a time just before the precipitous market drop that would see the Dow Jones Industrials average plummet from a high just below 1000 that February to 740 in the ensuing months. As March drew to a close, one large broker issued a report that said, "This is the time to consider adding well-selected, quality securities to portfolios—at unusually attractive prices." Two months later the investor could have found those prices even more attractive.

The Cruelest Months

April was a good month in the market (just before the bottom fell out), and what made it particularly good for the color TV group was a rash of good earnings reports for the first quarter. RCA, for example, announced on April 7 that its profits for the period were a record. Net income jumped 24 percent, with sales up 21 percent. Executive Committee Chairman Elmer Engstrom and President Robert W. Sarnoff said that color television continued to play a key role in the uptrend, according to the *Wall Street Journal* of April 8. The company also said that its backlog for color TV cameras (sold to stations) was growing. Electronic components, which included color TV tubes, went up by 30 percent, which showed that they at least contributed their share to the profit rise. RCA also later projected (as reported in the *Wall Street Journal* of April 12) that it would make "more than 2 million tubes" in 1966.

At Zenith, President Joseph Wright noted that "inventories are still very low." He said, "We've had less than a week's supply in the hands of our dealers for many months. We usually try to have five or six weeks' supply, and we prefer seven to eight." They were selling them as fast as they came in—even faster. Would demand ease off? Mr. Wright said he didn't expect any change in the market "for the balance of this year and into next year sometime. . . . We have persistently underestimated the strength of our demand."

Meanwhile, capacity was being built up at Admiral, Sylvania, RCA, Westinghouse, GE, and Zenith.

Inventory at Asher Cole's stock portfolio was having its own housecleaning, as he sold twenty-seven thousand shares in four days in early April, as did other NVD insiders Harold Cole (seven thousand shares), A. D. Giacchetti (who traded in forty-seven hundred for some fund stock), and Robert E. Scharfe who sold twenty-eight hundred, all in April. Could they have seen the handwriting on the tube?

Zenith had sold at $60 a share only a year earlier, as it began April with a tag of $159. This did not go unnoticed, as later in the month their company president, Joseph Wright, sold 3000 shares, with a value of $204,000. A two-for-one split was to be voted the same month. It was during this period also that three officers of RCA sold stock and none bought. The biggest seller was Robert L. Werner, who slid out of 9200 shares.

Perhaps the sellers were aided by another article out of the *Magazine of Wall Street* on March 19. The article said, "Fueled by a broader selection of color programming by the major networks, the demand for color should also be influenced by the following economic factors:

1. As total [consumer] income rises, so does discretionary income (amount left after basic necessities are allocated).
2. Ten years ago only one-quarter of the consumer's income was discretionary, while in 1965 the figure rose to nearly three-eighths, or 37%.
3. Gross national product should rise about 7% during 1966 to the $725 billion level.
4. The propensity of the consumer to spend has been increased by inflation fears."

Noting that Zenith was voting on its split soon, the magazine said, "Furthermore, management is sharing success with stockholders by increasing the quarterly dividend rate from 35¢ to 50¢ with the March 31 payment."

Now, wasn't that nice of Mr. Wright and the other insiders? Oh, by the way, another insider in Zenith, Sam Kaplan, couldn't be blamed if he took a little himself when he sold the split stock on March 31 (three thousand shares); a company director, Hugh Robertson, also sold three thousand shares the same month. That followed Mr. Grossman of NVD again, who had eased out of five thousand the prior month.

Bloom off the Rose?

On May 25, Zenith and RCA raised a few eyebrows when they announced that they were cutting some prices on their new twenty-five-inch sets.

"The move," said the *Wall Street Journal* the next day, "by the two industry leaders ran counter to industry predictions as recently as last month that rising costs would make it difficult just to hold the line on color TV prices."

Aside from the apparent about-face of industry group sentiment, this item illustrates another warning investors might take note of—that is, despite statements to the contrary, such as "We're cutting prices to broaden the market," it appears that *generally, cuts in prices are a sign of deteriorating demand.* Prices are usually cut to entice wary buyers. Prices are raised generally when demand outstrips supply.

On June 7, prices of the color TV groups stocks dropped precipitously, but they rebounded the next day when their trade association, the Electronic Industries Association, released an estimate of a two-billion-dollar increase, to $19.3 billion in electronic sales that year. The organization also said it "raised its estimate of color TV sales to 5.4 million sets, in line with producer projections," as reported in the *Wall Street Journal* of June 9.

Business Week noted the price reductions, with some soothing words by the setmakers:

"I think it's going to be two, three, four years before we get enough capacity," said RCA's W. Walter Watts. "I do not see anything on the horizon until then that is going to affect demand." Perhaps he was trying to influence his dealers. But if investors were tuned in, it just might have had a reassuring effect. It is also possible that potential investors read into his words the thought that profits would go on climbing for the long term, and bought stock.

Also helping out was a report by RCA (announced on July 7) that its second-quarter per-share earnings rose to forty cents from thirty-two cents in the comparable period the prior year, a 27 percent rise. Further, sales for the first half were announced as topping one billion dollars, an all-time high for six-month results.

"Assuming a continuing favorable economic climate, we anticipate that RCA's record of profit improvement, now in its sixth year, will continue through the balance of 1966 and will be maintained in the promising years ahead," said Executive Committee Chairman Elmer Engstrom and President Robert W. Sarnoff in a joint statement.

Undaunted by the excellent record the company was making, Mr. Engstrom sold twenty-five thousand shares of RCA stock twelve days later on July 19, grossing about one million dollars on the deal. I guess that required real courage in the face of the news. Perhaps he had personal reasons for the sale. In any event, it could be observed that the net effect of the publicity surrounding the group facilitated the sale and price he got for his stock.

The Drumbeaters

On July 27, National Video sent out a press release that caused some stir in the stock, but not as much as might be expected. It read:

"NATIONAL VIDEO AND MOTOROLA
SIGN FIVE-YEAR CONTRACT

"National Video Corporation has announced the signing of a five-year contract to supply Motorola, Inc., with a substantial number of color television picture tubes. The agreement replaces an informal working arrangement which had been in effect since development of the rectangular color tube by the two firms in 1963.

"Asher J. Cole, National Video president, explained that the Motorola contract is the largest thus far. Similar agreements had previously been reached with Admiral, Magnavox, General Electric and more recently, with Westinghouse. All but the three-year Magnavox contract extend through calendar 1970."

This had followed by two days another handout that blared:

"NATIONAL VIDEO COMBINED SET SALES INCREASES TO A RECORD $88,758,203"

More good news upon more good news. . . . Why?

"Why?" is a question far too few investors ask. Was the good news "priming" investor interest?

The news of the color TV group was as good as the prices the insiders were getting for their stock. The *Wall Street Journal* of August 4 reported, "Zenith Profit [had] Climbed 85%, Sales [had risen] 60% to Highs in 2nd Period." President Wright was reported to say that all Zenith consumer products showed first-half increases. The *Journal* reported,

"Mr. Wright noted that Zenith's color receiver sales in the second quarter were substantially higher than the company's total consolidated sales of $76,465,000 for the second quarter of 1964, two years ago. The company's color receivers remain in short supply with combined factory and distributor inventories continuing at levels substantially lower than a year ago, the executive said."

One might have wondered why, if things were so good, were Zenith insiders selling? Presumably it was pure coincidence that Zenith's Hugh Robertson took the opportunity to sell fifteen hundred shares the same month.

By the way, the day the statement appeared on the Dow Jones news ticker, the stock rose twenty-five cents a share, to 65½. Nine days later NVD also picked up, rising 7½ points to 88.

The Annual Report

If the officers and directors of National Video were to issue annual reports on their own profits in the stock market (or make public their income tax statements), they would make good investments if publicly traded. But rarely are individuals traded on major exchanges—stocks are. And annual reports are issued by corporations that make for good or bad reading to investors. The problem is that the reports are, by their very nature, self-serving documents, highlighting what management wishes to highlight and playing down what they wish to understate. And then there's the president's statement (often called his "message"). In this form management may also emphasize or de-emphasize, or sometimes give insights into plans the company has for the future in a more editorial vein than the drier stuff accompanying corporate statistics. Thus, these "messages" often make interesting reading.

National Video's annual report came out in the summer of 1966, since their fiscal year ended on May 31. And it made good reading for the optimist, fascinating reading to the cynic. Asher J. Cole told stockholders that he was delighted with the year's results, calling it "by far the greatest in our history." Among other things, Mr. Cole stated that Motorola had received its final reimbursement for its initial investment in the color tube program. An optimist would interpret this bullishly, since this final "payoff" would presumably lead to greater profits for NVD, as they would keep a greater share of the proceeds from additional sales. The pessimist or cynic reading this might question that now that Motorola was not getting any part of the profits, would they look for other sources (including their own research) to buy their tubes?

Mr. Cole pointed with pride at earnings of $88,758,302 for the fiscal year, as compared with $29,277,884 in 1965—and who wouldn't? Yet the cautious investor might have asked, "How long can they keep that furious pace up?" If he had asked the question, Mr. Cole had an answer: "Motorola, as well as Admiral, Magnavox, General Electric, and Westinghouse, have signed long-term contracts to purchase color tubes from us."

Unfortunately, too few investors even bother to read annual reports, but those who had could hardly be blamed for licking their chops at the following item in Mr. Cole's statement:

"Each of these contracts contains reciprocal provisions for adjustments of tube quantities to conform to the customer's requirements, our own production capacity, and prevailing market prices. Subject to these possible adjustments and assuming all tubes are delivered within the contract periods, these contracts represent, at today's prices, *potential aggregate sales volume for color tubes of approximately $850 million for the five years ending December 31, 1970*" (emphasis mine). I wonder how many people were directly or indirectly influenced to buy the stock because of a statement like that. If stocks were to be bought on this basis, why not buy General Motors, which during the next four years could show sales in the many billions? And these sales were more assured than National Video's. NVD's sales projection was based, to be sure, on the postulate that firms like General Electric could not make their own tubes. Yet it was not long before they would. And they apparently found a clause that enabled them to be released from the contracts.

The August 24 issue of *Financial World* magazine seemed, judging by a lead to an article, to be wondering about the TV group's stocks.

"COLOR TV-GROWTH OVER?" it asked.

"The Industry's greatest period of expansion may well lie ahead, but rising output will bring supply-demand balance and price competition," the subhead read, and one might have gotten a bearish impression. However, swinging into the body of the piece, the reader-investor may have been reassured in his bullishness by, "The Color television boom may pause for breath, but it has a long way to go before it comes anywhere near exhaustion."

Distribution Complete

By the fall of 1966, the distribution, as some Street observers are wont to say, from strong hands to weak was well nigh complete. Magnavox had split in May, Zenith in June. The good news had spread all over the financial press, and the insiders had sold a great deal of their stock, accompanied by excited price runups. So what's new? Very little, apparently. The insiders had more selling to do (neither they nor anybody else knows "the top"), but for all intents and purposes, the boom and bust cycle of stock prices for the color TV group was headed for the bust phase. National Video began the fall television Season at 77, somewhat off its high of 81. Zenith traded in the 50s in September (all prices adjusted for their splits), Magnavox in the high 40s, Admiral in the middle 30s. Only RCA hit its high during the period (at 65), with the rest having come off earlier highs.

On September 6, the set producers did a flip-flop on their prices (not for the first time), and (according to next day's *Times*) were revealed as raising retail tags, confusing some (including me). This story in the *Times* appeared alongside another saying that the SEC was investigating possible price-rigging in Westec Corporation stock. This brings to mind the thought that all of the preceding selling by corporate officials and directors in the face of apparently good news was not at all illegal, as price-rigging is. Indeed, this writer saw letters from National Video's law firm to the American Stock Exchange duly complying with SEC and exchange regulations by reporting insider stock transactions carefully and punctually, as I'm sure was the case with the other companies. The informed minority doesn't have to cheat. All their stock market profits are made right out in the open, thanks to the aforementioned agency's vigilance. If the investor chooses to ignore what may be construed as warnings about his stocks—*c'est la vie.* But the investor doesn't have to—and really never had to. The information is readily available.

Not Quite Finished

There was still some selling to be done, and remarkably, more good news to come out, though as later events revealed, the ball game was really over. During the week ending September 10, when set makers raised their prices (RCA announced officially on the ninth, following Motorola, Zenith, and Admiral's action), *TV Guide* sent out its set buyer's guide. In an article there by David Lachenbruch, it was reported that color sets were being bought by Americans at the rate of twenty thousand a day. He noted that in the prior year (1965), only about 8 percent of homes had color sets, whereas the figure for the current year was 14 percent, and this could double by 1967.

On September 20, the *Times* reported a statement by Asher Cole, NVD president, on the effect of a strike in the fiscal quarter that had ended on August 31.

"Earnings could conceivably equal the 1965 period, but it would be a miracle if they did," he said in a refreshingly candid vein.

Elsewhere, mimeographs were still churning out things like the seven-month report by the Electronic Industries Association that sales of color TV sets had doubled over the similar period in 1965.

Analysts, brokers, investors, institutional investors, and plungers were now expecting unremitting growth from the color TV group. There are few things sweeter to investors than the sound of the word "doubling," unless it be "tripling." The implication might have come to some that the group's stocks would also double. And if they didn't? Since the stocks had been bid up in anticipation of such growth, what would happen to stock prices if the expected turned into the unexpected? The thought perhaps entered into some of the minds of the informed minority. They were selling—abetted, unwittingly, by the financial press.

Zenith's president, Joseph H. Wright, told the *Wall Street Journal*[5] that his company's third-quarter and total sales and earnings would set highs, and pouring on the optimism, he said, "I don't see any reason that 1967 should depart from that pattern."

Who could ask for anything more? The stock reacted by rising $2.40 a share the day the item appeared on the Dow Jones news ticker, to close at $63. Yet, in the pattern of smart money distribution of securities from strong hands to weak, the group's stocks had been slipping. Even Zenith's $63 was substantially below the $85 of just a few months ago. Bullish statements by corporate officials were lately having a merely transitory effect on their stocks. It was all over.

Color Blinded

On September 27, Zenith's Robert Galvin addressed a meeting of security analysts, who inched forward in their seats expecting to hear words that would justify their rampant optimism about the stock and others in the group. Most such meetings are rather bullish affairs.

Mr. Galvin told the assembled that[6] "his company's earnings this year would be no more than $5.40 to $6.00 a share, against $5.23 in 1965." That might at first glance seem quite good, but, as the *Times* pointed out, "Analysts had been predicting as much as $9 a share."

Mr. Galvin attributed the disappointment in part to a labor shortage "fraught with high rates of turnover and absenteeism."

Mr. Mills felt the same way.

[5] This appeared on the Dow Jones (the *Journal's* parent) news ticker on September 26 and written up in the paper the following day.

[6] New York *Times*, October 16, 1966 (in a summary of recent color TV events).

"We've already gone through this and we know that the predictions of others in the industry will have to be tempered by the labor problems they are bound to meet," he said later.[7]

Mr. Truesdell claimed that he had previously gone on record as saying that the industry would be "hard-pressed" to reach the five-million mark.

Oh, oh—a specter from overseas appeared on the horizon that had sent well-deserved chills down the spine of many a Kodak executive. It was the appearance of the Japanese—who saw an opening in the line and ran through it. Mr. Kyutaro Isomura, president of Matushita Electric Corporation of America, which distributed Panasonic sets here, said,[8]

"We are thinking about different sizes than are offered by United States set makers. We intend to hit at the untapped market with color sets having 12-inch to 16-inch tubes. The 1967 Christmas market should be very good for our plans."

Few American setmakers were naïve enough to think that "new" buyers would appear to take the new sizes. Panasonic had already sold sixteen thousand nineteen-inch sets and was to lure (along with Sony) enough set buyers away to dent the heretofore impregnable defenses of the likes of Zenith, RCA, and Admiral.

Yet the official word from the setmakers was still basically optimistic. Sure, we are not going to meet our earlier targets, they said. But as soon as our troubles are straightened out, watch our steam.

"Executives seem completely surprised by the lack of investing faith by the public," the *Times* reported.[9] "There is little pessimism in the industry." Convinced?

By October, even late-rising RCA had started to fall, but not before Mr. W. Walter Watts (remember him?) had sold fourteen thousand shares on the open market. Was he less optimistic than before? Who could say? Perhaps his reasons were personal. But could *all* the insiders mentioned have had personal reasons?

By mid-October, some of the brighter sales forecasts by the group were beginning to temper. In the week ending October 14, Steven R. Mihalic, marketing manager for GE's television receiver department at Syracuse, had told the New York *Times* in a telephone in-

[7] Ibid.
[8] Ibid.
[9] Ibid.

terview[10] that by the end of the decade, "at least 70 per cent of all households will have at least one color television receiver."

"This means," he said, "that television manufacturers must produce 8 million sets a year from here on in to meet that demand."

Yet the same week, the executive vice president for consumer products at RCA, Delbert L. Mills, said that the earlier sales estimates of 5.5 million sets being sold in 1966, had to be cut to "between 4.7 million and 4.8 million color sets. The 1967 demand should be about 8.5 million color sets, but the industry will do good to get out 7.5 million sets."[11]

There were problems. There were not enough picture tubes to go around, nor components, nor trained workers. The investor had problems, too. It was not whether projections would be slightly up or slightly down. His problem was—and is—one of buying stocks in anticipation of rising sales or earnings, whereas the stocks had already risen to compensate for the news. Further, when the news is too good . . . watch out for surprises!

There is, at various times, a corporate picture of wildly jumping sales, sometimes due to consumer demand entirely, sometimes partly due to "pushing." Big sales in a period often represent sales contests. Perhaps excessive growth in a single period takes sales away from succeeding periods, to an extent. Many companies in various fields run contests for their sales force. Thus, the men push extra hard to pull business from, say, weaker buyers. They win cash or points toward gifts for achieving record sales. So what do they do for an encore? Many of the customers are "used up," so to speak—and cannot be hit again for business soon after. This is particularly true for big ticket items such as autos, refrigerators, and television sets. And not many of these facts get into the financial press, unfortunately.

A longer-term problem is that of increasing competition in a highly profitable field. How long did it take the Japanese to develop and export cars of their own, or high-priced cameras, or what have you? When a business is doing overly well, new competition enters to get a piece of the action. This increased competition leads to price-cutting and eventually to reduced profits. Businessmen generally understand this. Investors less often do.

[10] Ibid.
[11] Ibid.

Not Going up Any More

The November 12 issue of the *Magazine of Wall Street* hit the stands with an analysis of color TV stocks. Zenith by this time had dropped to the 50s, RCA to the low 40s (from an earlier high of 60), and Magnavox did about the same (60 to 40).

"There's no doubt about it—demand for color TV continues to explode. Nine-month sales were 72% ahead of the comparable 1965 period, despite the severely limited supply," the magazine said.

"What's more, nearly every student of the color TV market agrees that demand will continue to rise. There are many reasons to think so," it felt.

After going into the reasons, the magazine said,

"A stockholder of any TV company who has read this far is probably thinking, 'If things are so good, why am I losing money?' It's not an easy question to answer. The stocks of TV makers outperformed the market by a wide margin from late 1964 until April 1966, but since then have done even worse than the general market."

The article went on to point out that by now, most of the industry problems, such as parts and labor, had been ironed out. They said that *"The boom in demand could have several more years to run before price cutting develops and demand plateaus—the usual bear arguments"* (emphasis mine). Even if the TV business of the industry was to peak, they might well come up with another hot item, such as home video tape recorders, said the *Magazine of Wall Street,* and it concluded that at these price levels, the stocks "have merit for businessmen's risk type accounts. As always selectivity is the key."

It turned out that selectivity would have ruled out buying *any* color TV stock.

With the group's stocks down considerably from their highs, the good news that had sparkled from the media's black-and-white pages earlier, continued to turn gray. *Business Week,* in its November 19 issue, discovered some "snow" on their screens. It seemed that television retailers were watching their inventories build up. The sets that once had sold themselves now needed more than a gentle push. The dealers were worried, said *BW*. However, the magazine noted that "in contrast to retailers, the manufacturers were playing it very cool."

"No one professes anything less than satisfaction with the level of color sales," it reported. Mr. B. S. Dumont, president of RCA Sales Corporation, was even quoted as saying that there was nothing to worry about. The difference of opinion between the retailers and the manufacturers made for an interesting story to some readers, if a confusing one to those who were also owners of the stocks in question.

Meanwhile, back at National Video, they were still turning out press releases, the one dated December 5, 1966, stating,

"NATIONAL VIDEO TO ADD THREE NEW TUBE SIZES

"Plans to introduce three additional sizes of rectangular color television picture tubes were announced today by National Video Corporation. . . . Until now, the firm has been producing the 23-inch rectangular color tube which they developed three years ago."

The release went on to note that NVD was supplying its twenty-three-inch tubes to thirteen manufacturers; also, that the wider variety of sizes would aid in meeting industry requests so (in quoting Mr. Cole) "as to attain its estimated sales figure of 7–8 million color sets, in 1967. We hope that with these additions, National Video will be able to contribute about 1,750,000 color tubes to next year's goal and substantial production level of 2 million tubes thereafter."

Wow! Couldn't NVD be a buy now—now that it was only $46 a share (down from $120 a scant five months ago)? The stock did go up right away, to $49. But by month's end it was down to $38. Did you buy on the good news?

If you didn't, perhaps other investors did buy on the *Times* story on December 10, "Sales of Color TV Score Sharp Gains": "Volume in First 10 Months Soars above '65 Level—November Record Seen." This harks back to the *Magazine of Wall Street* article about "If things are so good, why am I losing money?" The answer is, *The prices of stocks often discount the future, rarely the present.*

Admiral had announced the day before that sales of color sets to their dealers "from Oct. 1 through Nov. 18 period, were 73 per cent above the like 1965 period." Motorola, according to S. R. Herkes, their marketing vice president, were "up to our best expectations," the *Times* reported. Sylvania said that its sales through October were 115 percent above the same period of the previous year. RCA was reported as registering its best month of the year in November. And Westinghouse's W. C. Fortune, marketing manager of the radio-TV division, said that their color sales had run "300 per cent higher than in November, 1965, with the year to date well over 73 per cent higher." Motorola's Herkes perhaps was the most ecstatic of the group. He said, "We're moving sets as fast as we can make them. . . . Anything selling at under $650 is snatched right off the dealer's floors right away."

1967—Going South

The year began with National Video selling at 38⅝, its short position at 157,000 shares. The other color TV stocks showed Magnavox at around 40, RCA in the middle 50s, and Zenith at 48. Admiral had had a particularly bad drop from its 65 (adjusted for a split) the previous year to now only 30. *Forbes* magazine began the year with a rundown of the industry that seemed less than optimistic. This was too late for some investors, unless they were willing to sell out at in some instances severe losses. As *Forbes* magazine said on January 1, 1965, "Sure the industry was booming, but there were some confusing crosscurrents." Those "crosscurrents" were to stock investors running downstream.

Mr. Engstrom was proud of RCA's achievements, as he was quoted by *Forbes* in saying, "Because of our unique length of experience and broad base of operations in color, we have been less subject than others to some of the ailments."

The ailments looked more like cancer, with the stocks of color TV manufacturers going downhill, not excluding RCA. And this was curious, because the news was still basically good, though not as good as in 1965. Witness the New York *Times*, which featured a story on January 9 telling of the continued squeeze of demand upon supply. Makers of color sets were said to be having the enviable problem of not producing sufficient sets to keep up with demand. Industry officials were quoted as still being bullish. Ross D. Siragusa, president of one of the two companies whose stock had plummeted lately (Admiral), said, "The industry expects to sell 7 million color TV sets this year against 4.7 million in 1966."

RCA, too, remained as buoyant (officially) as ever about its prospects, with its year-end statement saying, as reported by the *Times* on January 9, "manufacturing capacity this year will be three times that of 1965, and we anticipate that every bit of it will be needed to meet the continuing demand for color."

Perhaps some investors bought color TV stock on the basis of statements like that? And if they read that on January 22 some five hundred Sylvania employees were laid off from color TV production, they might have been reassured by the *Times* report two days later that "Layoffs in color television picture-tube production are not anticipated by the Radio Corporation of America and the General Electric Company, two major producers." The *Times* might not be faulted for this report, since it was merely quoting company denials.

The bullish pronouncements (though now heavily spotted with some bearish news) emanating from RCA might well have been reassuring—particularly if one did not notice that the aforementioned Mr. Watts reported that he had sold another two thousand shares in November of 1966, and another officer, Mr. H. R. Wege, disposed of the same amount that month. Mr. Robert L. Werner could point to his picking up stock, presumably below the market price on options in January of 1967, similarly to Mr. Engstrom in February. But few shares were being bought at prevailing prices in the open market, though one could not with assurance say that there was any connection. Nor should it matter if there is, as long as the reader notes that usually informed minority selling precedes (and later accompanies) stock price drops.

Incidentally, Mr. Ungaro over at Magnavox sold three thousand of his holdings on December 6, 1966.

As for the sets themselves, producers were now selling lower-priced models, which when freely translated into business means lower profits, but again the stock market prices had anticipated the move, for as *Financial World* pointed out in early March of 1967, "Magnavox is 43% under its old high, Zenith has shaded 37% from the top; . . . Radio Corporation, 22% and even blue chip General Electric is off 28% from its 1966–67 summit." Nonetheless, RCA officials were still bullish, the magazine stated. If they were, this bullishness was amid the sale of 29,500 shares by an officer and director of the company, Mr. Charles M. Odorizzi, in the first two days of March. Mr. Wege saw fit to sell another thousand in the same period.

Now that the stock of color TV producers had fallen drastically, some more bad news crept into the picture in March. Almost exactly two months after RCA denied its intention to lay off some workers, fifteen hundred men were laid off from the color TV assembly plant in Bloomington, Indiana. Mr. Delbert L. Mills (the same) explained that these were "season layoffs."

Better Times Ahead

If the news on the color TV group was beginning to go from indifferent to poor, there was always another quality to nurture the hopes on investors—that being, hope. Perhaps, now that the color group had taken a good right to the jaw and its knees were buckling (witness the price declines their stocks had taken), there was always hope that the next round would see the set manufacturers come up with a secret punch that would send its bearish opponents wheeling. Voltaire defined it in describing optimism as "a mania for declaring when things are going badly that all is well."

That mania came out in the form of an apparition that appeared in *Forbes* magazine on March 15: "The color-TV boom, though faltering a bit right now, is only the beginning of a tremendous future for electronics in the home," it said. It was perhaps influenced by a statement in its pages on the first of March by an executive of Texas Instruments (which makes electronic components), "Homes of the near future could contain on average as much as $10,000 in electronic devices." And who would make these devices? RCA, Magnavox, Zenith, et al. The basic error in this calculation was that the managements involved failed to foresee where the biggest jump in home electronics really was to come—in high-fidelity phonograph equipment. The big names in this group in 1972 are Marantz, Scott, Fisher, KLH, Dual, Elpa, Garrard, Benjamin, Shure, Kenwood, Pioneer, etc., with nary a big American electronics firm represented. They had the resources, but they lacked something else. As it is said of the fumbling end who drops the pass thrown right at him, "It hit him in a bad spot—right at the numbers."

A publicity handout emanated from National Video for release on March 21 giving nine-month earnings results for the company in the period ending February 28. NVD had shown a disappointing

$1.48 total per share, as against $1.81 for the comparable 1966 period. However, National Video's president, Asher J. Cole, explained,

> The current lag in consumer purchases of color television sets reduced the demand for picture tubes and as a result the company's sales and earnings for the quarter were lower than expected. However, we are encouraged by the news of a recent survey in an industry trade publication which shows set manufacturers' forecast for the year still centers around 6.5 million set sales, a healthy 38% over 1966.

Mr. Cole apparently was not sufficiently encouraged to buy any stock in the company.

The release went on, "Mr. Cole observed that if this holds true approximately eight million picture tubes must be produced to satisfy pipeline, inventory and replacement needs. Additionally, since the penetration of color televisions into the home is only a meager 16–17%, there are 45 million or more families as potential buyers."

And further into the release, it was stated,

> As a means of combating overhead and manufacturing costs during this slower period, the National Video chief executive stated "more effective use of manpower and equipment allowed us to trim our labor force and initiate a long-planned five-day week without overtime expense. We will endeavor to maintain this policy even after *the anticipated upturn again calls for increased production schedules*" [emphasis mine].

Things had slowed down a bit, but they were going to get better, right? They didn't get too much better for the stockholders.

Not Finished

Relentlessly, insiders kept up their selling. Nathan W. Aram sold one thousand of his Zenith stocks on June 21, Bennett Cerf another thousand of RCA on June 7, and two of NVD officialdom dropped some the same month. One insider, George H. Fezell, bought some Magnavox in June, but the majority vote clearly favored "sell."

If the informed minority was selling, who was buying? For a possible answer, we turn to the popular advisory service, *Value Line,* which on June 2 rated National Video in its V, or lowest category for performance during the next twelve months, but gave it a II rating for 1970 to 1972 potential, a category the service says is "above average" for performance in the market.

Value Line pointed out that it had been right in its prior report (March 3) in rating the stock as a "below average" performer for the near term, whereupon it fell some 30 percent. It continued for hold out little promise for the stock in the near future. But, they added, perhaps the steady growth projected for the color television market would make the stock a good bet over three to five years. The service indicated that the stock was suitable only for speculative accounts, which in retrospect turned out to be an understatement.

While indicating that NVD's share of the market might be reduced, *Value Line* rounded out its review by forecasting earnings of *$3.50 a share for 1970–72.* This report proved to be somewhat optimistic, with the company going out of business and into bankruptcy in February of 1969. You can't win 'em all. By the way, the stock was selling at $27 at the time of analysis, and *Value Line* projected a $42 price as "normal average price," considering the earnings predicted.

It may be noted here that two more corporate officials at RCA sold stock in April: Mr. Corin 4881 and Mr. Karns 2331 shares after the company announced layoffs. Is it possible that they didn't know what Mr. Engstrom and the others knew? Or perhaps it was better late than never, as Mr. Malcarney, another officer and director, might have said as he sold 35,000 shares in May. And then there was General Sarnoff, who sold 4000 the same month. It was not all one-sided, however. A Mr. Farese picked up 1372 shares just as General Sarnoff was selling.

NVD and Motorola Shift

You recall the optimism that Mr. Cole of NVD had about his potential business. This may have been tempered somewhat when, on May 3, National Video announced that it and Motorola were modifying their agreement. But let the press release speak for itself:

> Mr. Cole explained that under the new terms of the tube pur-

chase agreement, a specified quantity of tubes to be bought or sold is no longer one of the provisions. "This does not mean that either one of us will stop doing business with the other," he emphasized. "In fact, barring continuation of the present softening within the color TV market, it is still Motorola's intention to purchase the quantity specified in the original contract which extends to December 31, 1970."

Mr. Cole also noted that other customers having similar long-term tube purchase contracts with National Video will be offered the same amendment.

The investor's reaction to that one might have been, "Oh, oh, here it comes!" And on May 4 the stock fell 2⅛, to 28¼. By this time, incidentally, the short interest was over three hundred thousand shares, thus it would appear that the shorts, far from covering, were selling even more shares short on the way down.

After National Video received the modest advisory service endorsement, the informed minority sold the TV stocks as before (we're not saying there was a connection), as Sam Kaplan and Robert Alexander of Zenith unloaded some seven thousand shares in July.

The above came after Gene Smith of the *Times* did a good reporting job in announcing RCA's price-cutting moves at its annual convention for dealers in Las Vegas. Checking with some producers, he found that they were admitting too that some dealers were discounting, something that was unheard of, naturally, when the sets were hot items.

This was the same month that *Consumer Reports* zinged one at RCA's new fourteen-inch set. "Those who have been waiting for a fully satisfactory small screen color TV set to come along will have to keep waiting." It remained for Japan's Sony Corporation to do that a few years later.

They're Still Selling

In August, Mr. Hugh Robertson, who was not new to this sort of thing, sold another three thousand shares of Zenith, while Mr. Jack W. Schrey of Magnavox eased out of one thousand of his stocks. The biggest buying at the time by the smart money I observed was the two hundred shares picked up by a new director of NVD, Allen P. Stults.

As for National Video, their May 31 fiscal year for 1967 did not turn out as well as '66. Whereas the earlier year saw the company report $2.66 per share, it dropped to only $0.81 in 1967. Mr. Cole still had good things to say:

> Although I do not want to minimize present conditions, we still have every confidence in a return to a more favorable climate. Through early June, 1967 cumulative sales of color sets in this country were only about 11.7 million, or approximately 20% of the estimated 59 million households. It is anticipated by most industry experts, therefore, that color TV will enjoy increasing penetration in the years to come."
>
> We believe that National Video will share in the industry's expected resurgence. Lower production schedules of the past year gave us ample time to install new equipment and modify existing machines for the introduction of two new sizes of color tubes. The thoroughness with which this conversion was accomplished should be reflected in improved efficiency and lowered costs once a more realistic production rate is established.

So who was being unrealistic the previous year? Mr. Cole, of course.

Value Line *Re-evaluates*

In a report dated September 1, 1967, *Value Line* advisory service appeared to downgrade its expectations for National Video Corporation. Although the stock was selling for $34 in the rally of a mortally wounded shark, it was now expecting earnings to be little changed from the past year. Thus, though it was looking for a below-average performance for the stock for the near term (the stock had risen since *Value Line's* last poor near-term rating), it no longer felt that the long-term picture rated II (above average), downgrading it to a III (average). *Value Line's* longer-term outlook for NVD was still not quite bearish for they saw an expanding color TV market which would make it "at least an average holding" into the early 1970's.

As for finances, the service did indicate that the company's strong financial position would enable it to "endure the growing pains of the industry and be in a position to participate in the expansion projected in the years ahead." (NVD's subsequent plant closing may have put a crimp in their expansion plans.) Additionally, *Value Line* felt that the "normal average price" of the stock was $42 (estimated) for 1970–72. Stockholders who waited for this price to be reached may have to look into the hereafter if there is a Wall Street in the big tape of the sky.

Earnings Worse Than Expected (by the investor)

With all the hoohah about the fantastic growth of color TV and how the stocks would benefit from it (as the smart money apparently left the scene), many investors were shocked to find that the set producers turned in lackluster profits for the first six months of 1967. For example, Admiral, whose stock had done so badly, had a deficit of $0.64 against a profit for the like 1966 period of $1.32. Magnavox showed up with $0.65 against $0.84, and Zenith only earned $0.71 vs. $0.98. RCA, in its nine-months fiscal report, had earned $1.47, down from $1.49 for the similar time in 1966. Surprised?

Still, stocks of the group picked up in August, as later observed *Financial World* magazine: "Disappointing results in '67 seem fully discounted by investors now bidding up set makers' shares on hopes for a better '68." Those hopes were reflected in higher prices for the group over the summer.

Rising Prices Bring on Sellers

The treasurer-secretary of NVD, Mr. Joseph Grossman, wisely took advantage of his stock's rise by selling another thirty-five hundred shares. As the advance in the group basically continued into September, the public's "hopes for a better '68" enabled various insiders like Mr. Truesdell of Zenith to sell another one thousand; in the same company Mr. Robertson sold two thousand and Jesse Brown a similar number. Indeed, it appeared a curious happenstance that Mr. Brown, Mr. Robertson, and another insider, Karl E. Hassel, all sold some stock on the same day, the thirteenth of the month.

Meanwhile, back at the RCA ranch, Bennett Cerf was selling a few acres, pardon, a few shares (one thousand) on September 8, joined by Mr. Bilby with thirty-nine hundred and Delbert L. Mills, again, who gracefully loosened six thousand as the stock boomed to a new high. The stock was hot, so what better time to sell? And at NVD, Harold Cole was selling thirty-three hundred shares of his stock.

With the color TV group going so well again in the market, undoubtedly some investors bought in anew, having missed out on the 1966 "action." Holders may have felt reassured—and the sellers may have felt sorry. One group of sellers did not feel sorry—and you know who they were.

Financial World, in its October 25 issue, observed a "better picture for color TV," typifying the financial media's renewed bullishness for the group. The magazine noted that "In the hope of participating in a renewed color television boom, investors have been bidding up the makers' shares." Mr. Bennett Cerf was not one of those investors, as the RCA director unloaded another thousand on October 31. And RCA was still over fifty-five dollars as our friend Mr. Watts really moved, disposing in the open market on November 1 twenty thousand shares with a gross valuation of over a million dollars. It was almost as if he couldn't believe how strong his stock was.

Slipping

As the year drew to a close, the stocks dropped. But as they did, Mr. Frank Friemann showed up again with a tasty morsel for still bullish investors, selling his lovely Magnavox stock on November 28 for a gross intake of over eight hundred thousand dollars in a single day. Though "Maggie" rose again in early 1968 and RCA rallied briefly in April with Admiral following suit, the TV industry was fast losing its color. For a moment, it had made a comeback. The fading actress was heavily made up for the part. But it could not last. The wrinkles became more pronounced, the skin texture sagged. It would take more than brewer's yeast to hide the fact that she (the TV set industry) would have to settle for grandmother parts.

The year 1968 was not too good for the group. All the good news the companies could muster did little for the stocks—Zenith, for example, was reported on in the *Wall Street Journal* of July 30 in a sparkling story.

> Zenith's Second Quarter Earnings Tripled,
> Sales Soared 40% from '67 Period to High.

Who could ask for anything more? The stock did rise at that juncture, from $55 to as high as $71 on September 22, whereupon it commenced sliding till year-end, closing almost where it began on the magnificent earnings statement, finishing out 1968 at $57. It seemed finally that the Street didn't believe it could last. The hot lights of the market were causing her makeup to run.

National Video—The News Isn't All Bad

On November 2, 1967, NVD said that it and Franklin National Bank of New York had concluded an agreement for Video's borrowing up to $3 million "as additional working capital is required." Score: NVD 7, Franklin 0. As National Video drew the curtain for 1968, the stock appeared at the ignominious price of 22⅞, following some mighty poor earnings statements. Still, there had to be some buyers around, for the stock did move up to 24¾ on January 31, though it closed the day considerably lower, at 22¾, trading 106,000 shares. Perhaps some "tape readers" bought the stock during the day on a "breakout," but expert technicians (precious few of those around) noticed that all the stock was hitting the market, and the issue closed considerably below its day's high. In February, the stock drifted to around 20 most of the month, and in March it dropped even farther, fueled by a press release of March 22 that read:

> Sales and earnings of National Video Corporation for the third fiscal quarter and nine-month period ended February 29, 1968 showed decreases compared with results of a year ago.

The release did not go further into the earnings specifics, leaving that to page 2, which had a statistical table. Instead the statement went on:

> National Video Corporation recently was granted a basic pat-

> ent for a three-point suspension system for rectangular color television picture tubes. This system is used almost universally by color television picture tube manufacturers. Letters have been sent to all such manufacturers indicating that National Video is willing to license them under this patent, Asher J. Cole, president, said.

It was not long before that, that NVD could have sent these letters to itself, since hardly any tubes were being produced except by it and RCA.

Continuing, Mr. Cole had more good news for the investing public:

> The company, in its first diversification move, became the major stockholder in a new subsidiary, Precision Ultrasonics Corporation of Garden City, Long Island, New York. The new company is providing ultrasonic equipment. It will service such fields as the automotive, aircraft, aerospace, appliance, electronic, packaging, photographic, medical and garment industries.

With all that glamor, how did the garment business sneak in? Mr. Cole really should not be blamed for his optimism, for it is part of the American dream. Still, some wags in the Street said that NVD was producing more press releases than color tubes.

Oh, yes—on to page 2 of the release, which listed net sales of $27 million against last year's $72 million, both figures for the nine-month period closing at the end of February. However, in the 1967 period NVD had earned $4 million net after taxes, or $1.48 per share. The 1968 nine-month report showed a net loss of $3 million.

The market responded to all this with a half-point drop for the next four trading days in March. Perhaps it would have been worse if that exciting acquisition had not accompanied the earnings, but this is only conjecture.

In April the Sylvania Division of General Telephone & Electronics Corporation sued National Video, charging patent infringement. This did not help the already beleaguered stockholders of Video, some of whom had watched the stock fall from as high as $88 to $15, where it finished at the end of May 1968. There was little to help Video now, for the financial press, particularly the magazines, were printing much less about TV stocks since they had cooled down. After all, what is exciting about erosion and lassitude—two characterizations that could be made about the entire group during 1968?

A little late but better than never was the story in *Merchandising Week* on June 3, 1968, that stated, "Color TV Retailers Expect Big Fall Season to Be Highly Promotional." This last phrase translates to "discounts coming."

And this from the same publication on July 1, "Retailers Holding Up Heavy Buying of Color TV, See Price Breaks Coming."

The number of financial press stories about color TV in 1968 paled in comparison with those in the years that TV was hot—and this is part of the "game."

National Video Strikes Back

On June 26, 1968, NVD announced that it was countersuing Sylvania, alleging infringement of its patent and antitrust violations and requesting triple damages. Stockholders did not count the money Video would make if it won the suit—for the stock still languished in the $15 area.

The reasons that National Video lost $5 million for fiscal 1968, as opposed to a profit of $0.81 per share for fiscal '67 (announced on July 30) were given by President Cole:

1. Set manufacturers reduced their production of new sets until their large inventories existing at the beginning of the period had become more manageable.
2. The original twenty-two-inch rectangular tube developed by NVD became obsolete with the advancement of the color TV set art necessitating write-off of certain equipment, parts, and supplies.
3. Color tube price reductions.
4. Lower production requirements increased unit costs.

These were cited by Mr. Cole along with other interesting tidbits. National Video said in its annual report that it had been granted a patent for something called a "three point shadow mask suspension mounting system for rectangular television picture tubes." Despite NVD's claim that the system was almost universal for tubemakers, what was the result of the promotional letters they sent to prospective buyers? Sadly, NVD said, "no request for such a license has yet been received."

Still, the company had *some* good news. In addition to retelling about the loan agreement with Franklin National Bank, the company said it had purchased the 160,000 square-foot parking lot they were using adjacent to the main plant! To counter this wonderful news there was the admission that the Precision Ultrasonics Corporation investment of $100,000 was not exactly panning out.

The annual report said of this deal, "It has become apparent that Precision Ultrasonics will require additional capital and National Video would be required to increase its investment to maintain its position of ownership in the company. We feel that at present it would be unsound to make any additional investment, therefore, we are in the process of negotiating the sale of our interest." So much for the NVD's initial attempt at diversification.

But what of 1969? Might not things get better?

"Current economic conditions make it difficult to forecast the extent of consumer demand in fiscal 1969, although the industry is cautiously optimistic." Mr. Cole was not exactly a pessimist either. The report continued, "Normally television set sales increase in an election year." It concluded by rather meekly citing such variables as the income tax surcharge and higher interest rates. "These and other conflicting indicators will need continuing evaluation in the months ahead." Mr. Cole also expressed his appreciation for the support the customers and shareholders showed in the past year. He didn't mention the support shareholders gave his stock so that he was able to get nice prices for it when he sold, but this is rarely expressed in annual reports.

Mr. Cole could not be charged with only selling on "good news," expecting it to turn bad. In fact, he could never be charged, to my knowledge, with any securities violation, for we have noted continually how the firms' legal counsel repeatedly have complied with SEC requirements as to reporting statements and insider selling. Note that even with the stock and the earnings having fallen mightily, Mr. Cole disposed of additional shares in October of 1968 numbering some 22,340. He still retained 98,200. We mention this "remainder" pointedly. When we have cited smart money selling to investors who were "bullish" on a stock, they would counter with,

"But look at how much he had left!" Our experience is that it doesn't matter how many shares the company officials have left after they've sold strongly. Indeed, it is rare that company presidents ever sell *all* their stock, for they wish to retain their interests.

Harold Cole also sold some NVD stock in October of 1968—4900 shares, to be exact, on October 11, a day after he left his position. Asher J. Cole was elected chairman, retaining his title as chief executive officer, and Robert G. Scott was named president.

Two months after the sales by the two Coles, NVD announced six-month results for the period ending November 30. The company had lost $2,576,934, a bit less than the $3,028,408 for the same six-month period of '67. National Video closed on December 31, 1968 at 13⅞, still retaining a short position of 249,000 shares. The shorts apparently expected still worse—and they were right. Zenith finished '68 at 55¾, RCA had dribbled down to 46 (and wasn't Mr. Cerf glad he sold, not to mention Messrs. Truesdell, Watts, Mills, Sarnoff, et al.). Magnavox did not do as badly as the rest, closing at 58.

The Postelection Blues

The first part of 1969 was not too good for many stocks, let alone the color TV group, but not too good was a mild description for holders of National Video. The year began auspiciously enough for the company, as it tried another merger. The press release dated January 6 said that they had picked up Acorn Sheet Metal Manufacturing Company, which made metal cabinets and other components for the television industry and other items. Acorn also made those shadow masks Video had talked about, and they said, "The acquisition of Acorn will provide National Video Corporation with its color picture tube shadow mask requirements at a significant savings in the cost of this major component."

Acorn would have had some trouble collecting (the deal didn't go through, anyway) for the New York *Times* of February 27, 1969 reported the following disastrous news for the remaining Video shareholders and the Franklin National Bank:

"The National Video Corporation, manufacturer of television picture tubes asked the United States District Court today (Feb. 26) for permission to reorganize under the bankruptcy act.

"The corporation listed its total assets at $20,286,429 and its total liabilities and stockholders equity at the same figure . . . . the corporation announced yesterday that it is suspending manufacturing operations."

This followed a story in the *Times* by two days announcing that tube production had ended at the company. NVD was described as "once one of the color TV industries' high flying stocks." And so it had been. Though trading was suspended on all exchanges, the story of NVD was the story of the color TV group, only more so. Many of its investors were hurt badly, but so were those who had bought the "better quality" stocks. Yet the disaster was presaged from the very beginning. The pattern is that of most fads—informed minority buying, scarce news. Then the news gets better and better, the informed minority selling. Then a profusion of splits, accompanied by increased dividends and more informed minority selling. Frenzied price advances and big trading volume activity. Thence the decline, accompanied by more informed minority selling. Sometimes a brief respite, a rally that seduces the "John," who is bushwhacked. More price declines, bad news—and the morning after. The girl is not what you thought. Perhaps you see her again on her pale horse with her makeup removed or faded. Was she to blame? Or was it you, who hoped for what couldn't be? Perhaps you won't do it again. Perhaps.

NATIONAL VIDEO CORP. "A"

ase
NVD

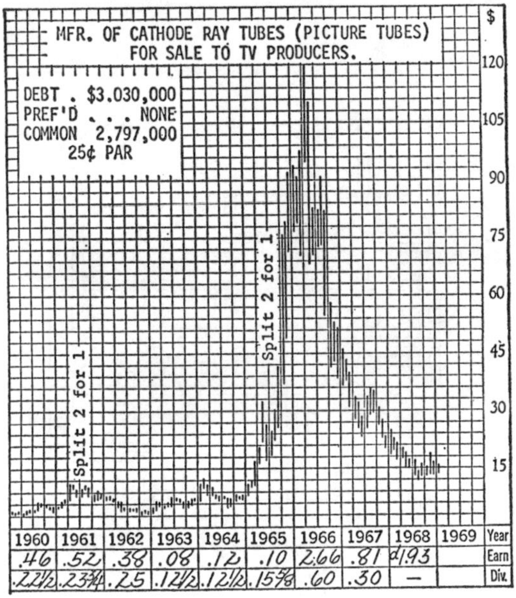

Company filed reorganization petition in Feb. 1969 in Federal Court at Chicago under Chapter 10 of Federal Bankruptcy Act. - Common dealings suspended from the American Stock Exchange in February 1969.

Chart courtesy M. C. Horsey & Co., Inc., Salisbury, Maryland 21801

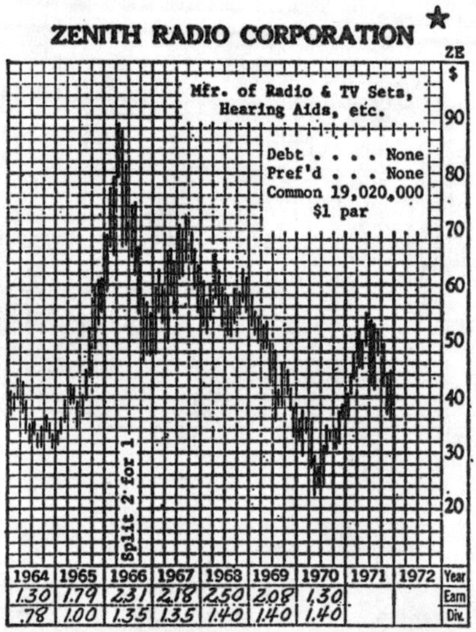

Chart courtesy M. C. Horsey & Co., Inc., Salisbury, Maryland 21801

MAGNAVOX COMPANY

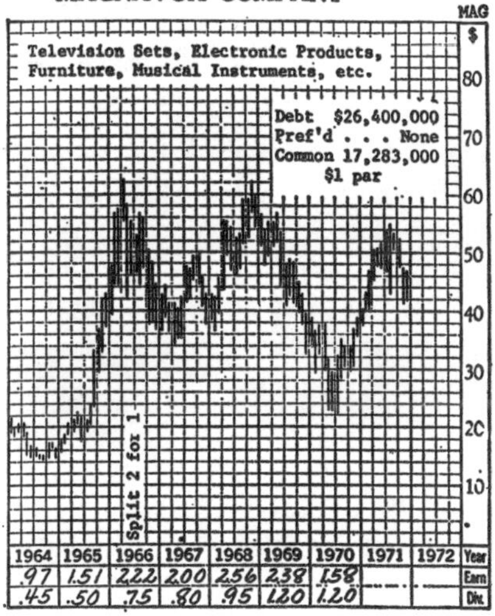

Chart courtesy M. C. Horsey & Co., Inc., Salisbury, Maryland 21801

six

Why You Lost–Wall Street's Cultural Hangup

"We studied in business school how companies compute the cost of money. It was quite complex. After graduation, I went to work for one of those 'giant corporations.' Three years later as a 'junior executive,' I asked the chief financial officer what he figured was the cost of money to the company. He told me 'around 9 percent.' I asked him how they arrived at that. He answered, 'It seems like a good figure.'"

—*A business associate*

Those present and former bachelors who frequent the canyons of the local supermarket after a while get to know how to shop for bargains, for fun and small profits. Shopping at the egg section one soon comes to the realization that generally, white eggs sell for about two cents more a dozen than brown ones, that is, in the northeastern part of the country. In Texas, however, the reverse is true. Is there any difference in food value or taste between white and brown eggs? None—only the price varies as reflected by the supply and demand relationship and their regional popularity. There are lots of other "attitudes" about food, such as the notion that toasted bread is lower in calories than the untoasted kind. And that raw carrots are better than cooked (the vitamin A is absorbed better after cooking), that lettuce has food value (it's 99 percent water), and so on.

I could never eat grasshoppers, though I understand that members of other national groups do, likewise raw fish. Why? It's my cultural hangup. You know, of course, that cultural (learned) attitudes determine our feelings about other races, the opposite sex, marriage, work, and play. Even in spectator sports, fans' attitudes vary widely from our own, say in South America. And as close as Mexico, cockfighting is approved. Does it all matter? Only when a cultural attitude affects the efficiency of our work or our health or our enjoyment of life.

Our attitudes toward corporate finance are really *learned* beliefs, often differing as day to night from what happens in the real business world. Institutional money managers with whom I deal would most likely scoff at the thought that companies are run for the benefit of the little old ladies in Keokuk. Yet many others get caught up in the euphoria of exciting stock price rises as they try to catch the shooting star. Instant performance is often their game, though some have admitted its tenuousness. Though the motivation may be the same, the informed minority's time frame is more elongated, thus more successful. The corporate president who takes on the job usually has two goals, maybe three, in varying proportion:

1. He hopes to accomplish a change in company fortunes for the better, thus gaining an ego gratification in doing a job well.
2. He gains the prestige accompanying the appointment, something he may have craved as he fought his way to the top.
3. He hopes to make a lot of money, principally by the capital gains route.

The first two are generally recognized, the latter is more often ignored by analysts. Insider buying and selling studies have proven efficacious (in studies by Perry Wysong, by individuals at the University of Chicago, by Portland State University, and others, as shown in Chapter One). We have done studies that with the proper lead time show even more dramatic improvements in stock profit performance. Try as I have with evidence in hand to convince money managers that their stock is in danger because of the persistent pattern of insider selling, few have taken heed. It takes a few Kentucky Fried Chickens, Four Seasons Nursing Homes, Penn Centrals, Fotochromes, National Videos, Littons, Automatic Sprinklers, Ling-Temco-Voughts, et al. to bring them around, if ever.

But the body of belief regarding traditional fundamental analysis dies even harder. What are some of the things one looks at in evaluating the worth of companies? Well, let's try *return on equity*—or *profit margins*—or *earnings growth.* The analyst who does not study these things would figuratively be thrown out of the analysts' society. *The question is: Do we know what we are looking at when we study these phenomena?* Do these factors bear any relationship to future stock prices? Do we care?

If supposedly the analysts' tasks are to find qualities that uncover "values" in stocks that will ultimately be reflected in market price, why do we not try to find fundamental factors that do indeed affect stock price? That is, find out if in fact there is a relationship. The tests may also be worth the effort if we discover that there is no relationship between recognized fundamentals and stock price. Maybe there is, maybe there isn't. Isn't it worth finding out? For many analysts there is the reply I recently got from a midwestern money manager, "I can't help it. This is the way we work in this shop."

Perhaps he wasn't the chap who woke up one day to find his Upjohn had fallen 50 percent, so had his Miles Labs, his Mohawk Data, and his Teledyne. We all have our "bag jobs," but some try to find out why. It is to these I address the following studies.

The first is that of "return on equity"—a measurement of management effectiveness, right? Maybe, but what does superior return on equity mean to the stock's price? The list below is of the top twenty companies in 1967 that had the best return on equity of the leading corporations. We used a five-year compounded figure to smooth out possible "odd" years. One might reason that the more consistent the return, the more effective the management.

Company	*% Return on Equity*
Xerox	47.4
Avon	42.9
Ethyl	37.6
Gillette	34.9
Smith, Kline	34.4
Bristol-Meyers	32.7
Magnavox	31.7
General Dynamics	31.7
American Home	30.2

Delta Airlines	28.4
National Airlines	27.8
Polaroid	27.7
Northwest Airlines	27.6
Ling-Temco-Vought	27.4
Sterling Drugs	25.9
Continental Airlines	25.2
General Cable	25.1
Eastman Kodak	24.8
Warner Lambert	24.6
Gulf & Western	24.6

Now we list the same companies with their corresponding stock prices at the end of 1967, the last day of December 1968, and the last of June 1969. Under the columns for the last day of December 1968 and of June 1969 are indicated in parentheses the percentage in price changes, plus or minus.

Company	*Last Day Dec. 1967*	*Last Day Dec. 1968*	*Last Day June 1969 (18 mos.)*	*Last Day Dec. 1969 (2 yrs.)*
Xerox	101	89(−12)	96(− 5)	105(+ 5)
Avon	142	127(−11)	154(+ 8)	171(+21)
Ethyl	37	36(− 3)	29(−22)	24(−49)
Gillette	62	51(−18)	52(−16)	52(−16)
Smith, Kline	50	51(+ 2)	39(−22)	50 −
Bristol-Meyers	74	68(− 8)	62(−16)	75 −
Magnavox	39	55(+41)	46(+18)	37(− 5)
General Dynamics	66	46(−30)	30(−55)	27(−59)
American Home	57	60(+ 5)	58(+ 2)	71(+25)
Delta Airlines	34	37(+ 9)	35(+ 3)	30(−12)
National Airlines	34	40(+18)	49(+15)	23(−32)
Polaroid	125	112(− 6)	118(− 6)	125 −
Northwest Airlines	43	43 −	31(−28)	28(−35)
Ling-Temco-Vought	125	95(−24)	40(−68)	25(−80)
Sterling Drugs	52	37(−29)	34(−35)	42(−19)
Continental Airlines	24	23(− 4)	16(−33)	12(−50)
General Cable	39	35(−10)	21(−46)	19(−51)
Eastman Kodak	75	73(− 3)	75 −	82(+ 9)
Warner Lambert	45	58(+29)	59(+31)	70(+55)
Gulf & Western	59	49(−17)	26(−56)	18(−69)

The average price change for the first period, December 1967 to December 1968, *for all twenty* is minus 1.95 percent. The Dow

Jones average during the same time period showed a price *advance* of 4.3 percent. Thus it can be seen that the group underperformed the Dow in a mildly bullish swing. But what happened during the eighteen-month period of December 1967 to June 1969, when the Dow *fell* 3.5 percent? The group of stocks with supposedly excellent management fell 12.8 percent! Only six of the twenty managed to advance in the twelve-month period, December 1967–December 1968 as did a like number during the eighteen-month period December 1967–June 1969.

All of which is not meant to say that one automatically avoids all stocks whose companies showed "good" return on equity. Though we have developed statistical studies that show "ideal" returns as well as (pragmatically) "poor" returns, the study merely shows that little in the stock market can be taken for granted, especially in terms of "formal" economic attitudes.

Growth Stocks

The word "growth" has in Wall Street an almost mystical quality (except possibly during bear markets), suggesting wealth, power, success. What is more appealing than watching your children develop their speech, their locomotion, their understanding? Growth! What is more attractive than watching the teen-ager bloom into womanhood, yet retaining her shyness and femininity? Growth! And what is more satisfying than building a company from a dream into a reality with wide-reaching markets, contented employees, and useful products or services? Growth! The growth stock has taken on during the past ten years all the desirable attributes the society confers upon the fortunate. Not the least is the satisfaction it affords those who pick them and ride the rainbow to financial success. The money manager who buys and holds them (and buys on dips) enriches the shareholders, the fund managements, or the trust accounts and the bank—and ultimately himself. But how do you find these growth stocks? It was somewhat easy in the fifties and sixties. Just keep buying Xerox or Polaroid—they always come out. And there is (or was) University Computing, Memorex, and Mohawk Data, and how many money managers were lured into them at high prices? Of course, if they did turn out to be the Xerox's of the future, why not?

The question you are expecting is, What is the relation between earnings growth and stock performance? This is a nasty question. Below is the list of the twenty stocks showing the greatest five-year compounded growth in earnings as of 1967. The next column shows the stock price on the last day of that year, and the price 18 months later. The last column shows the price change percentage, plus or minus.

Company (listed in order of growth amplitude)	*Price Dec. 1967*	*Price June 1969*	*% Change*
Teledyne Inc.	70	30	−57
Gulf & Western	59	24	−41
Continental Airlines	24	16	−33
United Airlines	66	36	−54
Ling-Temco-Vought	125	39	−69
Northwest Airlines	43	31	−28
National Airlines	34	39	+12
Xerox	101	98	− 2
Polaroid	125	118	− 5
UF	60	47	−22
Trans World Airlines	50	37	−26
Consolidated Freightways Inc.	33	27	−18
Twentieth Century-Fox Film Corp.	31	22	−29
Controlled Data Corp.	136	149	+ 9
California Financial Corp.	17	26	+53
Delta Airlines	34	35	+ 3
Texas Gulf Sulphur Co.	42	25	−41
Penn Centrals	62	49	−21
Kaiser Industries Corp.	18	18	0
Cerro Corp.	43	25	−41
Braniff Airways Inc.	15	14	− 7

The average decline for the twenty-one stocks is 21 percent, which compares with a drop in the Dow Jones for the same period of only 3.5 percent. By the way, we have run a series of statistical significance tests validating the conclusions. Our computer has some value, after all.

You are probably aware that similar results were obtained using "profit margins," another sacred cow to the fraternity. Of course, one may ask whether all this has any value to the business of picking stocks; or to put it another way, do I have the gall to suggest that stocks should be sold merely because they have "good" fundamentals? No, not really. Parameters must (and have been) established to determine at just what point profit margins are unsustainable, likewise earnings growth and so on. And further, can one tell by statistical means when growth will moderate and earnings slow down? To a certain extent, dear reader, to a certain extent.

seven

"Get 'Em While They're Hot!"

SOME PEOPLE do not know when to quit. Seeing their winnings pile up, they envision their "lode" rising again and again, as if the world existed merely to enrich them, as if the law of averages did not apply to them. So it was that one brokerage firm kept recommending Kentucky Fried Chicken (KFC) stock to its institutional clients in March of 1968, with the stock at $57 a share. The firm predicted earnings for KFC of $1.65 in 1968 and $2.70 for 1969, which, they said, did not even reflect "a number of 'kickers' which could well propel fiscal 1969 earnings significantly higher." The firm told its fund clients that though the stock was selling at thirty times earnings, it would continue to do so because of the "predictability" of its earnings. Whether or not the "predictability" would remain clear, three months before this report Mr. Jack C. Massey, the largest single stockholder, sold ten thousand shares to fund and individual alike, and was joined in selling of lesser amounts by President John Y. Brown and Messrs. Hitner and Matthews, both directors. Whether their actions "predicted" anything about future earnings is not a question often asked by analysts. Their selling followed a three-for-one split, which made the stock more accessible to the little guy, no doubt. The brokerage report noted that Mr. Massey "purchased the parent concern for $2 million in 1964 and which at the writing has a market value of approximately $230 million." So—that's not enough?

With this and other brokerage firms recommending the stock, the chicken fat was really in the fire. Advisory services, investment counselors, and other high types waited on line for their piece of chicken. Mr. Brown gave it to them—perhaps he felt the stock was a bit overdone? Whatever the reason, John Y. Brown dutifully reported to the SEC that he sold 110,000 shares on April 11, 1968. The shares weren't very difficult to sell. If the investors (large and small) did not bother to read the insider reports, they could drive by the roadside stands and see the populace line up for Colonel Sanders' specials. The kindly looking old gentleman beckoned them into the shops—and didn't the chicken taste good! It was a "hot" franchise time, and it would not cool yet. Joining the parade to feed the hungry multitudes chicken and stock certificates were also Chicken Delight, Minnie Pearl's Chicken System, Honey Fried Chicken Corporation (Yogi Bear label), and so on.

Mr. Brown and Mr. Massey were capitalizing on a boom. Whereas many of the less savory types were up the river or awaiting trial for fleecing the innocent of their life savings in franchising con schemes, they could enjoy the respect and even awe of their confreres and the comforts resulting from the fact that even up to this point they had realized $27.6 million. The two were part of a group[1] that had invested $2 million just four years earlier. They played a clean game as compared to the con men. But for thousands of investors who bought the stock because of a combination of its being "touted," "promoted," and being the object of reams of publicity generated at them, being "recommended" by advisory services, etc., the outcome was similar. The "public" who lost money and/or esteem in this game is a synonym usually applied to the small investor. The "public," in reality, is everybody *other* than the smart money, and they include the financial institutions, strangely enough—though *they* are misled on a higher plane, that is, in a "nice way." For we are all "customers" to be shorn—and sometimes stockbrokers unwittingly hand the scissors to the shearer.

It is interesting to note that the press sometimes aids and abets the shearers, too, possibly unknowingly. Yet occasionally it grabs the scissors and throws them into the nearest stream. Thus did *Forbes* say on June 15, 1968, "This wild runup [Kentucky, Minnie Pearl, and Dunkin' Donuts] in the shares of these purveyors of cheap, everyday dishes has ominous overtones. It equals anything

[1] *Forbes* magazine, June 15, 1968.

seen in the uranium boom of the mid-Fifties or the more recent run-ups of bowling and publishing stocks." And the "public" ran after the scissors, picked them up, and handed them back to the sheep men.

"Probably the hottest fad around is in the franchising stocks," said Clem Morgello in the July 8, 1968 issue of *Newsweek*. A chart showing the price rises of the group was shown under the heading, "Nourishing Investments." Who was being nourished was another question. The magazine tallied Denny's Restaurants as having risen 576 percent above its 1967 lows, Hardee's Food Systems 313 percent, International Industries (House of Pancakes) 1020 percent, and Lums, the same. Staid old Howard Johnson, which had sales ten times Denny's and nine times International Industries and stockholder's equity twelve times Kentucky Fried Chicken, had risen only 28 percent during the period! Mr. Morgello pointed out that the franchising group was selling for an average of forty times earnings and was "vulnerable to sharp declines if market psychology in general deteriorates or if the fad changes." "Give me back those shears," cried the masses.

How It Was Done

How was the franchising group able to obtain such remarkable price rises in its stocks? The cynical might assume that it was done solely by a combination of manipulative practices, assuming for the moment that public relations would fall into this category. One might assume that it was done merely by public hysteria, greed, and "follow the crowd" activity, aided and abetted by naïve or unethical stockbrokers. It could have been another "tulip craze," but it wasn't. If the smart money hadn't learned anything from history, we'd have to drop the appellation "smart."

The smart money does it all legally. They do it respectably, with "earnings." Although many of the stocks that rode the coattails of the franchise boom had precious little of the latter, others turned in fat per-share earnings jumps. What stock buyers, be they banks, insurance companies, investment counselors, or mutual funds, could fail to be impressed with companies whose earnings leap from, say, \$.20 to \$.50 to \$1.50 to \$3.00, all in a few years? What advisory services could not be seduced by such "fundamentals"?

The problem was that the "fundamentals" so assiduously followed by security analysts were suspect. Banks are paying higher and higher salaries to beginning analysts in a search for better performance for the trust accounts, pension funds, and college endowment funds they manage; but those analysts were all trained at the same business schools and come out of the same naïve milieu that does not understand the basic operations of smart money. They are all looking at so-called fundamental factors such as earnings, profit margins, return on equity, and the like without the slightest thought that it may all be one large con game, in which conners are immune from the law, since the law does not consider anything amiss in these practices. Even if they did, white-collar crimes, as you know, are not prosecuted as vigorously nor punished as harshly as blue-collar crimes, the latter referring to common theft. The law, and one says it with tones of grandeur normally reserved for the most holy implications, is courting disaster in its inequities.

What Kind of Earnings?

The best way, of course, to make your stock go up fast (so you can sell out at high prices) is to show dramatic earnings rises. Doubling and tripling can be quite impressive. But how can this be achieved, since to accomplish it would be to open a hamburger joint every ten minutes, what with large staffs (overhead) required to sell the buyer, and advertising to entice him. Further, there is the matter of the time it takes to build the units, hire and train the staff, etc., not to mention the selling conferences, legal work, and building permits. It is all depressingly slow. Besides, even if time stood still, would business be that good so the restaurants and drive-ins could be spaced ten abreast? No, obviously, the roadside stands would become so numerous that they would eventually have to depend on each other's employees, who would get tired of the same fish or chicken meal three times a day.

Here's the way it has often been done. The enfranchiser sells the franchise to the buyer for, say, fifty thousand dollars. He hasn't got fifty thousand dollars? That's easy. We can finance it for him, or use our giant credit power to get him a loan at the local bank. All he needs is ten thousand dollars down, the rest being paid off in, say, ten years out of income. We can always promise him an income of forty thousand dollars a year, so he can obviously make the payments and still buy the chickens. Now we take the fifty-thousand-dollar selling price into current income. If we sell ten units, that's five hundred thousand dollars; one hundred gives us five million dollars. It's easy this way to show a spectacular earnings rise, merely by selling more units. If things slow up and we can't find enough buyers, simply lower the down payment, even to one thousand dollars, *still showing the fifty thousand dollars per unit as income.* Sell more units, and earnings per share rise dramatically. Of course, there's a catch. What if the franchise buyer finds he can't pay off the 10 to 12 percent interest, still pay his help the wage rises they are demanding, pay more for the chickens, for local advertising, etc.? Well, then he loses. But you, the enfranchiser, can't lose. You see, by the time this happens in quantity, you've already sold enough stock to retire—or to try another scheme.

There were those franchise businesses that used "conservative" bookkeeping practices, like Kentucky Fried Chicken. There were those who sought public money to organize their operations, thus transferring much of the beginning risks to the public, while retaining substantial equity for themselves and keeping their eventual right to sell out to other segments of the public if and when they were successful. This is called eating your chicken and having it too, or heads I win, tails you lose, if I may be so trite. There was even one that "went public" with the name of "Frank N' Stein Systems" (hot dogs and beer), noting in their offering prospectus that "working drawings of a model of a Frank N' Stein Restaurant have been completed." If this would seem scant experience on which to go to the public trough, it was not an unusual case. Within one month of opening their first "Tony Bennett Spaghetti House," the backers claimed they had sold 250 franchises. "Lum's," another beer and frankfurter emporium, opened 140 units in 1969, but they were old hands, having sprung forth three years prior.

What with pancake griddlers, pizza bakers, taco cookers, steak broilers, hamburger joints, chicken friers, and sandwich makers proliferating over the landscape, it would seem that the saturation point was not far off. By September 1968 there were, by *Barron's* magazine's[2] count, about 250 firms selling franchises to individuals. Publicly traded companies numbered some fifteen in 1968, about thirty

[2] September 15, 1969 issue.

more had registered their intention to follow suit with the SEC in succeeding months, and the magazine estimated that the total would reach around four hundred by the end of 1969. "As long as they're buying," the enfranchisers seemed to be saying, "we're selling." The financial journal seemed to be sounding its customary warning, but who was listening?

Cashing In—Kentucky Fried

Most gastronomes would agree that the colonel's chicken was a good product, particularly in contrast with some of the vulcanized birds then being offered. The chickens were meaty and were not too heavily coated with flour. Further, they were fried in soy bean oil, which was changed frequently. A healthy product all in all, not that most people care what they put into their stomachs. It was easy to sell, what with the price of a bucketful (fifteen pieces) being six dollars and serving some four to six good appetites. To aid the process, KFC spent eighteen million dollars on advertising in 1968.[3] The question now was: How do you sell the stock? Oh, any insider can sell a few thousand quite easily, but what about two hundred thousand? And what about the prices one would get for them?

Members of the New York Society of Security Analysts might have twitched nervously when Board Chairman Jack C. Massey told them on May 31, 1968:

"We at Kentucky Fried Chicken are very conscious of the importance of you people of the financial community and are quite aware of the influence that you have on opinions about our company and on the actual market for our securities. *You have been good to us during the time our company has been publicly owned* [emphasis mine], and we appreciate your interest and your support and we try very hard to keep you supplied with information you need and to cooperate with you in everything you do. . . . Our purpose here today is to tell you about our company; how it has grown, how it operates, where it is going and what you can expect from it in the future." I have no evidence that he had a more sinister purpose, i.e., unloading his stock upon the financial institutions and the investing public, using the analysts as a conduit. If there were

[3] Ibid.

proof and it were offered, would the analysts believe it? Hardly.

When evidence was provided of patterns of smart money behavior and the resultant action of the securities involved to financial institutions, more than a hundred termed the evidence "technical." Still, more than thirty are now utilizing these techniques, so there's hope.

I'm reminded of an anecdote about Mr. S, chief executive of a large company with which I've had some dealings. Though his office is in a large midwestern city, he knows few brokers and does not socialize with them. By chance, then, he was cornered by the managing partner of a regional brokerage firm, who asked him plaintively, "Why don't you talk to our analyst——. He knows a great deal about your type of business, is a bright fellow, and quite nice." Mr. S responded, "Why should I talk to him? I'm not ready to sell yet."

Back at the Chicken Farm

"We have had a history," Massey on May 31 told the assembled analysts, who represented a cross section of the fund, bank, brokerage house, and investment counselor fraternity that make up the investment community. Any hundred-member turnout could possess the buying-power clout of three billion dollars. Mr. Massey noted that he had spoken to other (regional) societies around the country. He apparently considered it part of his function to keep them "informed."

Mr. Massey noted in his talk in fume city that the initial public offering had been made in 1966 at fifteen dollars a share, and that it had sold the same year at thirty-six dollars, whereupon he split the stock five for four.

"By April of 1967 the price had climbed to fifty-two dollars, by July to seventy-four dollars, October to eighty-five dollars, mid-December to one hundred thirty-two dollars. We split the stock again, three for one, and it went back to fifty dollars. In January it hit a new high of eighty-one dollars, and in the ensuing months it has sold in the seventies, on up to the eighties." Mr. Massey was obviously a chartist.

A bit of mathematics would show that the stock had risen some 900 percent from its initiation in 1966. Readers should realize that no matter what was coming in the company's future, a 900 percent rise in two years should surely discount a great deal of it. In other words, the rise had taken into account virtually all the bullish possibilities, unless the company was another Xerox. I heard of one fellow who, jumping off the Empire State Building, landed on the wing of a passing plane. His chances of repeating the feat are roughly comparable to finding another Xerox. It did happen that KFC rose another 40 percent in the ensuing year, to its peak. But what were its chances of rising another 900 percent as against dropping at least half of the prior gain? As a matter of fact, after the modest rise following Massey's talk, the stock eventually fell 70 percent *from the price at which one might have bought it during the analysts' meeting.*

The experts present at the session came to hear what the marvelous future had in store for the holders (and buyers) of Kentucky Fried Chicken. Mr. Massey introduced Kent Prestwich, "to tell you about our new roast beef program." Mr. Prestwich was a former franchisee, now vice president of KFC in charge of the roast beef sandwich promotion. Mr. Massey said that Prestwich "is doing a fantastic job."

Mr. Prestwich told of his first operation in Las Vegas, which had produced a net profit before taxes of eleven thousand dollars on gross sales of sixty-nine thousand dollars, or about 17 percent. Later experience showed that the location of the first roast beef spot proved an apt one. Mr. Prestwich showed a photo, blown up movie screen size, of the Las Vegas operation and said that KFC planned "three hundred such outlets within a twenty-four-month period."

Mr. Massey then introduced John Y. Brown, the company president.

"It's great to be No. 1 . . . and still growing. And it's a pleasure to be here with you today, to explain why we continue to grow, and how we are going to grow in the future." Mr. Brown told about the company's spot TV commercials and showed them to the assembled multitude. He told them of a new outlet in the Philippines and of two in Australia, and mentioned their man in Germany. He said, too, that he hoped to have two hundred company-owned stores by the end of the following year, and indicated what these would bring in terms of profits.

"To save you the trouble of multiplication, two hundred stores averaging $250,000 would produce annual gross sales of fifty million dollars, and pretax profits of at least ten million dollars." To save the reader the same trouble, that's five million dollars taxed, or fifty cents a share.

After his talk, the audience was asked for questions. The first query was how Mr. Prestwich was going to motivate the employees to sell roast beef. The questioner should have realized that motivation was one of KFC's fortes, as this meeting may have attested.

Another question elicited the response that the company was netting in excess of 10 percent after taxes. How many in the audience realized the unsustainability of this figure? But the reader can, and should.

Another questioner asked if he could really meet Colonel Sanders. Shut my typewriter if the old colonel, a director now and, more importantly, symbol (at a sixty-thousand-dollar salary), wasn't there in the corner, and he was greeted with the kind of applause usually reserved for heads of state. He responded with becoming modesty.

There were other questions, such as how many units did KFC have abroad? Nobody, of course, asked the real question: "What are we doing here?" At any rate, Mr. Brown smiled, Mr. Massey smiled, Mr. Prestwich smiled, and one could see the twinkle in the colonel's eye as they wended their way out.

A Bit Optimistic?

Mr. Prestwich had said that 109 present chicken franchisers had signed up for the roast beef operations, and that, apparently, was just the beginning. He had also said that a $4000 franchise fee would be paid by each outlet opened. And new franchises would have to pay $10,000 apiece.

"A unit grossing $40,000 a month, or $480,000 annually, will pay royalties of $14,400 a year. A hundred units then would pay royalties of $1,440,000 a year. We know that each unit will make a significant contribution to the corporate net income."

What analysts present would fail to be impressed with such numbers, particularly since this was on top of the already dynamic growth the chain had achieved? Mr. Prestwich further said, "We conservatively plan three hundred outlets in operation within a twenty-four-month period." Just how conservative Mr. Prestwich had been could have been challenged by a statement in *Barron's*[4] subsequently, "Yet the beef outlets cost twice as much and yield 35 percent lower returns." A KFC official, said the magazine, reported "They're averaging about 12 percent pretax, against the 18 percent a good KFC chicken-store operator can point for." Aside from Mr. Prestwich's possible overoptimism, if the chicken business was so good, why would the company go into another field in which the risks might be greater and rewards fewer? Hard to say, except that one may note that Mr. Prestwich transferred 11,719 shares a little over a month before the analysts' meeting, according to SEC reports. George Rood of the New York *Times* wrote in the *Magazine of Wall Street* in July that at some point the "chicken war" might develop into a cockfight with the proliferation of roadside stands. This was the same month that Corporate Secretary Murine F. McGuire sold fifteen hundred shares and Treasurer Kenneth J. Coomer slid out of a thousand. At prices then prevailing, it would give the latter some $80,000 and the former some $120,000. Soon after, chairman Massey told *Investment Dealer's Digest*,[5] "We have some eighteen hundred retail outlets today, and we have plenty of room to expand. We believe that there will be four thousand outlets by the end of fiscal 1975." In addition, he said that seventy-five stores were projected for foreign markets by the end of 1969, not to mention negotiating "a tie-in agreement with major oil companies to build units at major gas station locations." The article was headed, "Kentucky Fried Chicken Corp. Flies High over Wall Street," and Mr. Massey forecasted "continuing increases in sales and earnings." The *Digest* readers (brokerage firm employees) could presumably sell the stock to their customers with the confidence that the bird would continue to soar. Even *Business Management*, in its August 1968 issue, pointed out, "Franchising—and franchise firms—can be downright profitable. And they can get that way fast." The insiders had found another way to make money—convert their low-cost stock certificates into cash—and they had a lot more to go.

[4] September 22, 1969.
[5] July 29, 1968.

The Purveyor of Information

Board Chairman Jack C. Massey continued his program of enlightening the investment community with a talk before the Investment Analysts Society of Chicago on September 19, 1968. "Many of you may recall that we were here for another type of meeting a few months ago, and several of you were in that group." It was nice of Mr. Massey to be so accessible and informative, don't you think? However, one might note that Mr. Massey had plenty of time for educating the masses. He was in a relaxed frame of mind, you might say, since he had cashed in some *seventeen million dollars'* worth of certificates in a secondary distribution[6] through Lehman Brothers and Goodbody & Company and over a hundred other brokers a few months earlier. Thus Mr. Massey could spend his time enriching mankind's store of knowledge rather than on more crass pursuits. "We have occasion to speak to groups such as yours with some frequency," he noted.

"On each occasion, we must truthfully announce that sales and earnings have again increased over the same period of the previous year by 80 to 100 percent." He noted that the stock price rises had merely kept pace with the earnings rises, and "This is one reason that so much of our stock is held in funds, where portfolios are managed by professional investors."

What is meant by the appellation, "professional"? Webster's New Collegiate Dictionary, briefly stated, defines professional: "1: of, relating to, or characteristic of a profession [which tells us nothing]; 2: participating for gain or livelihood in an activity or field of endeavor often engaged in by amateurs [true]; and 3: following a line of conduct as though it were a profession." Judging by the performance cited by two Wharton School studies of mutual fund activity (showing that investors would do about as well investing in most funds as in portfolios without such "professional" management), one might vote for the third. Specifically, in early 1968, with the stock selling at around thirty dollars a share (adjusted for

6 Brokers line up customers for a large block of stock sold by insiders. The customers do not pay the usual commission; rather, in essence, it is borne by the sellers.

all splits), only two funds owned Kentucky Fried Chicken.[7] In the second quarter, with the stock selling between thirty-five and forty dollars, seven funds owned it. Enterprise Fund, which had owned 170,000 shares, increased its (your) commitment by over twenty-seven thousand shares. Total fund ownership amounted to 7 percent of the number of shares outstanding, versus 4.6 percent in the first quarter.

After more brokerage firms recommended the stock and Mr. Massey helped to inform Wall Street about KFC, the Diversified Growth Stock Fund made its first commitment, fifty thousand shares. The stock ranged between thirty-six and forty-five dollars during the period. Funds do not often state their purchase and sale price for equities, for if they did it might prove embarrassing to some. Enterprise added a bit and Fletcher Capital added 14,100 shares to the twenty-eight thousand bought in the previous quarter. Putnam Growth Fund saw the "growth" in Kentucky and bought seventy-seven hundred shares to bring their total to 37,700. It was obvious that while the informed minority was selling, the uninformed majority was buying.

If the analysts present on September 19, 1968 had been cautioned by the New York *Times*' caveat on June 23 of that year concerning get-rich-quick speculation and the point made that the price-earnings ratios of 50 to 70 prevalent in the franchising group "puts them in a class of such market superstars as IBM, Xerox, and Polaroid," why not pay that price if, as Mr. Massey told the assembled multitude, "There is a great deal more growth left in Kentucky Fried Chicken Corporation than it has already had"?

Mr. Massey quoted *Institutions* magazine to the analysts as estimating total volume for the corporation of $360 million, though how they could know more about KFC than its chairman of the board, I fail to see. Perhaps it was just modesty on Mr. Massey's part. Though he was the great information provider, even he could learn from a trade publication. Mr. Massey provided many figures on the company's operations otherwise, and he really hit home with the information that in Chicago there were fifty-three KFC units, with twenty-eight more to be in operation by February.

"I hope that all of you are regular customers of one of our Chicago

[7] Fund data supplied by *Facts on the Funds* (New York: Weisenburger Services, 1 New York Plaza, N.Y. 10004).

stores. You will find a coupon good for a bucket of chicken on the table in front of you. I hope that you will use this to treat your family to a Kentucky Fried Chicken dinner as our guests."

Mr. Massey did not say he hoped they would buy his stock. Nonetheless he closed with the mention that they had just filed an application for listing on the New York Stock Exchange, and "Hopefully, by November 1 you will be able to follow the KFC symbol we have requested on the Big Board."

As Indian Summer rounded the bend and leaves took on rosy hues and the breeze brought with it a chill nip in the air, the chicken stock did what a real chicken rarely does—it started to fly. Spurred by the "realization" in Wall Street that KFC was a corporation that might grow and prosper, investors thought to fly along with it. Advisory services recommended it, bankers noticed it, analysts saw its possibilities—and there is little that excites analysts more than "action" in a stock's price. Merrill Lynch advised in October, "We believe that the company will extend its excellent growth record by opening more Kentucky Fried Chicken units in large communities, by its entrance into smaller communities with outlets carrying roast beef sandwiches as well as chicken, by emphasizing company-owned units in its expansion, and by acquiring previously franchised stores." The growth-oriented booklet in which this quotation appeared listed thirty-seven investment opportunities, among which were such as Loew's Theatres, Zenith Radio, Twentieth Century-Fox, Restaurant Associates, and RCA. The firm was among the foremost in "full disclosure," and noted that it owned *for its own account* or that of its officers or voting stockholders over one hundred thousand dollars' worth of the stock.

Banks were putting the pension funds they managed into stock; investment counselors were buying the stock for their accounts, along with some others, such as Four Seasons Nursing Homes, Mohawk Data, and Levin-Townsend Computer. When some were concerned that they might be exposing clients to undue risk, they chose American Can for balance, which, though it might not go up much, probably would not go down much either. KFC stock broke through to fifty dollars (on a split basis) for the first time. Mutual funds, which along with others had been somewhat responsible for the rise with their concentrated buying, owned 819,764 shares, representing 9.1 percent of the total issue, as the year drew to a close.

Director Pete Harmon (the owner at one point of ninety-two KFC outlets) saw his way clear to sell 10,600 shares in November, according to SEC reports.

"Get 'em while they're hot!" the hot dog sellers howl at football games, but few frankfurters ever got as hot as the chicken stock. With the arrival of 1969 and the impending New York Stock Exchange listing of KFC, George Rood interviewed President John Y. Brown for the New York *Times.* The January 5 article told readers that "KFC stock reflects the company's success story." Mr. Brown revealed that "We're already making plans for a string of outlets in Europe—we've got two in Germany now—and we're looking into other areas, too."

In a personal note, Mr. Brown, it seemed, had been No. 2 man on the University of Kentucky's golf team behind Gay Brewer, the Masters champion, though he wistfully said he had "no time for golf any more."

"I love the chicken business," Mr. Brown said, and well he might. The investment community loved the business too, although each had their own reasons. Five new funds bought in during the first quarter of 1969: Colonial Growth Shares, Financial Industrial, the Hedge Fund of America, Putnam Vista Fund, and the giant Investors Diversified Services, through its Progressive Fund. With its vast resources of analysis, IDS could spot such exciting investment opportunities. Who could blame any of them? They were joining the thundering multitude caught up in the euphoria of a hot stock. Even Mr. Brown may have wondered about it, as he told the *Times,* "I'm not saying we can keep doubling like this forever, but over-all things look pretty good."

The new year did not witness a diminution in the "franchise opportunities" offered investors through ads in the *Wall Street Journal,* New York *Times,* and countless other papers around the country. In the words of one such ad (in the *Wall Street Journal* of January 15), "Picking the proper franchise is not simple. It's simply puzzling" (Franchises International, a subsidiary of City Investing). Judging from the subsequent name-calling between City and Franchises, either Franchises found its choice of a merger partner also "difficult" or City Investing found its franchise acquisition quite "puzzling." It may be noted that City was a multimillion-dollar outfit, and if they found it disappointing, what of the ten-thousand-dollar investor? Franchises International noted in the ad that they were No. 1 in the business, one may add.

The day KFC was listed on the New York Stock Exchange, January 16, 1969, it traded thirty-three thousand shares and closed at 46⅞. The analysts had all day to share in the excitement of watching the KFC symbol cross the tape, and if vicarious thrills did not appeal to them, they could always buy the stock for themselves or recommend it to their fund managements.

Those financial institutions whose appetites had not yet been whetted for Kentucky Fried had another opportunity to be titillated when a conference was held at the New York Hilton Hotel from January 22–24 under the auspices of *Institutional Investor* magazine. The publication is a highly successful one distributed to the stock-buying financial community and is festooned with ads from those who would get their business. Somehow KFC didn't make that conference, though International Industries (House of Pancakes) did. So did Holiday Inns, whose graceful signs dot the tawdry landscapes astride the highways of our nation. Howard B. Johnson of the chain of the same name was there too, though he was most candid, in keeping with the more conservative nature of his stock. Mr. Johnson pointed out that Dun's *Review*, in their January issue, estimated that "four thousand of this year's new franchise ventures are doomed to failure."

The Stock—What's Happening?

With all the promotion the franchise industry was getting, by the end of February KFC was selling at only forty dollars a share, this despite two weeks in the month in which over one hundred thousand shares changed hands—and this despite another plug for the stock in the February 5 edition of *Investor's Reader,* a Merrill Lynch publication. Articles were selected for their "news or general interest," the magazine said, and not for their investment characteristics. Still, it couldn't hurt, *n'est-ce pas?* The article had a photo of a pretty girl between President John Brown and the septuagenarian colonel. The reader might assume that the girl was a paid model, for she was looking at the colonel.

"Handsome, thirty-four-year-old boss Brown," said the magazine, was looking into the motel field, and "we're interested in continued earnings growth but we want to build a sound business operation and don't intend to rush into anything without being prepared." That was good to hear, said some, and hadn't Brown and Massey proved it by their fantastic success with KFC?

With March coming on, the winds of doubt began to swirl among some traders. "What's keeping the stock down?" one tape watcher asked his neighbor at the back of a Chicago boardroom. He had not been one of the more than 650 shareholders who attended the company's annual meeting, but he had just received the report of the event from Kentucky Fried. Mr. Brown had told the assembled (and was telling all shareholders through a folder report) that, in the words of Victor Hugo, "there is nothing so powerful as an idea that has come of age." He (Brown, not Hugo) related the remark to the chicken business, which indeed had come of age. Investors who bought the stock at fifty dollars only to sell it out later on for much lower prices might have felt that the chicken stock already had arthritis.

"Today, all of us happen to be a part of one of the great success stories in American history," Mr. Brown said. "One filled with truth, romance, nostalgia—one built and developed in the true Horatio Alger fashion, one that is truly the fulfillment of the great American dream."

The mutual funds wanted to become a part of that dream. American Express Special Fund bought 16,000 shares of KFC, Colonial Equity Fund picked up 30,400, Commonwealth Capital bought 22,000, and IDS added 50,000 between two of its funds. Now the portfolio managers of these and three others could watch the tape and see KFC cross it with heightened interest. They could also see it cross more frequently, as weekly volume soared to 200,000, and yet the stock rose to only $50 a share. If the stock was to fulfill the dreams of fund managers it would have to do better than that. It wasn't as though they weren't trying, what with Manhattan Fund buying 131,000 shares alone. Keystone's Low Priced Fund (designated S-4) hoped the stock would become a higher priced one as they picked up 105,000 shares. The brokerage community's ardor for the stock had not cooled yet—and a smaller brokerage firm suggested "purchase in aggressive accounts." Noting that Jack Massey and the Massey Foundation had filed intent with the SEC to offer 400,000 shares in early May, the firm said, "We do not expect the secondary to be a depressant on the performance of the stock." That would be true, of course, if enough enthusiasm, excitement, and "dreams" were extant to cover the sales by Mr. Massey, who, along with Mr. Brown, was given to more realistic business appraisals, as witness the success of their venture. Plainly, they were not dreamers.

Why the Institutions Bought

The funds, the banks, and the insurance companies that bought shares in Kentucky Fried are no different from you or me. They are groups of human beings who act rationally sometimes and irrationally at other times. The problem was that to be consistently successful in investments requires, in addition to other attributes, that one be *in*human. It is human to be caught up in the speculative fever that accompanies wild price rises in stocks. It is human to want to "get in on the action." It is inhuman to stand aside and say, "If that many people want in, I want out." It is inhuman to be unmoved by public passion, whether it is in political movements, manners of dress, or stocks. The mob[8] is invariably wrong. I recall recommending a stock to an analyst with a major fund. He turned it down, citing among other reasons, "If Morgan Guaranty, IDS, and Fidelity buy it, I'll look into it." Having a mind of his own would have been helpful, or perhaps he was illuminating his own insecurity. Indeed, I know of two funds who bought KFC, partly on the basis of their inbreeding conversations with other institutions. They too are part of the "crowd."

Money managers no less than other people (unfortunately) are influenced by the media, which envelop them in a blanket of mass images. *Time* magazine, in its April 18, 1969 issue, was one of many publications that heralded "Franchising: [the] New Power for 500,000 Small Businessmen." It was around the time franchises were being offered in everything from shoe-repair shops to dental-technician schools to a system for correcting bed-wetting. The news media were infected with the same franchise frenzy as the funds and the banks—and their excitement rebounded off the money managers to the media to the public to other publications to the money

[8] The investor is advised to read *The Crowd*, by Gustave LeBon, an excellent treatise on mass psychology, and, in the same vein, *The True Believer*, by Eric Hoffer.

managers to the brokers and back again. The exhilaration of the boom was self-feeding, and, ultimately, self-defeating, as it led to excess. It was under the strength of all the euphoria that the informed minority were able to get good prices for their shares, since they are more hard-nosed than investors.

To the informed minority buying stock was just like any other business. Buy stock with good prospects and public indifference and sell it at high markups to an eager multitude. The institutional buyers are yesterday's odd-lotters. They have become "the little guy" of the fifties, if not in their money power, then in thought and action. By the way, KFC treasurer Charles Hitner sold again on April 29, grossing some $450,000 on the day. This was during the period that the funds' position jumped 50 percent—with eight of them assuming brand-new positions. If they were a little late for the gravy train, this would not be a novel position for them. I recall the grin Robert Bofrou of Central Penn Bank and I had at the prospect of their future embarrassment. No, rather than a grin, make that a sigh of resignation.

There were, of course, many who did not go along. I recall Ralph O'Brien then of State Bond & Mortgage (New Ulm, Minnesota), Donald W. Ellsworth, Sr., of the Axe Funds, and Dave Pettit and Monty Zinc of Steadman. And three others I knew bought despite evidence to the contrary. It seems that their boards of directors liked the stock, and they were powerless to refuse. It may surprise the reader to know that internal politics often decide investment policy among institutions, and sometimes the freedom of the manager has a direct relationship to fund performance.

Uncle Sam Steps in

On May 7, 1969, the Federal Trade Commission announced that it was investigating the franchise business and that fifty organizations had been ordered to file special reports. How many franchise buyers had lost how many millions by then was incalculable. As far as KFC was concerned, its stock was not affected since it was one of the "clean" ones. The money managers continued to buy as the insiders continued to sell. Company director Ervin E. Hanks eased out of some six hundred thousand dollars' worth during May, the same month that the New York *Times* (on May 26) featured the success story of Patrick J. O'Hanlon, who left a small farm in County Armagh, Ireland, to find riches as a purveyor of donuts in Wilmington, Delaware. The *Times* noted that "There is presently a lot of concern in the franchise industry that fast food systems will soon crowd each other so severely that there won't be enough business to go around." If that worried the investment community, the *Times* said, however, "the stronger ones will no doubt survive." Thus the investor (and by proxy the institutional investor) did not have to work the seven days a week that Pat did. He could make it easier and faster in the market. Why not? Didn't KFC earn fifty-two cents a share for the recent six-month period, against thirty-three cents for the previous year's comparable time? Didn't Messrs. Brown and Massey say that KFC in addition has "concentrated on building for the future," and was moving into further diversification by acquiring a fish and chips operation, H. Salt, Esq., and reveal that KFC had built its first motel, the Colonel Sanders Inn?

All that "good news" no doubt impressed the financial institutions. Investors Diversified Services may have been influenced, for the second of their funds, IDS New Dimensions, bought 28,400 during the second quarter, a period in which some more insiders did a bit of unloading. They included Harland Adams, K. J. Coomer, and Leon Harmon's wife, the latter selling twenty thousand shares, almost as much as the IDS fund bought.

Broiling

The franchise boom was at its zenith—and new issues were being floated to an eager public at a phenomenal rate. The stocks were rocketing upward immediately the day they started trading. Sambo's Restaurants opened at nineteen dollars and closed out the week at twenty-six dollars. Mr. Steak came out at fifteen dollars and jumped to twenty-seven dollars. Church's Fried Chicken went from seventeen to twenty-seven dollars in a single day. The brokers were doing favors for their clients by letting them in on a good thing—and wasn't this an easy way to make money! Famous names were being attached to fast food operations, and this did not exactly hurt their stocks, since the investor could not only "make it big" in a hurry but went the autograph hunters one better. Instead of getting their signatures on a piece of paper, they could "own a piece" of a star, in a sense. Thus Pat Boone had his Favorite Foods of America, Eddy Arnold his Tennessee Fried Chicken, Al Capp his Li'l Abner Restaurants, Mickey Mantle his Country Cookin', not to leave out Sammy Davis, Jr., Willie Mays, Hank Williams, Jr., Ernie Ford, and Johnny Carson. Stars these days found it *de rigueur* to have agents, voice coaches, P.R. men, *and* franchise consultants. Not a few of the latter took advantage of their clients' business naïveté to cash in on the boom.

The infection had become a plague, with large and small investors not immune to the glory and the gold. Still, some analysts told their managements that perhaps the shadow of a Ponzi could be seen in the dim recesses of the buying panic. One "technical"[9] analyst told his fund portfolio manager to sell KFC stock. He was ignored. When I inquired as to what happened to the manager, who did not sell until much later (and lower), I was told that he had been fired. "They fired him, for only one mistake?" I queried. "No, he made many of them, just like a lot of us. His personality just didn't fit in," said the technician. "Is personality more important than ability?" I asked. "No, but there are more nice guys than those with talent," was the reply.

On June 16 (the story appeared on the seventeenth), Mr. Brown told the *Wall Street Journal* that "We're a young, hungry crowd, and we've got the management expertise to move into growth-oriented fields." There were some dissenters among the brokerage community. "The way things are going, we'll soon have a food franchiser in every backyard. There doesn't seem to be any end to them," said one. Yet Mr. Brown said that the fast-food industry "still has great opportunities."

Mr. Brown may have been helping Mr. Massey spread information about Kentucky Fried. And he was aided by the bulls on the stock among some brokers. The fund managers were typified by Larry Rader of Enterprise (which owned 398,000 shares), who said[10] he was "very positive on the group—long and short term."

[9] A technical analyst is one who uses price charts, trading volume, or other devices to determine that a stock should be bought or sold, rather than the more popular approach of observing earnings and supposed prospects for corporate growth. There are, of course, both good and bad technicians, though there are more of the latter.

[10] *Wall Street Journal*, June 18, 1969.

By "the group" he meant the franchisers, but especially KFC, Hardee's, and American Snacks.

Keep the Faith, Baby

On July 14, 1969, *Institutional Investor* did another clever thing with a "Videoforum," a closed-circuit television setup, and invited John Brown and two broker-analysts. George Goodman (Adam Smith) of the magazine moderated, but had his licks at the guest. In discussing the food chain's current practice of buying back franchises from their holders and paying for them with stock (at five times earnings), he asked Mr. Brown, "The owner/operator that sold the thing back to you has got a block of Kentucky Fried Chicken stock and can sell it at any time [can't he?]." Mr. Brown's reply was a gem. "I'd say that is a problem but they have such great faith that we're going right on up to the sky that they don't want to sell, and we're still keeping them motivated at the present time." Mr. Harmon may have been motivated, for he bought back five thousand shares in the open market. One of the presumed motivators, Jack Massey, had just sold 350,000 shares through a secondary, bringing him some *seventeen million dollars,* which may say something about who does better, the motivated or the motivators. It may all be purely coincidence, however. And Mr. Brown did say at the forum, "Well, of course, we can't expect to double every year *ad infinitum;* but we do feel we've got quite an aggressive growth program ahead." The reader will please note that the emphasis was Mr. Brown's, not mine.

After a brief discussion on the question of KFC raising their own chickens, Mr. Brown really laid it on the line with this blockbuster, "I don't know of a business in America that has less downside risk than Kentucky Fried Chicken." From Los Angeles to Chicago to New York, institutional investors heard that remark and saw Mr. Brown make it. Perhaps he did not mean to say it so strongly, but could the analyst fail to be impressed by such a statement?

Analysts viewing the event were split in their views of KFC as an investment. Indeed, seven funds did some selling during the third quarter. But many more bought, to bring the total to twenty-three in all, holding 16.1 percent of the outstanding shares. The figure was higher counting bank purchases. Another insider, George W. Baker, sold seventy-five hundred shares during the period.

Going Nowhere

United Business Service said on July 14, "Now 41, the stock is worth holding as a long-term speculation. Competition in the food-franchising field is thickening, but management is obviously optimistic about the industry's future." Obviously.

As July drew to a close, KFC stock was selling at forty-four dollars a share, disappointing considering the buying thrust provided by institutional investors during the summer. The technician again told his fund manager to sell the stock. His plea met deaf ears—"What could *he* know?" The investment chief was being informed (indirectly) of the company's progress, and he noticed the "visibility of the earnings."

In Des Plaines, Illinois, a suburb of Chicago, clear to anyone's visibility were twelve fast-food places in a three-block area on Route 83. A *Wall Street Journal* reporter saw them, and was told by Leo Carli, owner of a Burger Chef franchise there, "It's a dog-eat-dog deal. If one more hamburger place comes here, we'll all be dead." Mr. Carli was looking to sell out, said the paper on September 10. "Yet even as he speaks, contractors clear the ground for a new hamburger drive-in, a new fried chicken unit, a new roast beef stand and a new doughnut operation—all on the same three-block strip."

Though some analysts worried about overconcentration, most were bullish on KFC, "because it's a strong operation." Hardly noticed were the spiraling real estate costs in opening new units. And KFC was committed to continued expansion. They certainly were not cutting back on their public relations efforts—and another payoff (apparently) resulted when the New York *Times* on September 15 ran a substantial story on a successful KFC franchise in Warsaw, Indiana. Mr. and Mrs. Earl Smalley had switched from a luncheonette, which brought them three thousand dollars a year, to Kentucky Fried, which gave them fifty thousand dollars. Mr. O'Hanlon and Mr. Smalley could not be begrudged their success. Mr. Smalley and his wife both worked sixty hours weekly the first year. Stock investors hoped to make it big with less effort. And institutional investors sometimes bought stock with little more care than "the little guy."

How many bothered to check the insider trading on KFC? Informing them of the fact found one as welcome as a Western Union boy with a wire about a dead relation. They never learned about the operations of smart money in business school, and they were not about to learn now.

One of the institutional brokerage firms that had been following up on its earlier recommendations of KFC now (in September) said, "We would not be aggressive buyers at this time. On a longer-term basis, however, we continue to regard the shares as attractive, and a year from now could see the stock perhaps in the mid-seventies, assuming a 25 price/earnings ratio, if prevailing Street estimates of three dollars a share pan out." This could give the stock a 50 percent price rise, the broker said. Another recommendation in the same report favored Parvin-Dohrmann (seventy-seven dollars at the time), a good way to buy Denny's Restaurants (with which a merger was contemplated), another food chain. We all have our little disappointments.

The advisory services were warm on the stock, too, as *Value Line* rated it as "average" in potential appreciation over the next twelve months and "above average" for the 1972–74 period. The stock was selling at fifty dollars at the time, October 3, 1969.

The P.R. mill kept churning away as KFC announced that it had made a deal for development of stores in Japan and the pickup of operations in Britain. This was in mid-October, and five days later they said KFC "has agreed in principle to acquire an Alabama poultry producer" *and* made a joint-venture agreement to establish two hundred fish and chip stores.

Down the Stretch

Despite some reservations in Standard & Poor's *Industry Survey* of October 23, KFC, which had lain dormant in price over the summer, gained new life. Several banks added to their holdings, and others bought for the first time. Fund buying remained feverish, though some did sell. Enterprise held on to their huge commitment, but Channing Growth unloaded their 125,000-share position. IDS's feelings were ambivalent, with one fund buying, then selling (or was it the other way around?) and another of their funds buying. Investor's Variable Payment picked up 150,000 shares and Manhattan sold 75,000. The net result was that the funds held 1,547,000 shares, slightly less than they had the previous quarter. They now owned 15.6 percent of the stock. Some smaller funds, more speculative than the larger ones, "took a flyer" (as one put it) and bought. His was a "hedge" fund, meaning that he could go short[11] if he were bearish. He should have been. Perhaps he, like some bank trust departments, was influenced by KFC's nine-month pamphlet report, which showed profits of eighty-five cents a share versus fifty cents a share for the same period in 1968, and which said, "We are most optimistic about the growth opportunities in the years to come. The continued support and interest of our stockholders is greatly appreciated." No doubt.

On September 4, the same brokerage firm that recommended Whittaker and National Student Marketing turned a bit cooler on Kentucky. Two other stockbrokers were more bullish, one of whom had suggested Levin-Townsend at between forty and fifty dollars. If the reader is not familiar with all these issues, he can note that the above was told to me by a very bitter fund man. The brokers, it seems, were all "institutional" in their research, though some fund managers were thinking of another type of institution when they recalled the recommendations.

Boiling Over

As 1969 drew to a close, the chicken pot was still boiling, though cracks were beginning to appear on the kettle's surface. Erstwhile politician John Jay Hooker's Minnie Pearl operation, which had been offered to the public at $6.75 in May of 1968, had slumped to $3. Five Wishbone Fried Chicken stores had closed in Memphis, Tennessee, and Chicken Delight's wings were clipped somewhat with the 660 stores in 1966 having their ranks reduced to 553. *Newsweek* told of a Burger Chef franchise holder, James Donovan, who had dropped nearly $45,000 in the hamburger war. Still, the magazine asked itself the question, "Is the great franchise game, then, all over?" It answered optimistically, "The answer seems to be, probably not—at least not yet."[12] Nevertheless, by the end of 1969, *New Issue Performance* directory (published by New Issue Out-

[11] One does this if he expects the stock to go down and profit by it.

[12] Wishbone, Chicken Delight figures and the quoted material from *Newsweek*, November 10, 1969.

look of New York City) listed the price action during the year for stocks that had been offered to the public. The top percentage loser in the country was Cobbs Co., Inc., which had gone public in March with plans to develop a franchise chain. The stock had fallen 95 percent.

Other disasters, pricewise, were Unitas Quarterback Club, down 82 percent, Mickey Mantle's Country Cookin', down 77 percent, and Al Hirt's Sandwiches, down the same. Chicken Chef Systems and Mr. Swiss of the East were close competitors for big-loser honors, with 76 percent and 75 percent drops, respectively. Beefy King, Mr. Steak, Inc., Broadway Joe's, Hamburger Hamlet, and Church's Fried Chicken did somewhat less badly, hardly a solace to disgruntled investors who plunked down their hard-earned shekels in a vain attempt to participate in a boom that may have been over before they found out it had begun. They were picking the chicken bones of the franchisers, and the bell was sounding for KFC. Yet the pallid butcher on the pale horse had not yet reached Kentucky Fried. The distant hoofbeats were heard by but a few.

On December 8 *U.S. News & World Report* headlined a story, "A Business of Your Own, The Growth of Franchising." "It's catching on everywhere," they said. David Slater, president of the Mutual Franchise Corporation, was quoted as saying, "Franchising has had its share of growing pains. Right now, it is plagued by tight money, heightened competition, and rising costs. Still, I can't think of an area with more promise for people who are willing to work hard and stick with a venture until it begins to pay off."

One of the institutional brokers who had recommended KFC in mid-December said, "While KFC remains one of our favorites for longer-term growth, we would prefer new commitments at current levels in *International Industries* (41) and *Lums* (22)." The emphases were theirs, and so were the prices. They did not remain at these exalted levels for long.

The broker of Whittaker National Student Marketing fame was again saying nice things about KFC, which may have heartened the institutional buyers, but it had little effect on Vice President Donald D. Greer apparently, since he sold 31,500 shares valued at some $1,364,000. Mr. Harmon appeared to be unaffected as he resumed his selling ways during the month with 6200 shares, and

Jack Massey's foundation the next month traded 10,000 shares for $450,000 of a more liquid species. Possibly they did not know of the continued recommendation by the prestigious stockbrokers or perhaps they did—and sold because of it. One of the few bears on the stock from a lesser-known firm among the Wall Street community approached many institutional investors with his tale of gloom for KFC. But "it was," as they say in Kentucky, "like spitting into the wind."

Wings Clipped

Harland Adams was another insider who was oblivious of the more popular bullishness in the Street, perhaps, for he grossed $1,440,000 for his February 1970 sales. In fact, February looked like a chicken coop during a fox raid as Messrs. Baker, Harmon, Barlow, and Thomas sold stock. This did not exactly help the price of KFC, which during the month slipped below $40 for the first time in a long time. Even some of the funds sold. Yet as many bought as sold —even more, in fact. The first quarter ended with total fund position in the stock back at 18.6 percent of the outstanding shares. When the stock cracked $40, then $38, then $36, many financial "experts" felt that they had a "bargain." They may have been cautious at $50, one Street observer said, "but now the stock was cheap." It was to get cheaper. The fund with the bearish technician "averaged down," thus reducing its average cost. After the stock had fallen to around $37, the chicken was let out of the bag. That marvelous growth image got a bit singed. It was announced in August that net profits for the June 30 quarter dropped from $.36 a share to $.31. As for the chain's grandiose plans, Mr. Brown told Dan Dorfman of the *Wall Street Journal* (August 13, 1970 issue) that fiscal 1970 was "a year in which we're catching our breath." As to the motel operation, "At this time, we're in a holding pattern." The roast beef? "It hasn't been successful." KFC's average cost was to go still lower, and the fund sold out below $20. The bearish broker was, at $40, yelling his lungs out. The bullish institutions could not hear him. In one case a fund blamed him for the stock's drop. Others did not return his calls. He embarrassed them, particularly at $15. Among those who were not embarrassed (though they didn't care about the broker either, they had their own reasons) were insiders Adams (again), Vice President Martin ($500,000),[13] and Haddon Salt, who got his stock when fish and chip joined the KFC menu.

The Game

According to the International Franchise Association,[14] more than a hundred enfranchisers raised money from the public to begin their operations (or planned to) during 1969. Then they sold franchises to other segments of the public, thus stretching their capital further by using the franchisers' money to open retail units. The units sold merchandise (or occasionally services) to the public, and many eventually sold their low-cost stock at higher prices to another segment of the public, though of course there was overlapping. The same investor might serve more than one function to the enfranchiser. But the buck stopped with insiders' stock selling, which reaped the largest gains. In the current stock market, dominated as it is by larger investors, the payoff is often made at the expense of the institutions, who of course in many cases got their money from the public anyway. In this case, workers' pension fund money, trust fund contributors, "special situations"[15] fund investors at banks, mutual fund purchasers, etc., provided the money power that enabled the stocks to rise, or to stay high while insiders were able to get good prices. This is not a one-for-one situation, since it is difficult to say exactly who bought whose stock. It's safe to say at least that KFC, for example, would not have gone up as far as it did or stayed up as long if the more than 1.5 million dollars' worth had not been gobbled up by the funds. When the *Wall Street Journal* (on November 11, 1969) added to the old stock market story of the fellow who was shown stockbrokers' yachts and asked, "Where are the customers' yachts?" they used the expression, "Where are the [franchise] dealers' yachts?" At that imaginary boat basin, they all belonged to the franchise company insiders.

Investors in KFC stock might have been chewed up somewhat, but they could rest assured in the knowledge that the colonel would go on. A younger Colonel Sanders, reportedly a nephew (the real

[13] During 1970 there was some buying by insiders in KFC, it should be noted. The selling was far heavier, however.

[14] *Wall Street Journal*, November 11, 1969.

[15] A general term. Each bank has its own expression for more speculative types of investments.

one is over eighty) was unveiled at a "finger-lickin'" picnic for employees at the ground-breaking of new corporate headquarters in 1969. The "new" colonel would presumably carry on inveigling the faithful, replete in the same double-breasted suit, string tie, and goatee, a source of joy to hungry Americans and sorrow to (now) poorer ones.

A Lesson

One of the lessons of this chapter for the investor is to scan the mutual funds' position list[16] to see their holdings. It has been my observation that while an increasing number of buyers may add impetus at first, when they all begin to climb on the bandwagon, get off. Or better yet, don't get on in the first place.

[16] *Facts on Funds,* cited earlier, is a handy source. *Barron's & Financial Chronicle* publish such lists regularly.

eight

Why Penn Central?

"WHY PENN CENTRAL?" is what my editor asked when I discussed including the story in this book. After all, we have already covered the Jimmy Ling encounter, the color TV stock boom, the "Kentucky Frying" of investors.

There are, to be sure, many fascinating and some ludicrous facets to the Penn Central investor railroading. In the first half of 1966, the Pennsylvania Railroad, pride of the East, earned $41 million, or $2.97 a share. On February 1, 1968, a long-awaited merger took place between the Pennsy and the New York Central, also a previously profitable road. It was a "dream" situation for Wall Street, and investors large and small rushed to buy. The combined management projected savings of the merger at eighty million dollars, plus a brilliant future. Yet two years later the Penn Central had to seek protection from the courts (bankruptcy) and in the process hundreds of millions of dollars were lost by investors all over the world. Railroad buffs saw the dissolution of such storied trains as the *Wabash Cannon Ball,* commuters suffered mightily before and after the event, the pension funds of thousands of workers with both blue and white collars were damaged, the financial markets were shaken, and the federal Administration tried to step in, in a clumsy effort to shore things up (some said merely to help the banks, using public tax monies).

The amount of material available to the researcher is vast, thus allowing for considerable detail of the alleged workings "behind the scenes" of the "little train that couldn't." Further, the investigative work done by such as the U. S. House of Representatives Banking and Currency Committee, the U. S. Senate Commerce Committee, and the Interstate Commerce Committee (the regulatory body for the transportation industry),[1] if proven true in court (three of the participants in the Penn Central case have been indicted on criminal charges), show the investor for whose benefit corporations are often run.

Although much of what went on at the Penn Central may appear rather flagrant, it is really a view like Blake's "seeing the world in a grain of sand." Although the PC should perhaps be likened to a rock, the story of what happened is herewith set forth as the symbolic embodiment of what is wrong in the corporate world—illuminated vividly and meticulously by investigative bodies commanding resources never before (to my knowledge) assembled to diagnose a widespread malignancy.

This story highlights classic mismanagement, miscalculation, and internal feuding that contributed to the railroad's collapse, a story so bizarre in parts that it could provide script material for a score of Hollywood films, but it does more. It may also have its benefits —hopefully, it may bring about a new awareness on the part of investors as to what the game is really all about—and some would say that it helps dispel some of the naïveté investors display about their corporate participation.

In short, the informed minority method is here demonstrated with spotlighted inquiry by objective sources. For, though certainly the indicators that tracked the operations of the informed minority could never have predicted a bankruptcy, they did point to serious trouble within the subject.

As we shall see, without any inside information, one could have observed indicators of a substantial stock price drop. These and other indicators throughout the book may help the investor to be forewarned about future stock price disasters. Although quite a number of stocks fell precipitously in the 1950s, '60s, and '70s, few of the companies actually went bankrupt. This provided little solace for those who invested in such as Boise Cascade, Milgo, Memorex,

[1] This writer covered some thirty-four hundred pages of testimony, analysis, charts, and appendices; conducted interviews with participants and observers; and collected material from over one thousand newspaper and magazine clippings.

Telex, and Mohawk Data. And there have been better-quality issues, such as A&P, which sold for as high as $70 in 1961 and slowly spoiled down to $18 in 1971; Otis Elevator, which went "up" to $82 in 1961 and then "down" to a low of $44 in 1962; Con Edison ($49 in 1965) which dimmed a bit to $32 in 1966 and $23 in 1970; Campbell Soup, which sold for $43 in 1961 and slurped its way slowly down to $28 in 1972; Kennecott, which was way up there at $55 in 1970 and copped out to $20 the following year; Scott Paper, which excited investors as the bluest of the blue chips in 1970 and got torn up a bit to fall to as low as $14 the next year. And there was P. K. Wrigley, which sold for as high as $188 in 1971, only to get chewed up within three months down to $120.

The point is that "quality" in a stock is little protection against stock market losses, but checking the informed minority indicators may offer defense. And, as particular informed minority indicators popped up in Penn Central before its collapse, so they will in other stocks, some of which you may contemplate buying—or already own.

The problem is that the investment community presents the façade of a people's capitalism. Participants in it mistakenly think they can get rich. Why should it be shocking that most people are more concerned with their own welfare than with yours?

What the Penn Central story illustrates, to a great extent utilizing the investigative resources of Congress and the Interstate Commerce Commission and presenting their opinion and observations, is that the suspicion the informed minority has as a prime concern the feathering of its own nest is not an idle one. The full realization and embodiment of this should benefit the investors' objectives and should help the investors look at the corporate public relations machine for what it is.

The Penn Central idyll also hints at the behind-the-scenes forces that act upon the stock market—for the informed minority does not always parade itself in the media shop windows.

And last but not least, it may help illuminate the passive role played by the financial institutions who miscalculated in their investment research and bought and held the stock—the process by which these large investors play into the hands, albeit unknowingly, of the informed minority.

For years good children in Philadelphia "were taught to pray for the Republican Party, the Girard Trust (Bank) and the Pennsylvania Railroad."—Nathaniel Burt, *The Perennial Philadelphians*

Cast of Characters

The participants in the drama included:

"Kindly old" *Howard Butcher III,* stockbroker and director of the Penn Central, who advised such venerable institutions as the Presbyterian-University of Pennsylvania Medical Center, the Philadelphia Museum of Art, and the University of Pennsylvania to buy PC stock (they eventually lost over three million dollars collectively, the *Wall Street Journal* said).[2]

Railroad man *Alfred E. Perlman,* who began as an engine wiper and rose to be president of the New York Central. He thought he "merged" into the Pennsy, but on reflection later described the deal to a Senate committee as a "takeover." Was he taken?

Stuart T. Saunders, former board chairman of the Penn Central, who told stockholders at the 1966 annual meeting, after reporting that first-quarter earnings were up 19 percent, [This rise] "strengthens our belief we will be able to continue [the] upward trends that have occurred in the [past] five years."[3] He proved to be as apt a prophet as (in the minds of some shareholders) he was a corporate executive, as he later presided over the road's bankruptcy. Long before this cataclysm, Mr. Saunders had pushed the road's diversification program, which cheered Wall Street and temporarily helped the stock. Representative Wright Patman, chairman of the House Banking and Currency Committee, later said, "This program, rather than financially supporting the railroad's operations, proved to be a

[2] July 13, 1970.
[3] Philadelphia *Inquirer,* May 10, 1966.

very serious drain on the railroad's financial resources, amounting to at least $175 million, and contributed significantly to the Penn Central's ultimate financial collapse."[4]

David C. Bevan, chairman of the Pennsylvania Railroad's Finance Committee. Representative Patman's committee staff said that in at least one instance of the diversification program, Executive Jet Aviation, $5 million of Pennsy's funds "had been funnelled into EJA before the Board of Directors even knew PRR investments were being made to EJA." Executive Jet's activities were in violation of the law, since a railroad cannot have control of an air carrier without CAB approval, which it did not obtain. EJA later was penalized by the second-largest fine ever levied by the CAB. The financial aid to EJA, said the House Committee, [was made] "with the full realization on the part of Bevan." A letter to Pennsy Treasurer William R. Gerstnecker from a lawyer hired by the railroad described the EJA business:

"As it is, the whole picture is one of amateurish intrigue, vividly colored with the devious, that suggests a consciousness of guilt deeper than is justified by the bare facts."

The Pennsy paid EJA $395,330[5] for flights made by executives and board members of the road. A total of $234,148 of this, or 60 percent, was charged for flights by Bevan, Charles J. Hodge (see below), and Gerstnecker during a five-year period. Some of the trips were made from Philadelphia to Boca Raton, Florida, at a cost of $1350 per flight. Boca Raton was the site of another Pennsy subsidiary—and also where Bevan and Hodge maintained condominium apartments.

Charles J. Hodge, former chief investment adviser of the railroad and a principal officer of Glore, Forgan, a brokerage firm that later merged with E. I. DuPont, a combination that was later bailed out in a last-ditch massive transfusion of cash by Texas multimillionaire Ross Perot. Hodge and Bevan engineered the diversification program of the Pennsy before the merger with Central, and also were the most active participants in a private investment group, Penphil. Interestingly, Penphil's investments in common stocks often paralleled those of the Pennsy's, the latter's under the supervision of Bevan in his capacity at the railroad and of Hodge in his

[4] Part I, staff report of the committee. November 2, 1970.
[5] Staff report of the committee, December 21, 1970.

advisory role. The Committee on Banking and Currency of the House of Representatives said of these activities:[6]

"Charles Hodge and/or his investment banking firm were (1) the principal investment advisor to Penn Central; (2) investment advisor to and broker for the Penn Central Supplemental Pension Plan and the Contingent Compensation Fund; (3) investment banker for Kaneb Pipe Line, Tropical Gas and Great Southwest Corp. [three companies whose stock was bought by the Pennsy and which were subsequently acquired by the road]; (4) a director of Great Southwest Corp., Arvida Corp. [another acquisition] and Tropical Gas; and (5) holders of substantial investments in Kaneb Pipe Line, Tropical Gas and Great Southwest [by virtue of his activities in Penphil, in which he had a personal investment]."

"How," the committee asked, "could Charles Hodge give sound objective investment advice to clients of Glore, Forgan concerning their investments while being so personally involved in the management and control of these significant corporations?"

The committee also questioned the propriety of Penphil's buying stocks in companies during the same period as the railroad did.

Just a Little Ol' Investment Club

Just what was Penphil anyway? The House Banking and Currency Committee thought the subject so provocative that it sent its bloodhounds loose on the trail, producing a sixty-one-page report on Penphil's varied activities. Among other things, the following letter dated July 31, 1967 was turned up, from David Bevan to Charles Hodge:

". . . actually we are thinking in terms of having a large number of shares of Penphil outstanding and going, you might say, public ultimately with Penphil and turn it at the same time into an aggressive acquirer of other companies so that we can build it up into a very substantial conglomerate holding and operating company."

Three years later Mr. Bevan, in testifying before the Commerce Committee of the U. S. Senate on August 6, 1970, said:

"The Penphil Corporation was a small, informal investment company set up by a number of us who were linked by friendship to

[6] Part III of the House committee report, February 15, 1971.

invest for capital appreciation. It was a very small affair and run quite informally. I was a stockholder."

One is tempted to say, "You pays your money and you takes your choice," of the two descriptions, but this might prove painful to those who paid their money to buy Pennsy stock and subsequently got bombed. Though we cannot say that Penphil contributed to the Pennsy's collapse (though that may be reasoned too), the affairs of the two entities were strangely intertwined.

The Beginning

Penphil was incorporated as an investment company on July 10, 1962, with sixteen members. According to William Gerstnecker, treasurer of Penn Central and one of the sixteen, most were friends of David Bevan and members of "The Silverfish," a fishing club. It was not the sort of "mutual fund" one ordinarily reads about. Nor was it the type of "affinity" group that forms around fraternal, neighborhood, or job investment clubs for investment decisions on information normally found at their local broker's.

Of the sixteen, one was David Bevan; another was his brother; three were also officers of Penn Central: Paul D. Fox (retired), Robert Haslett, and Gerstnecker; there were Hodge's wife and Mrs. Dorothy H. Warner, wife of another officer. More people joined "the club" later, among whom, curiously enough, were also officers of companies whose stock was bought by the Penphil group: Angus G. Wynne, Jr., president of Great Southwest; Fred H. Billups (now deceased), president of Tropical Gas; Herbert E. Fisher, chairman of the board of Kaneb Pipe Line, and, like Hodge, an officer of Glore, Forgan; Hobert C. Ramsey; Brown L. Whately (he joined in 1968), president of Arvida Corporation; and Joseph W. Davin, another Arvida director, who joined late. How'd you like to have that lineup in *your* investment club, particularly in view of the fact of having invested in some of these same companies?

The House Banking Committee, in its reports, was of the opinion that all of the group's investment decisions were steered by Bevan and Hodge, a pair whose financial advice was singularly effective in view of the subsequent price rises in their stocks. Or was it? If the investor wishes to emulate this pair, he might ponder some of the coincidences that worked in Penphil's favor. Bevan and Hodge were responsible for initiating investment decisions for the Pennsy as well as for Penphil. The railroad and Penphil had a number of parallel investments, e.g., Great Southwest, Tropical, and Kaneb.

The Patman House Banking and Currency Committee said, "... a number of the situations described in this report[7] raise serious issues concerning the use of insider information to benefit the members of Penphil. This includes the purchase by Penphil of Great Southwest Corporation stock and its subsequent sale seventeen months after Penn Central gained control of Great Southwest. On this sale, Penphil realized a net profit of $212,500, a 130% return on its investment in less than 2½ years."

On a presplit basis, Penphil bought 10,000 shares of Great Southwest on July 18, 1963, according to the committee. On the same day the road purchased 4000 shares and continued to acquire GSC common stock and by July 1964 had acquired direct majority control. It would be handy to know that your investments were preceded by, and would be followed by, buys in the same stock by a giant corporation—that is, if such were the case. Of course, we cannot say for a certainty that such was the case in this instance.

David Bevan, in his capacity as chief financial officer for the railroad, also oversaw the investments of its supplemental pension plan. The plan involves the pensions of about 21,700 active and 15,300 retired employees of the road and its subsidiaries. The Tropical Gas purchase may not have been one of those decisions made by a blindfolded professor at a dart board, for five of the ten directors of Tropical were members of the Penphil group. It would be difficult to make a case for the road's use (through its pension plan) of "inside information" in doing the buying in a twenty-five day period in September and October of 1968, for Tropical Gas had planned to make a stock offering on October 15, 1968. Often, stocks go down on such news, since new stock issuance represents a "dilution" of the existing stockholders' equity. If Mr. Bevan had such "inside information" in view of his relationship with his fellow Penphilers, why would he cause the pension plan to buy the stock? Either he did not have such information, or possibly he was careless with the investments of the pension plan. Of course, it may have all just been a mistake—and we can forgive such things. The House

[7] Part III of the committee report (February 15, 1971).

committee took the view that "Bevan and Hodge, members of Tropical's Executive Committee, knew of plans for the new issue before the Pension Plan started buying Tropical stock in September 1968 but did nothing to prevent this harmful action from taking place." If this were true, one wonders whether they would have been so negligent if those investments were made by Penphil.

An interesting complication was raised by the immediately subsequent attempt by another company, Mapco, to take over Tropical Gas. The committee wondered "whether Bevan and Hodge were using the Penn Central pension fund (1) to protect Tropical Gas from a takeover rather than managing the pension fund strictly as an investment for the best interests of the beneficiaries of that fund, and (2) [to] help maintain Penphil's ability to control Tropical."

Another of Penphil's buys grew by over eight hundred thousand dollars, or more than 191 percent in a little over three years, the committee reported. It seems that Penphil fortuitously bought stock in two banks in Boca Raton, Florida at a time when a Pennsy subsidiary (Arvida) was developing real estate in the area. Bevan's and Hodge's uncanny timing and judgment would make them welcome on any investment team—that is, if there weren't those bothersome doubts, wouldn't you say?

So Where Do We Get the Money?

All in all, Penphil investors did somewhat better than mutual fund buyers, garnering some 600 percent on their investment in under eight years. In addition to the two principal members, Bevan and Hodge, one other factor was required to achieve this end—and that was money. The group did not have far to look, for one of the larger creditors of Penn Central came to their aid to the tune of $1.8 million, according to the House committee. The line of credit was obtained "on an unusually favorable basis" from the Chemical Bank in New York.

"Unusually favorable" it was, in the sense that there was no formal repayment schedule, the money was advanced (over a seven-year period) at the prime rate[8] and no compensating balance[9]

[8] The prime is the rate of interest granted to very large and credit-worthy accounts, such as, say, General Motors or Standard Oil of New Jersey.

[9] For the privilege of granting large loans, banks often require that non-interest-bearing deposits be maintained at their office, thus in effect raising the

had to be maintained. Why did Chemical provide such peculiarly attractive terms for its loans to a group of "fisherman friends"? In the words of the House committee, "In effect, it was *Penn Central's* compensating balances, interest payments and deposits that were subsidizing the Penphil line of credit for the personal profit of Penphil members" (emphasis mine).

An interoffice memorandum written by C. A. McLeod of the bank to W. S. Renchard (now chairman of the bank's board of directors) and to M. A. Chamberlain, vice president of the bank's Metropolitan Division, read in part:

"David Bevan, financial vice president of the Pennsylvania Railroad Company, called me on the telephone today and said that he and a group of friends, totaling about fifteen, are planning to organize a corporation to purchase a substantial block of common stock of Kaneb Pipe Line Company [Penphil's first investment]. The group will include Charlie Hodge of Glore, Forgan and Company, Benjamin F. Swain, President of Provident Tradesmens' Bank and Trust Company, Messrs. Gerstnecker and Haslett of the Pennsylvania Railroad's financial staff and others.

"Frankly the rate on the proposed loan [the prime rate] is too low, but, in view of the size of the deal and the fact that it has such good friends connected with it, WSR [W. S. Renchard] felt it was preferable not to quibble with Mr. Bevan over the rate."

Subsequently, as late as June 1970, the rate went to 1 percent over prime, due to the credit squeeze then extant. It was even then a very sweet deal indeed. Mr. Chamberlain admitted to the Patman committee that normal loan requirements were not applied to the Penphil loans because of "other" considerations that compensated the bank, among which was Bevan's position with the railroad. The bank, however, did not always take such a benevolent attitude toward Penphil. After the railroad's collapse, the bank put the screws to the club to pay back some of its loan. Obviously a bankrupt railroad could not maintain the compensating balances that the Penn Central had done. The minutes of a Penphil meeting on October 5, 1970 read:

"Due to the fact that the Bank [Chemical] had expressed a desire

interest rate as much as 20 percent. Even the largest companies frequently face this requirement. Congressman Patman in a telephone interview railed against the practice.

for payment in reduction of the loan, the sale of the stock of National Homes and U. S. Freight pledged as security for the loan was authorized." National and U. S. were later purchases of the group.

Who, Me?

Great Southwest was a particularly blatant case in the acquisition program of Penphil and the Pennsy because it was the one in which even Bevan admitted a *possible* conflict of interest. In a letter written on July 21, 1970 he said:

". . . A few months later I expressed a desire that Penphil sell its Great Southwest stock so that we would be sure to avoid any future possible conflict of interest. My wishes were respected and the stock was sold at a price of $38. All members of Penphil made a sacrifice in this connection as the price of $38 compares with even today's very low price of approximately $60 a share since the stock was later split 10 for 1. Actually at its highest the stock sold at $430 a share, which was just over a little over a year ago."

The Patman committee pointed out that "The 'few months later' was actually 17 months." On page 31 of the report they facetiously ask, "It took Mr. Bevan that long to recognize the existence of a possible conflict of interest?"

I recall the time the lawyers for the Gulf Sulphur Company (later Gulf Resources) wrote asking for a retraction to my comment in a market letter that their president had sold stock in his company. Actually he had sold a year earlier. Many of the doubters of the efficacy of utilizing insider trading as a market tool point out that the stock often goes higher after they sell. Actually, it is *supposed* to go higher. How would it look to the SEC if a corporate official sold stock *weeks* before bad news was released by companies? But *a year later?* Jack Clark, for example, sold stock in his company long before it suffered a rather precipitous decline climaxing in bankruptcy. Oh, yes—the company name was Four Seasons Nursing Homes. Who could blame Mr. Clark? Could he possibly have known? No, his hands were clean. In the Penn Central case, as we shall see, their insider selling at one point was rather clumsy, but for the most part quite rewarding, one might say.

Back to Pennsy, the House committee pointed out that despite the "sacrifice," Penphil sold their Great Southwest stock for a profit of $212,500, a 130 percent profit in a bit under 2½ years. One is not committing libel in pondering whether a reasonable contribution to the price rise in Great Southwest was the buying by Pennsy, at the direction of men who also owned stock (through Penphil) in the company. It is true, however, that the stock did go higher after they sold it, a common phenomenon.

I recall a story related to me by Tony R., an amateur pilot. It seems that he had met at the airport on various occasions the vice president of a company listed on the American Stock Exchange. One day, Tony asked the corporate officer about his stock, having noticed its action on the charts. The fellow airplaner casually mentioned that he had just bought twenty thousand shares. Tony bought a few hundred subsequently and sold out later at a handsome profit. Yet, after a while, he missed the vice president. The latter, it seemed, had emplaned via commercial jet to Europe on an extended holiday and returned almost a year later.

When next they met at Zahn's Airport on Long Island, Tony inquired as to what the officer did with his stock. "Oh, I sold it at forty dollars." Tony noted that the stock went to forty-nine dollars after the insider sold. He had bought at twenty dollars or so.

"Really? That's nice," was the rejoinder, and the executive went calmly on with his check sheet before taking off.

What Happened?

"The rail industry's malaise has been forced upon the public's attention by the bankruptcy of the Penn Central Railroad. That the largest railroad and the keystone to rail service in the heart of the nation's population and industry should collapse provides solid ground for Congressional concern. The public deserves an explanation of the collapse and assurance that action will be taken to minimize any injury to the public interest that may result."[10]

Investors, shippers, rail travelers, and other air breathers have already been injured. Investors (including institutional ones) were lured into the stock or did not sell when they could have done so. Shippers have lost revenue because of lost cars and misrouted shipments. Rail travelers have obviously suffered—and will continue to

[10] Report of the Senate Commerce Committee, 91st Congress, 2nd Session, December 19, 1970.

do so, as the new Amtrak eliminates some unprofitable routes and others deemed less essential. The Penn Central's bankruptcy makes it "acceptable" to cut off rail services by muting the hue and cry such action would normally incite.

With special emphasis here to the investor, let us see what led up to the bankruptcy and perhaps learn some lessons in avoiding future "bag jobs."

Merger

Merging the Pennsylvania and the New York Central seemed like a good idea when it was hatched in 1957. They were, of course, competitors, and by joining they would effect cost reductions such as duplicate trackage and freight yards (can two run as cheaply as one?) and reducing personnel. The plan did wonders for the stocks—and who can say that that was not really its purpose? But then, in 1960, the Baltimore & Ohio and the Chesapeake & Ohio were brought into the picture to complicate matters. November of 1961 saw a rebirth of the merger idea, and the original two, Pennsy and Central, formally filed with the Interstate Commerce Commission (the regulatory body that had to pass on the arrangement) in March of 1962 (lawyers and papers and all that had to get together). By that time, the Penn Central (on an adjusted for split basis) was selling at around nineteen dollars. Public anticipation about the merger's benefits over the succeeding years propelled the stock to over seventy dollars a share by early 1966, as the commission gave its approval on April 27. Excitement was fueled by stock advisory publications, brokerage house recommendations, and other media entreaties, typified by this comment made two years later (on March 2, 1968) in the *Investment Dealers' Digest*, a trade paper in the industry:

"The merger of these two giant eastern systems constituted the major milestone, thus far, in the railroad merger movement in the U.S. As in the case of other merger proceedings in the industry, both the I.C.C. and the courts have given the carriers a green light to continue a movement which is destined to reduce substantially the number of individual carriers, strengthen the operating and financial position of the new systems and benefit the shippers, the public—the nation itself, and security holders."

Security holders who bought the stock at seventy dollars in 1966 or as high as eighty dollars in 1968 may not have done as well as Pennsy officer Allen J. Greenough, who sold six thousand shares in August of 1965 (according to SEC reports) or New York Central executives Walter R. Grant, Samuel H. Hellenbrand, Robert W. Minor, and John F. Nash, who sold stock in the same month and then again in October (joined this time by Central man Wayne Hoffman), nor Pennsy official Herbert M. Philips, who sold three thousand in November, the next month that Central bigwig Leo B. Fee sold a similar amount. Mr. Greenough didn't make much on the deal (nor may have some of the others), since he had just bought in the prior February. Considering, however, that he could have sold out eventually as low as six dollars (as against about fifty dollars then), a penny saved is a penny made in the market.

Of course, it may have been just coincidence, but as the public's fervor for the new entity's prospects heightened, the selling by insiders increased. Even David Bevan, the financial whiz who helped put the merger together, slowed up a bit and sold some in February of 1966, when the stock hovered in the seventy-dollar area. William R. Gerstnecker sold a little in April of the same year, as did James M. Symes, who had sold before.

It appeared to be a veritable stampede, as 1966 also saw Pennsy executives Henry Large, John D. Morris, and Herbert M. Philips sell, along with Messrs. Knight, Greenough, Cook, and Gerstnecker again. David E. Smucker sold six thousand shares, but he waited until January 25, 1967 to do that.

Why Did They Sell?

Was the merger really a good thing? The public (and this includes the financial institutions—the *new* public) seemed to think so, witness the price rise. This despite a court ruling that said that in order for it to approve the deal, the new road would have to take into itself the already bankrupt New Haven. After all, hadn't the ICC (using, to a great extent, the roads' figures) concluded that the Pennsy-Central merger would save eighty million dollars a year? Thus they could afford to undertake the New Haven's rehabilitation too. And hadn't the Central's reporting a first-half (1966) profit of $3.64 per share underscored its viability?

With all that good news, why did the informed minority sell? In some cases, there were "personal" reasons, though this phrase is sometimes a sham. I asked one Central man why he sold.

"I could see that there would be clashes. The personalities of the two roads were quite unlike each other. I could see who would win in a merger and it wouldn't be us."

Another felt that the merger wouldn't work on a mechanical basis. It was later admitted publicly that the computer systems the Pennsy had were not compatible with the Central's. It would be later compared to merging a General Sherman tank with a battleship that neither floated nor walked.

But whether the knowledge of what was going on inside the Pennsy affected the sellers' decisions was problematical. It is entirely possible that only Bevan and Hodge and a few others knew about the Executive Jet caper, a series of miscues that may have warned about the quality of leadership extant in the road. Investors found out about Executive Jet some time later, when for all intents and purposes it was too late.

The Little Jet That Never Was

"I would like to give you some of the reasons why the Penn Central Transportation Company, in my opinion, was forced into reorganization under Section 77 and to state what was done up to June 8, 1970, the date I retired as Chairman, to avoid this," Stuart T. Saunders told the United States Senate's Committee on Commerce on July 22, 1970.[11]

"Many of the reasons for this reorganization [bankruptcy] were beyond our control and by and large they involve problems not of mismanagement but problems which were unmanageable."

A few months later[12] House Banking Committee Chairman Wright Patman appeared to be disagreeing:

". . . the large non-railroad investments were a major factor in the collapse of the Penn Central Transportation Company. The [committee] staff study reaffirms this fact, but it [also] reveals a great deal more about the inner workings of Penn Central and the

[11] "Hearings on S.4011, S.4010 and S.4016," bills to provide loan guarantees to railroads, Part I, p. 298.

[12] Letter of transmittal to the committee in the staff report, Part II, December 21, 1970.

decision-making process of those officials who controlled the investment practices of the railroad."

Mr. Saunders continued, ". . . The railroad industry and the Penn Central in particular have been hit very hard by the recession, tight money, and high interest rates. First was the spiraling cost of operating the railroad. In 1969, our level of labor costs increased 7%, or $74 million . . . which was on top of a 9% increase in labor costs in 1968, or $90 million."

Among the other (preventable) situations was that of Executive Jet, a story that could serve as a basis for a 1940-style Hollywood script. One can visualize the part of General Lassiter being played by Jonathan Winters. A casting problem would be which character would be played by Groucho Marx.

Brigadier General (Ret.) Albert F. Lassiter of the Air Force had a beautiful idea. Have a fleet of small jet planes and pilots available for corporate executives who, on short notice, could be flown privately to their business destinations. The industrial companies therefore would not have to invest in their own jets, which might in any event have insufficient usage to maintain them (and their pilots) all year 'round. Spencer Tracy might have played flight chief if he were alive, and Cary Grant the dashing figure with a flaming red silk scarf could be a pilot.

"Thirty-three reporting. Just over Phoenix. Be down in five minutes. Who's next? Over."

"Okay, thirty-three. You've got a job in Denver in six hours. Forget that blonde in Phoenix," would be the reply.

"Roger, wilco," could be Grant's remark. He smiled to himself, "Tracy doesn't know about the brunette in Denver."

It was a romantic and possibly profitable idea. The general had done something analogous (without the women) in freighting around Air Force bigwigs, so why not corporate executive types in civilian life? According to the House committee, "Much of the groundwork and even the actual incorporation was accomplished while General Lassiter was still technically a member of the Air Force."[13]

What was needed, of course, was the money to buy the planes. Lassiter contacted an Air Force reserve officer and Washington attorney, Bruce G. Sundlin, who proceeded to raise the capital. Mr.

[13] Staff report, Part II, December 21, 1970.

Sundlin made the rounds of investment bankers, one of which was Glore, Forgan, which had been helping the Pennsy in its acquisition program with its General Hodge as the intermediary. It was 1964, and the railroad was hellbent on a program of diversification out of its basic business.

The board of directors of Executive Jet had a somewhat military caste, with two members, in keeping with the Hollywood analogy, actually being Arthur Godfrey and James Stewart. The latter two were both fliers and presumably could add their expertise. There was also Sam Hartwell, a Glore, Forgan partner; Hodge; Lassiter; Curtis LeMay, former Air Force Chief of Staff; Mr. Sundlin; retired Air Force General Perry M. Hoisington; Fred H. Billups, president of Tropical Gas Company; M. J. Rathbone, former chairman of the board of Standard Oil of New Jersey; and James Hopkins Smith, who had been an Assistant Secretary of the Navy. General LeMay, the House committee said, described Executive Jet as a small Strategic Air Command (SAC) operation. "It is hoped," the committee said, "that SAC, for the sake of our national defense, is operated more efficiently [than Executive Jet]."

The relationship between the Pennsy (which agreed to provide the money) and Executive Jet was a cozy one. Thus General Lassiter wrote to William Gerstnecker, treasurer of the railroad, on November 2, 1964:

"Dear Bill: Since you had the foresight and the interest to advance $275,000 for our project, I thought it important to give you some protection. Enclosed is a note for the proper amount with the interest blank. Thought you'd have a better idea on the subject."

In today's more *cinéma vérité* style of movies, this arrangement would not be believable in its casual approach to business arrangements. The fiction would have to be made more believable than the truth.

The Railroad as Sugar Daddy

As later revealed in a "conflict of interest" committee report by Mr. Basil Cole,[14] the road would make deals (through a subsidiary, American Contract Company) and have them approved at the next

[14] The Penn Central's board requested Mr. Cole to investigate certain activities of its officers, and his May 1970 findings are hereafter called the Cole Report.

board of directors meeting. These were generally once a year. And the Pennsy really poured on the coals. As Mr. Cole said:

"Although it is not possible to trace the original source and flow of all the funds which American Contract invested in EJA, it is clear that most of them came in the form of 'advances' from PRR or Pennsylvania Co. On June 23, 1965, Mr. Bevan reported to the PRR Board—and this is the first such report on EJA that we have been able to find—that the company [Pennsy] had advanced funds to American Contract, which had made loans in the amount of $4.7 million to Executive Jet and had paid $328,000 for nonvoting stock."

Why was the railroad pouring money into Executive Jet, a company that later turned out to be a less satisfactory investment (unlike the ones Bevan and Hodge made for their own company, Penphil). General Hodge was quoted in the House committee report as saying, "I screened and proposed EJA. I thought any railroad management not aware of what's coming in air freight was not doing its job."

"Despite [this pronouncement], the potential for entry into air freight business," the committee said, "was limited by a simple fact: *It was against the law.* An unsigned memorandum to the file in August 1969, presumably written by an officer of Penn Central sheds additional light on the railroad's motivation." And possible political clout.

The memo stated:

"The transaction was handled in this way [through the purchase of nonvoting stock] because of the fact that rail carriers, under law, cannot become involved in the operation of air freight service. The whole project was undertaken, however, in the hope that Executive Jet would expand into the freight area and at some future date *laws might be changed* so that Penn Central would move in" (emphasis mine).

Meantime, Stuart Saunders was making speeches urging that railroads be allowed to expand into other transportation areas. According to the House committee, "In one speech EJA was mentioned specifically as the vehicle through which the Pennsy would enter the air cargo business. This reference precipitated a stern memorandum from William Gerstnecker to the road's P.R. man, reminding him that no mention of their interest in EJA was to be publicly discussed."

Meanwhile, back at the railroad's treasury, money was flowing from it into EJA to the tune of seventeen million dollars through December 1966, not to mention the nonvoting stock purchases. And while the Pennsy was buying the nonvoting stock, they were joined by another buyer, Glore, Forgan—where General Hodge hung his hat, coincidentally. Why should Glore, Forgan buy these (Class B nonvoting) shares? Possibly they had the same idea as the road, since the Class B could be converted into Class A voting, if the law preventing the Pennsy's ownership of Executive Jet could be changed.

While (in our metaphor) the cameras were rolling at the Pennsy (the merger had not been effected), insiders were selling Central stock as indicated. This did not impress investors large or small, for Central prexy Alfred E. Perlman (an early seller) was publicly bullish; as reported by the New York *Times* on July 26, 1966, "at the annual meeting in May he [Perlman] told newsmen that April profits had been 30 percent higher than in April of last year." True to his word, the Central reported on July 25, 1966 (as reported in the *Times* the next day) an 80 percent increase in earnings for the first half of the year. For the quarter ending June 30, their profits "were the highest for that period in the company's history." As if to pour more coal on the flame of investor greed, "Mr. Perlman added that he believed that the Central could continue 'indefinitely' to report a 30 percent improvement in earnings for the subsequent months of this year," the paper said. It should be added that Mr. Perlman did not sell as much as other officers, whatever that says for him and the others.

Roll 'Em

By August of 1966, Executive Jet, fueled by massive injections of cash from the Pennsy and lesser amounts from the Philadelphia National Bank and the National Newark & Essex Bank, really started to move. The latter two loans, by the way, appear to have been granted from the power of the Pennsy to command the financial resources. In return, the road had to maintain compensating balances at the banks. Further, as with other subsidiary activities, this restricted the Pennsy's ability to borrow money for itself, thus weakening the road. This provides ammunition for those who, in opposition to Mr. Saunders, claim the acquisition program helped to bring on or hasten the railroad's eventual collapse. The following note dated September 19, 1969, from the files of the Philadelphia National Bank may be illuminating in this connection:

"We then discussed the company's [EJA's] relationship with PNB [the bank] and I pointed out that our loans . . . . were really granted at the request of the Penn Central and based on the balance treatment which we have from them."

In August of 1966, Executive Jet acquired 80 percent of Johnson Flying Service, a supplemental (nonscheduled) air carrier. While seeking new worlds to conquer, EJA was not doing too well at home. As of August 31, 1966, their twelve-month results showed revenues of $2.8 million and a net loss of $1.8 million. It's much easier in the movies, particularly in the 1940s, when the happy ending was *de rigueur*.

There was a question of CAB approval, but Executive Jet forged ahead. General Lassiter, David Bevan, and William Gerstnecker, the House committee said, "decided to commit EJA to the purchase of large aircraft, specifically two Boeing 707 and two Boeing 727 jets. The total cost on delivery was $26.2 million, with the first plane to be delivered in May of 1967 and the last in November of that year."

Executive Jet's *chutzpah* was alluded to by the committee:

"Unless and until the CAB approved EJA's acquisition of Johnson, EJA had absolutely no use for these planes. Because of this fact, the decision to purchase the large aircraft at this time proved to be a serious blunder. General Lassiter was also interested in purchasing the Lockheed L-500, the civilian counterpart of the C-5A, and at one point signed a letter of intent with Lockheed for six of them at a total cost of $136,500,000. He obviously thought the PRR [Pennsy] had an extremely deep pocket."

In movies there are only occasional breakdowns (with some engine trouble in flight providing footage with our hero wrestling with the stick to pull 'er out of a dive) and maybe a hangar fire started by the competition to temporarily bar the flight path to financial and romantic success. In real life, the massive red-ink problem finally precipitated a study by a chap at the Wharton School in Philadelphia. At Lassiter's pleas for help, Bevan suggested that the school and specifically W. W. Abendroth, executive officer at its

Management Science Center, conduct a three-month study on a private basis.

On February 13, 1967, Abendroth wrote to his contact at EJA, Vice President Frank Conace:

"Our efforts will be focused on the marketing, promotional, sales and price aspects of the business, including employee effectiveness and organizational structure."

A curious note was sounded by Abendroth to Conace five days earlier, as taken from the committee report:

". . . I've had an opportunity to meet with our Dean Willis Winn and David Bevan. The former is willing to have us offer our services to you individually, and the latter takes the position that as long as the confrontation is requested by Executive Jet Aviation, more power to them. He, of course, is bending over backward to avoid any implications of his requesting the effort." The House committee claimed that this "is another example of Bevan's efforts to maintain an illusion that the Penn Central was not controlling EJA in contravention of CAB regulations."

Abendroth's report recommended the appointment of a new chief administrator (releasing Lassiter for long-range planning, which the House committee interpreted as "kicking him upstairs"), the hiring of a marketing vice president and two assistant vice presidents (who would be contacting EJA's potential customers in the corporate world), a marketing analysis section, and a field sales force. Subsequently, the marketing vice president and sales force were hired, but Lassiter remained in his post. One can imagine another pilot, say, Ray Milland, storming into Winters' office and saying, "We're with you, Jon!"

On January 15, 1967, *Forbes* magazine presented a major study on the railroad industry, "The Comeback Is Getting Up Steam." The article noted, "This year looks a bit rough and there are blocks further down the track. But by 1970, barring a major setback, the industry as a whole should be earning 50% more than it did last year —which was, itself, the best in a long, long time. And after that? The potential is vast. It only remains to be seized."

It turned out to be more like a seizure in the medical sense for the Pennsy and the Central. While investors were as yet happy with the Pennsy and Central's stock performance, the biggest profit providers for the roads were less than ecstatic. Said one such shipper (as quoted in the *Forbes* article), "While there are some signs of a management improvement, the total industry effect isn't what you'd call excitingly obvious to the shipper. We'll do as much if not more to work with them as far as providing the technology is concerned. All we want is intelligent response. Instead, we get the same thing: the whisky at Christmas and the baseball bull session in April. It's not enough today."

On June 12, 1967, the ICC gave what was apparently a green signal for the merger. The anticipation in investor minds had likewise gone straight ahead, with the stock (adjusted) going from as low as forty dollars in 1966 to a high of seventy dollars in mid-1967. Other investors were selling—they happened to be Pennsy officers John B. Prizer, J. E. Chubb, A. J. Greenough, and A. Paul Funkhouser, according to SEC reports.

Together, at Last

One of the stumbling blocks to the merger of the Pennsy, the conglomerate, and Central, the profitable, had been the objection of other roads that felt the combination would be an invincible competitor. When a three-judge federal court on October 19, 1967, ruled that the merger should proceed posthaste, Stuart T. Saunders, president of the Pennsy, and Alfred E. Perlman of the Central jointly announced, "We are greatly pleased with what we understand to be its unanimous opinion." It was the Norfolk & Western Railroad people who were upset. The stockholders of the Pennsy-Central were jubilant. Market observers hailed the impending consummation as a "boon to shareholders." The only shareholder among the insiders at the two roads who bought any substantial amount of stock was a director, Walter H. Annenberg, a publishing tycoon and ambassador to Great Britain. The jubilation among the other insiders had to be measured in words rather than in dollars.

Some other words had been written: "There is no question but that the transaction will permit more economical and efficient use of applicants' transportation facilities. The economics realized will rebound in large part to the benefit of shippers and thus to the general public either through the improved services thereby made possible or lower rates."[15] These words came from the ICC, which had

[15] Quoted by Senator Vance Hartke of Indiana at subcommittee meetings of the Senate Commerce Committee, June 23, 1970.

also approved the merger, without, it turned out, even knowing who owned the railroads in question.[16]

It was a very exciting time on Wall Street. Investors were gobbling up the stocks of both roads as trading volume soared. Some of the investors were of the type the media refer to as "sophisticated." A close examination of these "sophisticated" types reveals that, according to Vickers service, an outfit that monitors these things, as of December 1966, no insurance company owned more than 3,000 shares of the Pennsy RR. By the end of 1967, one owned 149,000 shares, another owned 200,000, and a third had 800,000. Some, of course, had owned Central Stock—and unlike the *truly* sophisticated types, did not "sell on the news." And herein lies a lesson for the investor. When stocks rise, say, 500 percent over a period of time, and "news" comes out in momentous proportions, one can assume that most if not all of the rise had been due to anticipation of the event. A merger, split, an exciting new product, etc., would qualify for such treatment. The "new public"—the insurance companies, banks, and mutual funds—may not know this. The informed minority, the true sophisticates of the market, understand the principle—and you can too.

Flyin' Low

There were numerous benefits to the Pennsylvania Railroad (or at least to some of the insiders) in its position vis-à-vis Executive Jet Aviation. According to the House committee, a Pennsy subsidiary, Manor Real Estate, was utilizing EJA to ferry such executives as David Bevan, General Hodge, and Pennsy Treasurer William Gerstnecker from Philadelphia to Boca Raton, Florida. Of course, the Pennsy (through Manor) was *paying* for the flights, according to a study made by an independent accounting firm for the years 1968, 1969, and early 1970.[17] Why should Pennsy bigwigs ride the nasty, old, slow railroad when they could fly Lear Jets, Falcons, and Jet Stars? Why, indeed? Of course, it was a bit expensive—having a private plane ferry you around; witness the flight of David Bevan from Philadelphia to Pittsburgh on November 17, 1967 at a cost of $372.60; or on October 4, 1967, when Bevan and two others flew

[16] Cited throughout the Senate committee report.

[17] The study was made by Lybrand, Ross Brothers & Montgomery at the direction of William Sundlin, who subsequently took over from Lassiter.

from Newark, New Jersey to Philadelphia at a cost of $145.80. A typical flight from Philadelphia to Boca Raton cost the railroad $1160—each way. The excellence of the planes could be attested to the fact that they could jump great distances, like the time that President Saunders hopped from Santa Rosa, California to Philadelphia by Falcon on July 20, 1967, a distance of 2545 statute miles. Oh, yes, that trip cost the road just $5980.75, something more than the $200-odd it would have cost on a regularly scheduled commercial jet. Mr. Saunders went himself, but returned with an unnamed passenger ten days later for another $5000, billing his railroad. There is no evidence that the Pennsy bigwigs flew their dogs or cats at railroad expense. And there probably was a good business reason for Mr. Bevan to send, on April 10, 1968, a beautifully furnished Lear Jet from Columbus to Newark with a package at a cost of $658.80.

It was all very convenient. And if it did not exactly help the railroad's financial position, it certainly did not hurt Executive Jet—or did it? Despite all the revenues collected from the road for these junkets (estimated at $299,689 during 1968 alone), it may have sapped the energies of the sales staff, who knew that the planes needed to be available for Pennsy flights. Abendroth was called upon again, six months after the initial study. An internal memo among EJA personnel read in part:[18]

"A few days ago you [Lassiter] requested that we consider how EJA's P.&L. [profit and loss] performance could be improved. The three of us closeted ourselves (and Bill Abendroth) in the board room most of the day on November 15, 1967, and examined and discussed areas about what major changes need to be made.

"Our principal recommendations aimed at getting EJA into profit territory are presented below, in order of importance with respect to timing and the action itself:

"In the best interests of EJA we believe it is absolutely essential that final authority to make all decisions with respect to day-to-day, month-to-month operations of EJA be vested in someone else, whose qualifications should be from the business world, and someone who could devote most of his time to management problems in Columbus, the home office. It is our opinion that this change must be made in order for EJA to become profitable."

It was as though Cary Grant, Bill Holden, and Spencer Tracy were

[18] House committee report, Part II.

leading a palace revolt against Jonathan Winters. What bugged them? In addition to their feeling that Lassiter should be removed (or elevated), they felt that European business should be reduced as unprofitable, the stationing of jets on the West Coast be halted, various regional offices be dropped, and another Boeing 707 not be ordered. Also, they suggested reducing administrative (non-revenue-producing) flights and cutting executive travel expenses. These administrative trips should not be confused with those of the Pennsy officials, which were paid by the road, but referred to flights by executives of EJA. In one year, 1968, the House committee revealed that there were 668 such jaunts; 355 of them "were made by Lassiter himself at a minimum out-of-pocket cost of $132,000. . . . To these sums must be added revenue lost because aircraft being used for administrative flight purposes were not available for revenue flights," the committee revealed later.

Abendroth and the three EJA men zinged one at Lassiter when they said,

"We understand that you want to tackle this area yourself so we will simply point out here that the month-to-month executive travel expense in recent months had been running from $5,000 to $10,000, which is approximately 25 to 40 percent of the traveling expenses of all our airplane crews."

In Lassiter's defense it may be added that Pennsy executives had set him an example. If it was good business to be picked up promptly and deposited conveniently, why should not a general learn from his contemporaries? His activity also showed the zeal with which Lassiter was engaged in trying to build the business. Yet a month later another source complained—an investment management company that had been approached by Hodge to raise money for EJA. In a letter of December 19, 1967, James H. Orr, president of Colonial Management Associates of Boston, wrote Hodge,

"You have been aware of our concern over the substantial increase in losses in the business aircraft operation above those expected last summer. As a result, it is impossible for us to continue [implying that he had previously done so] to recommend the purchase of the 7½ percent Senior Subordinated Debentures of EJA to our clients without a change in the financing plans and management of the company.

"We feel the following changes must be accomplished if our purchase recommendation to our clients is to be maintained:

"The company must obtain a new chief executive officer and president with business experience who is satisfactory to us. The role of the present senior management would be determined by the new chief executive in coordination with the board of directors."

Orr also suggested the end of the EJA's European operations.

As with the Abendroth advice, Lassiter remained in command—and the money continued to flow from the Pennsy to Executive Jet. It was kept up through 1968.

Perhaps Mr. Orr was getting a bit uneasy—or perhaps his clients were. In any event, according to the House committee, Colonial Management had given a commitment for five million of a total of seventeen million dollars. Glore, Forgan (Hodge's firm) had put together a stock offering for EJA, filed with the SEC on November 7, 1967. Whereas Orr got cautious, Pennsy continued to funnel dollars through its subsidiary to EJA to the tune of over five million dollars in the year following the "disagreements" over Lassiter's administration.

One might attribute the continued support by Pennsy of EJA to any of several factors:

1. Despite the complaints and losses, Pennsy executives may have felt that by putting in more money, they could "turn the airline around."
2. It was all just a big mistake. Pennsy was not exercising sufficient control over EJA.
3. Lassiter had the confidence of Bevan and Hodge, and they did not want to admit any error in backing him.
4. The Pennsy was so big and disjointed that effective control over any of their investments was difficult if not impossible.

You lost your money (in Pennsy stock) and you takes your choice. But while the reader is deciding which if any of the above factors contributed to the problem, he should take note of another, shall we say, sticky business involving Penphil indirectly with EJA. Penphil, remember, was the private investment vehicle of Bevan and Hodge and their friends and associates.

Travel Is Educational

The Penphil group—no dummies—were aware of the worldwide boom in air travel and attempted to cash in on it by acquiring one of the largest travel agencies, Fugazy Travel Bureau.

While unsuccessful in this endeavor, they managed to pick up a Florida travel agency in 1967.

General Lassiter was also a member of Penphil, and he was contacted by a friend, Julian Lifsey, a Tampa, Florida, attorney, about the possibility of picking up a local outfit, Bowen Travel Services, Inc., owned by Mrs. Irene Bowen. According to the House committee report, Lassiter and three other Penphilers—who just happened to be Bevan, Hodge, and Gerstnecker—met with Mrs. Bowen and (through Penphil) ended up buying a 51 percent interest in her company early in 1968. The balance was held by Mrs. Bowen and the attorney, Lifsey. Penphil provided a two-hundred-thousand-dollar line of credit, the name was changed to Holiday International Tours, and it was moved to Miami. Mrs. Bowen was made president and Lifsey chairman of the board. The affairs of Executive Jet (and therefore the Pennsy) and Penphil were intertwined in a revealing manner.

Executive Jet, in possible contravention of CAB regulations, had gone on an extensive program of building a worldwide air carrier network. Like other such grandiose plans, they came to little except CAB irritation. However, one of the deals resulted in the acquisition of International Air Bahamas (IAB). That and another line, Transavia Holland, ran up enormous debts to EJA, which were later settled for a fraction of the face amounts.

At the time it looked like a good idea to all concerned, and it must have looked especially good to Lassiter, who now contemplated commanding a worldwide flight network. And tying it all into a travel agency that would book the flights seemed quite logical.

Lifsey discussed the deal in a letter to Hodge on March 26, 1968:

"Immediately after receiving your approval and authorization to proceed, we met with officials of IAB [International Air Bahamas] in Miami and were informed that the company had been capitalized and activated. In these initial meetings we were asked to act as the general tour operator [for IAB] and were requested to organize a tour program on a priority basis and to dedicate our initial first efforts to that program."

The arrangement as described by Lifsey had IAB pay all the expenses in exchange for Holiday giving the airline "top priority" sales efforts in its behalf. Subsequently, Holiday was asked to consider acting as IAB's general sales agent, helping out with the hiring of reservation personnel, ordering ticket stock, flight bags, baggage checks, boarding cards, "and so forth," for 3½ percent of gross sales.

"On Saturday of last week," Lifsey said, "at a meeting in Miami, we finally concluded our agreement with IAB, which agreement provides that for a period of 3 months we will dedicate the entire efforts of our staff to getting IAB off the ground. Since their schedule has not yet become operative we are to receive a fee of $5,000 per month for the initial 3 months, and they are to pay all expenses. The $5,000 fee is to be charged against the 3½% commission which has been established as our continuing fee for acting as their general agent."

This appeared to be a pretty good deal for the travel agency, since the five thousand dollars monthly it would provide "is the total monthly sum required to meet HIT's (Holiday's) projected salary requirements for 1968 and 1969," the committee observed.

A letter reprinted by the committee from HIT's attorney in Tampa to Thomas Bevan put the arrangement in sharp focus:

"As discussed with you on the telephone, the initial concept as outlined by General Lassiter was that Executive Jet Aviation would lease the airplane or airplanes to International Air Bahamas who in turn would fly them[,] and Holiday International Tours was set up to be the agent for the sales. Under this concept there would be no need for IAB to trouble itself with a sales manager or sales at all."

Executive Jet would apparently be backed up by the Pennsy's good credit. IAB would benefit from Holiday's possible expertise in arranging its tours. The travel agency would have most of its expenses paid from, it would seem, a "captive" supplier. And who owned the agency? Although there must have been two sides to the question and a case might have been made for its independence, one side could have charged that Penphil was the guiding hand behind the agency and a substantial stockholder in it. And of course, Penphil was controlled to an extent by the financial power structure in the Pennsy. The story would appear to get "curiouser and curiouser."

One of these who appeared to be troubled by his connection with part of the roundelay was the lawyer who had first approached Bevan to raise money for EJA and who served as its general counsel, Bruce G. Sundlin. Julian Lifsey of the travel agency asked Sundlin for his opinion as counsel, and Sundlin replied in a letter dated July 10, 1968:

"My chief problem with this agreement is that I do not know from which side to approach it, the IAB or HIT [Holiday] side. Actually, I represented EJA, and that company should have an interest in neither IAB nor HIT. On the assumption that some time in the future EJA may have a desire to acquire an interest in IAB, and the fact that EJA currently has close business relationships with IAB, I feel that the proposed agency agreement is excessively favorable to HIT and detrimental to IAB."

The agreement had not been committed to paper, but Holiday continued to provide services to IAB. In return, IAB was paying—but not up to the "oral" degree. Thus a meeting was allegedly held in Miami among Lassiter, Lifsey, Mrs. Bowen, Holiday's general manager at the time, Albert Engle, and the then general manager of IAB, Robert F. Blake. The House committee reported that Lassiter told Holiday that they should meet a loan request from IAB to the travel agency, whereupon they would be reimbursed by Penphil. Bevan had promised him this, Lassiter was quoted as saying. Subsequently, $40,000 was advanced by Penphil through a Swiss bank to Holiday, which used the money to continue its operations in behalf of IAB, the "delinquent" payer.

Subsequently, IAB and Holiday quarreled over the "oral" agreement between them, and IAB denied that a deal really was in force. I do not know which party is correct, but it all ended with an out-of-court settlement of $150,000 to Holiday by IAB and its subsequent owner, Icelandic Airlines.

Holiday had other problems, since there developed a clash over who was running things. In a memorandum, the lawyer for HIT, John Germany, described one meeting between Lifsey, Mrs. Bowen, and Lassiter. Reprinted, as were the other notes mentioned here, in the House committee report, it reveals that they also discussed Lassiter's contention that he personally was to receive 10 percent of HIT's stock. And, according to Mr. Germany, "General

Lassiter stated that he did not want to be shown representing 51 percent of the stock of Penphil." Though Penphil did control 51 percent, the committee believed that Lassiter wished to conceal the fact from the CAB, which would not look with favor upon the relationship. The committee was helped to that conclusion by a letter from Mrs. Bowen to Mr. Germany on August 12, 1968:

". . . General Lassiter has given strict instruction to both Lifsey and myself that all correspondence between General Lassiter and either of us must be addressed to his home and there must be no copies in existence anywhere. However, for what it's worth, there is a file of letters in the Miami office. Mr. Lifsey has most certainly not destroyed copies of these letters."

Lifsey's and Mrs. Bowen's quarrel was settled with Lifsey's departure from HIT. Mrs. Bowen had apparently succeeded in winning over Lassiter[19] to her side, and Lifsey complained later of Lassiter's alleged role in HIT's affairs.

On August 28, 1968, Penphil sold its 51 percent ownership of HIT to Mrs. Bowen. Executive Jet was at the time trying to acquire another airline, and it would be better, some would say, to "clear things up." The House committee felt that the sale was made merely to cover up the relationship between HIT and Penphil, citing another letter from attorney Germany on October 30, 1968 to Mrs. Bowen in which General Hodge "stated that while it appeared there was no legal requirement that Mrs. Bowen should return the stock [which she had ostensibly bought from Penphil] there was certainly a moral obligation for her to do so."

Albert Engle, who subsequently became president of HIT, told committee investigators that in September of 1969, David Bevan called Mrs. Bowen and demanded the twenty-five-thousand-dollar payment or the return of stock. Mrs. Bowen reportedly refused, claiming that her business reputation had been damaged by her association with Lifsey, Hodge, Lassiter, and Bevan. There was no indication in the committee report that rebuttal was offered by any of those charged in this matter, and, so, much of the foregoing must be labeled "one opinion."

[19] It should be noted in his behalf that General Lassiter denied that he represented Penphil.

Till Bankruptcy Us Do Part

The year 1968 was one of hope. Hope that the merger of the "diversified" (read conglomerate) Pennsylvania would marry the efficient, profitable Central and bring happiness in the form of stock market profits to the little old ladies in Keokuk, the mutual funds, the brokers who pushed the stock, the insurance companies who bought it, and the pension funds and trust accounts that acquired it after much fundamental analysis of the merger's benefits.

After all, Pennsy's Saunders had said almost two years before that although "It will be several years before we can realize the full benefits of the proposed merger [it is] far and away the best means of achieving economics and efficiencies necessary to produce a reasonable level of earnings and a satisfactory rate of return."[20] On the same day, the chairman of Pennsy's finance committee, David Bevan, told the stockholders that the merger provides a "golden opportunity not only to improve our earnings but to improve the quality of them."

The U. S. Supreme Court had given its approval for the merger, with one big condition: that the newly formed Pennsylvania-New York Central Transportation Company take on the rehabilitation of the bankrupt New Haven Railroad. The two merger partners also agreed, "pending their acquisition of the road, to lend the New Haven up to $85,000,000 over a three-year period. They have also decided to assume the losses of that line during the three years," reported *Investment Dealers' Digest* at the time (January 22, 1968).

It had been just over ten years earlier that the then Pennsy chairman, James M. Symes, reportedly stomped off the manicured greens of the Greenbrier (West Virginia) Hotel's golf course muttering, "We've got to do something drastic." Symes had retired from the Pennsy since then, but as the February 1, 1968, merger date rolled around, he recalled that "At the time, I thought it could all be done in three or four years at the most."[21]

His wasn't the only miscalculation, though it was certainly one of the least harmful. Merger savings over a three-year period were projected at over $40,000,000 and after five years could amount to

[20] Philadelphia *Inquirer,* May 10, 1966.
[21] *Forbes,* February 1, 1968.

$80,000,000. "*Annual* [emphasis ours] savings after eight years are expected to approximate at least $80,000,000," *Investment Dealers' Digest* reported in its January 22, 1968, issue. The same paper reported on a little-noticed expansion and modernization by Flying Tiger Line, Inc. (FLY), was to be a future winner, led by former Central man Wayne Hoffman. As is their wont, most investment analysts were buying the loser, or past winner, Pennsy, and ignoring the future winner, FLY. Of course, there was more enthusiasm for the former (read enthusiasm for earnings visibility, the current cliché) than for the latter. Contrary opinion[22] is a helpful approach for investors, I have found.

Financial institutions (aided by their typically hidebound research staffs) were buying Pennsy, and on the date of the merger, February 1, 1968, the new entity, Pennsylvania-New York Central Company, was selling at $59.50 per share, with the recent average number of shares traded daily being 15,000. It had already risen five dollars in little over a week—and 500 percent over its (adjusted) price a few years earlier. It rose another eight dollars in the ensuing two months, with volume virtually doubling, fueled by bank trust department, pension fund, insurance company, and mutual fund buying.

Twenty-two insurance companies held Penn Central stock at the end of 1967. During 1968, there were thirty-five holding the "investment."[23] But that was nothing compared to the bank trust departments, which partly due to government regulations, do not reveal their holdings. My understanding is that their holdings multiplied. It was at the time considered a "suitable" holding for pension and trust accounts, a bank man told me. Later I questioned an analyst at one of the largest, New York-based trust companies on her reasons for recommending a "buy" or a "sale" of a particular security. "I refuse to be intimidated," she declared. One can understand that delineating one's investment analysis could be self-incriminating in view of some bank investments.

Then there was the bank that bought Memorex Corporation stock at $160, only to watch it fall some 50 percent in the following year. One broker told me that he had recommended the stock to them at forty dollars, but it didn't meet their requirements for market value

[22] Seeking an opinion or thought opposed to the "popular" view.
[23] Statistics from *Vickers Insurance Company Guide*, section 2, August 1969.

then. You see, many trust departments (and insurance company stock sections), being of such immense size, cannot buy stocks where the market value of the shares is below a certain figure. After the stocks rise, say, 500 percent, they qualify. Accomplished businessmen howl with laughter when they hear of this "qualification," since it contradicts their market attitude of buying *before* the rise and selling *into it*, an informed minority approach. Bank trust and insurance company analysts, being academically trained rather than "Hard Knocks U." backgrounded, express puzzlement at this tactic. "If it's going to a thousand," they will say, "why not buy it even here?" "Dreamsville," reply the cynical. It should be noted that not all bank trust fellows run to form. Some Bankers Trust Company people provide a refreshing change, and I am sure there are others. I have heard talk that General Electric's investment operations and those of the Prudential sometimes break tradition with the investment company models.

I take the time to note the foregoing because the individual investor may approach the stock market with the feeling, "How can I make money in the market when I am fighting the big guys?" To him I say, read on. The growth of institutional investing in this country has not led to a greater sophistication—to the relief of the informed minority, who feed their naïveté.

A Rosy Future

As the reader shouldn't, the institutional investors may have been influenced by Mr. Stuart T. Saunders, the new sachem of the Penn Central, who was quoted by the *Wall Street Journal* on the day of the merger as saying, "We [he and Perlman] have a number of [nonrailroad] projects under consideration." Inasmuch as they had a tax shelter from previous losses, "Penn Central could acquire many profitable nonrailroad ventures and still pay no taxes for five or six years," the paper said. The latter statement would prove to be prophetic, to say the least.

Wall Street was appraising the Penn Central favorably at the time. "The Pennsylvania New York Central Transportation Company," said *Forbes* magazine in its February 15, 1968 issue, ". . . is much more than the biggest U.S. railroad. It is also probably the world's biggest private real estate company and may well one day become one of the U.S.'s biggest conglomerate[s]." Of course, "conglomerate" was not a naughty word at the time, but merely (in some cases) a synonym for "bag job." There would be others, but new words would be used as euphemisms. One advisory service backed the group using the phrase, "free form" company. It would not prove to be one of the best things in life.

"Some experts estimate that the Penn Central's realty holdings are exceeded in size and richness only by those of the Roman Catholic Church," the press was saying. Add to that the Pennsy's real-estate purchases "three of the most promising . . . in the U.S.," they said, referring to Macco Company in California, Great Southwest in Texas, and Arvida in Florida, each owned in varying proportions by the Pennsy. Of those, said Penn Central director and Philadelphia stockbroker Howard Butcher III, they "are only a wart on the pickle compared with the rest of our realty holdings."

The merger was a performance of great éclat. It was a great stone behind a glass window that shone with the brilliance of a magical diamond. The crowds of investors rushed to buy their shares, as if to own a piece of the diamond. The press marveled at the awesome sight. In the back room, however, the diamond cutters who knew it was all just glitter slipped away in embarrassment, making sure to pick up their checks in the process.

The Street ticked off its merits, like the twenty-nine acres the Penn Central owned in mid-Manhattan, appraised in 1966 by New York City for $227 million. "Some think the area is worth half a billion dollars," said *Forbes*. Then there were the 70 acres of freight yards on Manhattan's West Side; the Sunnyside freight yards in New York City's Borough of Queens ("air rights worth probably $40 million"); 80 acres of air rights in Philadelphia worth, some said, $70 million; 150 acres being developed in Pittsburgh, possibly $20 million. And the 25 percent interest the Penn Central would get in the new Madison Square Garden Center, then under construction, etc., etc.

"We are about the only large owners of undeveloped land in the center of big cities," said Treasurer Gerstnecker. "Naturally we want to see it properly developed."

"We can afford a really expert real-estate group," said Butcher. "The merger takes the lid off. Now we can really move." And then there was the Buckeye Pipe Line Company, owned by the Pennsy, and Strick, a truck-trailer builder acquired by Central, to throw into the deal. The diamond that was the Penn Central shone with a radiance that reached the investment corners of the nation. And "the new road will have plenty of cash [sic] to enable it to diversify further," said a financial publication. In the back room, it could be said, the diamond cutters were packing.

It would have been surprising to the bank trust analysts to observe that two months before the merger, Mr. Gerstnecker sold 1000 shares, director Eugene C. Pulliam sold 3000, and Leo B. Fee sold 1250 the following month to eliminate his holdings. Of course, they may have sold for "personal reasons," and in any event, I have found few trust investment "experts" who bothered to look or cared when they were told. They don't study such things in business school, you know.

Insider selling was not and is not used as a tool by the masses of investors and, from my experience when it is, it will be used inappropriately. It will, if it ever becomes popular on Wall Street, be used as an absolute, i.e., when an insider sells, you sell; when an insider buys, you buy. Not so, in my view. Insider selling and buying should be used as a warning tool. *Patterns* of insider selling take more time to study than chance observations. One should ask the questions: How many insiders are selling? How much are they selling? For how many months are they selling? When did they start? How many shares? (I regard less than a thousand at a time as not significant.) And the same goes for buying. Generally, the period of accumulation by the informed minority takes longer than the "distribution" phase. They have the patience that individual investors and many institutional ones do not.

Most of all, insider selling often reveals fundamental weakness within the corporation, fundamental trouble that will come out later, too much later; problems that research departments will discover *after* the stock has fallen 50 percent or more.

Take Penn Central, for example. I cannot say that insiders sold because of the quiet but pervading cancer that was spreading throughout the corporation. Some may not have known of it. One of the cancer symptoms discovered *after* the patient's death was that as of February 1, 1968, a total of 17,153 freight cars, or 9 percent of the entire fleet, was out of service for repair.[24] The national average is 5.7 percent.

During the same period that the Street was raving about the "fabulous future" of the Penn Central, Executive Jet was just one of the many leaks that were quietly eating up the profits. In 1968 alone, EJA lost about $4 million. In 1969, another $4 million loss year, it was alleged that Lassiter charged $11,500 to EJA for a New York apartment, $6240 for expense report reimbursements, $24,751 in expenses paid directly by EJA, $8965 in "accounts receivable," $88,077 "transferred" to Lassiter Aircraft Corporation, and $274,385 paid directly to Lassiter plus his $59,000 salary. This did not include $135,076 for "administrative flying." General Lassiter surely must have been a "fun fellow." At least the girls thought so. The subsequent management of EJA found photos of Lassiter with Linda Vaughan, his fiancée and former Miss Pure Firebird, Miss Atlanta Rockaway, and Miss Hurst Golden Shifter, in Rome, a trip paid for, they charged, with EJA funds. Lassiter claimed the trips were strictly business—to help the company win friends among racing drivers. It was just four years since General Lassiter had reportedly said to his sergeant major, Gus Rathberger, "Gus, come to Colombus [EJA headquarters] with me. We won't make any money, but we'll have lots of fun."[25]

Beneath the surface, all may not have been kosher with the Penn Central. The Street, however, was looking at the golden dollars they would make by investing in the new winner. While the stock was rising the ten points following the February merger, "seasoned analysts" were being quoted by the *Wall Street Journal* on March 27, 1968 as being bullish on PC. One broker noted an "awakening of fund interest and individual investor interest in the merged company's ability to diversify more widely and more rapidly." Vice President for Administration Paul D. Fox may not have been one of those, for he sold a thousand shares on February 21, 1968.

Another bullish broker was Butcher and Sherrerd, an old-line Philadelphia concern. Where else would you go for information on Penn Central? Further, Howard Butcher III was a partner of the firm *and* a director of the railroad. It was a time when acquisitions per se were considered bullish by the Street, whether or not the

[24] *Wall Street Journal*, September 8, 1970.
[25] *Business Week*, October 24, 1970.

management would know how to handle them once acquired. Growth was admired for its own sake. This mistake is not being made lately on Wall Street, but is being replaced with other miscalculations. The 1971–72 shtick is called "beta co-efficient," a statistical evaluation used to pinpoint a previously unsuccessful "relative-strength" syndrome.

Recently, more and more analysts have the suffix C.F.A. placed after their name. This is the leftover part of the accreditation syndrome that afflicted our society just before the recent Ph.D. glut. Whether passing a test designating the analyst as "Chartered Financial Analyst" added to his maturity and perspective is doubtful, but one of the more astute bank trust managers (there are some) recently told me it was a "license to steal." I would prefer to call it a "license to err." Some of the C.F.A. types recommended to their bosses investments in Penn Central after reading a report by the Philadelphia-based house that calculated the railroad had a tax shelter at four hundred million to six hundred million dollars.

"Taking into consideration all the things the company could claim—depreciation changes, investment tax credit, the right to charge off merger costs against 1967 earnings—it could be nearer six hundred million dollars," Mr. Butcher told the *Wall Street Journal* on March 26, 1968. This was bullish, because it would allow for more acquisitions, whose profits could be used against the tax write-offs. Thus despite any increase in profits from the additions, no additional taxes would be paid.

And here's the topper: "The Butcher and Sherrerd study," continued the *Journal*, "estimates that the company 'could be earning at an annual rate of approximately $12 a share pre-tax' by 1972." Further, tax liability would be small, as indicated.

"Maybe so," an investor might quibble, "but how about nearer term?"

The Butcher & Sherrerd study "estimates 1968 earnings at $4.50 a share," which it considers "conservative," said the *Journal*. In retrospect, we might choose another adjective.

Other euphoric estimates from Wall Street ranged from $4.50 to $5.65 per share, but most analysts were even more bullish on Penn Central's longer-term prospects, since they expected greater savings from the merger in 1969 and greater growth from acquisitions in the future. Inside the railroad, the only things that were growing were rust, decay, and acrimony.

"Even at the top," said *Newsweek* later, "the animosity between Saunders, Pennsy's shrewd lawyer, and Perlman, the Central's railroad man, is barely concealed."[26] They clashed over basic policy, with Saunders' Pennsy approach being volume business and Central's being more efficient marketing to bring higher profit, and lower sales volume. Further, Pennsy was the conglomerator that sought to expand into other businesses, a possibly favorable action if they had had the management talent to judge and run them.

Meanwhile, the analysts were not checking into what was happening out there in the boondocks where they moved the freight. Mr. C. R. Ellenwood, Jr., Manager of Transportation Services for the American Plywood Association, pointed out in a letter to Senator Warren G. Magnuson of Washington[27] how increased freight charges, requested by railroads and granted by the ICC, kept prices up and caused a divergence of traffic to other modes. One such rise resulted in a $10.5 million revenue loss to the railroads, he maintained. Other switches to truck transportation were prompted by a shortage of freight cars. Most businesses try to obtain the highest price that will *still retain the business,* one would think. Mr. Ellenwood also claimed that freight increases subsequently were given by the ICC to help alleviate the poor financial condition of the Penn Central.

"But again," Mr. Ellenwood wrote, "the entire shipping public was called upon to contribute to a railroad that, through poor management, had become, in a few short years, a financial disaster."

The investment community ignored or was ignorant of the quality of management more knowledgeable people saw as "poor."

All they needed, said some Wall Street analysts at the time, was a freight rate increase. "The railroads are confident they can demonstrate a vital need for another rate hike," said Paine Webber's Frank Straub, according to a March 13, 1968 article in the *Wall Street Journal.* "If successful [in getting the raise] they could show a strong trend in the second half." Mr. Straub was quoted as be-

[26] Hearings before the Sub-Committee on Surface Transportation of the U. S. Senate Commerce Committee, March 16 and June 23, 1970, p. 118 (Serial No. 91-78). Senator Hartke used the quote.

[27] Ibid., p. 145.

lieving that a recovery move "would include such 1967 laggards as Chicago & North Western, Great Northern, Illinois Central, Louisville & Nashville, Penn Central and Seaboard Coast Line." Fortunately, he did not single out PC for special praise.

"However, it will take some time for the new company [PC] to become the leader with respect to net income, though there is little doubt that within the next five years Pennsylvania New York Central's earnings will lead the industry," *Investment Dealers' Digest,* on March 4, 1968, seemed to echo the Street's majority view at the time.

Feeding the investment industry's popular attitude was PC's annual report for 1967, issued on March 15, 1968. Saunders and Perlman signed its opening letter to stockholders, which said in part:

"Although we are just getting started, the transition and progress of our merger has been smoother and more rapid than we had anticipated." Further,

"A remarkable spirit of cooperation and enthusiasm is manifest throughout our new organization."

"One of the great strengths of Penn Central lies in the fact that we are uncommitted to traditional approaches."

One would have to agree with that. Senator Hartke's Sub-Committee on Surface Transportation later charged:

"Some Penn Central Co. officials pushed a major diversification into the aircraft field (EJA) more for personal gain than for benefit of the railroad operations.[28]

Of course, that was only the senator's impression, you understand. For his part, Mr. David C. Bevan said, "I didn't have any basis or way whatsoever to gain" from EJA operations. He told the subcommittee he owned 3 percent of Penphil's stock. The senator was as piqued at the connection between Penphil and Executive Jet as was Representative Patman.

"Senator Hartke contended that the Penn Central officials pushed the $21 million investment in Executive Jet and were instrumental in its purchase of additional Boeing Co. 707 and 727 aircraft, although the planes it already had weren't being fully used," the paper reported. Even though EJA did not appear to have the "stuff" under its setup at the time to ever be profitable, Penn Central of-

[28] As reported by the *Wall Street Journal* on August 7, 1970.

ficials continued to push the investment in EJA, a "terrible" one, the senator said. Despite claims by the CAB (and later the House committee) that Penn Central controlled EJA, Mr. Bevan stoutly denied it. He stated to the Senate group that EJA's own management made its decisions.

The senator also propounded the thesis that the money poured into EJA could have been used for the railroad, possibly to improve its equipment.

Wall Street with Blinders

The investment community saw mostly the good in Penn Central. Perhaps they were influenced by Mr. Bevan himself, who at the time (April 16, 1968) addressed the combined meetings of the Investment Analysts Society of Chicago and the Transportation Securities Club of Chicago, Illinois.

Mr. Bevan began modestly:

"I am delighted to have this opportunity to discuss Penn Central before this important segment of the Chicago financial community, but I must confess it's a little difficult to know where to begin. Your brochure informs me to 'Please bear in mind that members . . . . are assumed to be reasonably well-acquainted with your company's history and recent events which have been reported publicly.'"

If Mr. Bevan was concerned about the nonpublic events, he could have rested easier. The "public events" are what analysts call "fundamental research." This is the kind that investment analysts find all too easy to obtain when the stocks are being "distributed" by the informed minority when the latter are selling—and all too difficult to obtain when they are buying. Breakdowns of company operations, rosy pictures of corporate development, and promotion by company officials are part of the information the Street calls research. It is at this time that "information" is spread far and wide about corporate workings, so that business-school-indoctrinated analysts may judge them. I recall the time a fellow proposed a certain stock to a certain "establishment type" expert who managed a mutual fund. He read the report carefully and rejected it.

"You don't give justification for the earnings projections," he said. "Why not?"

"The company didn't give breakdowns," the writer replied.

"Then how can I buy it?"

"I see what you mean," the writer said. Why bother to attempt to deflate his twenty years of analytical experience? After the stock tripled (a fluke, no doubt), the writer did not rub it in. If guys like the establishment type persist in their innocence, the informed minority can profit with impunity. The uninformed majority's artlessness gives the market its ingenuelike charm. Bayard H. Roberts, corporate secretary of the Penn Central, could not have been charged with such ingenuousness, as he sold 1800 shares (according to SEC reports) on March 21, 1968, at around $63 a share. Or perhaps he was lucky.

Penn Central had shown earnings of $3.10 from operations, as opposed to $6.44 the prior year. But Wall Street was expecting better things. After all, as Mr. Bevan told the assembled multitude in Chicago:

"The economic downturn led to a definite decline in traffic volume and a series of strikes in key industries further contributed to our lower 1967 earnings." He pointed out how low a rate of return the combine was getting on their investment, pleading for relief from the ICC. He was appreciative of "our banks," who were "extremely cooperative in helping us." They were not the only lambs around, and it would be a mistake to put the blame entirely on their investment analysis sections.

Mr. Bevan was guardedly optimistic. "Through a careful selection of companies, we expect to establish a long-term growth trend completely separate and apart from the cyclical characteristics of the railroad industry and iron out the wide fluctuations which have affected our earnings in times past." Later, the bankruptcy would be stabilizing in that if did not exhibit wide changes in corporate affairs.

Mr. Bevan went on to discuss how the company would attain a "constantly increasing upward trend in profitability.

"We have not been looking for weak companies with the idea of making them strong."

Yes, but sometimes it turned out the other way around.

"We are seeking companies with good management, with promising growth potential, with a proven ability to stand on their own, and most importantly, with earnings patterns that will supplement the cyclical nature of railroad income." He did not single out Executive Jet as a model. In fact, while listing such as Arvida, he noted that they "started clearing ground for a $500 million golf resort community to be known as Boca Raton West." Not only would it include the course, but 4000 apartments would be built on the 1450-acre site.

It might be illuminating to quote from Mr. Bevan's testimony later to the Senate Sub-Committee on Surface Transportation on August 6, 1970.[29]

> Referring to Arvida, Senator Hartke asked, "Who are Arvida's creditors?"
>
> Mr. Bevan replied: "The largest one is the Aetna Life Insurance Co., which has a mortgage on the entire property."
>
> Senator Hartke: "How about the First Bank & Trust of Boca Raton?"
>
> Mr. Bevan: "The First Bank & Trust did have a line of credit there, recently established, of about a million dollars."
>
> Senator Hartke: "How about the University National Bank of Boca Raton?"
>
> Mr. Bevan: "There is no connection as far as I know."
>
> Senator Hartke: "Does Penphil have any stock in any of these banks?"
>
> Mr. Bevan: "Penphil has stock in University Bank and the First Bank & Trust."
>
> Senator Hartke: "To what extent do you stand to gain personally from the operations of Arvida?"
>
> Mr. Bevan: "None."
>
> Senator Hartke: "Through Penphil or otherwise?"
>
> Mr. Bevan: "None."
>
> Senator Hartke: "None whatsoever?"
>
> Mr. Bevan: "Only to the extent that the general area prospers and the banks do well."

Now back to David Bevan's speech to the Chicago analysts:
". . . Arvida also announced plans for a $4 million condominium apartment building at Boca Raton, the fourth to be built since 1964. There is plenty of room for further development, since

[29] Part 2, Serial No. 91-90.

Arvida has a mile and a half of beach-front property on the Florida Gold Coast."

Mr. Bevan noted that Penn Central was the nation's largest real estate company. Another of its ingredients was Great Southwest Corporation, "an 80 percent-owned land company in the Dallas-Fort Worth area of Texas and in Atlanta, Georgia. It operated industrial parks and two "family recreation" parks, "Six Flags over Texas" and "Six Flags over Georgia," both of which, he said, "are highly successful."

Maybe so. But two years later, Senator Hartke pointed out that Great Southwest had a net loss on operations of $3½ million for only half a year.[30] "Is that true?" he asked Bevan. Mr. Bevan replied that he didn't know. Senator Hartke asked Bevan if he was really in charge of this operation until recently. After Bevan replied in the affirmative, Senator Hartke said, "I am rather surprised at an 'I do not know.'"

Mr. Bevan pointed out that when he was there, Great Southwest earned $34 million (no taxes were paid) in 1968 and $51 million in 1969. Before he left, it appeared that they were going to show a profit for the first half of 1970.

"My supposition—and this is the only thing I can go on—I heard they sold some properties to raise cash, and my guess is that they were sold at distress prices and, therefore, sustained a loss on them, but they sacrificed in order to raise cash," Mr. Bevan said.

The senator seemed perplexed. How could Great Southwest be making all that money and still need to raise cash so badly that they had to sell properties at a loss? If he was troubled, imagine the financial analysts who did not know of the internal cash troubles of this Penn Central subsidiary and had only to go on the bullish statements of corporate officials. One would hope that they would gain analytical maturity from the experience, but my discussions with many would seem to yield little hope. As a group, they are "believers."

The Great Beyond

By the end of March 1968, it was all "go" for the shares of the powerful new steamroller with the wheels of clay. The stock was

[30] Commerce Subcommittee, cited previously.

selling for sixty-seven dollars a share, no doubt helped by the blandishments of Mr. Bevan. Behind the scenes were General Lassiter and Executive Jet, draining the precious financial resources of an already cash-thin engine. There was the sticky business of Holiday International Tours, but Spencer Tracy might patch it up, even if he needed help from Pat O'Brien, who could do a "Knute Rockne" to pep up the boys.

There was the rather confusing business of a missing four million dollars that a Swiss moneyman seemed to have "misplaced." There is no point in going into detail on this matter, for it would take another chapter just to explain it, before which I would have to understand it. But the Street would hear only the "good" news and pass the exciting details to their confreres, who bulled the stock even more. In the next two weeks, the stock rose another five points, with average daily volume of about twenty thousand shares. Insurance companies abandoned their restrictions against common stocks (at the wrong time, of course) and were buying. Bank trust departments had been setting up special funds to handle those who had only twenty-five thousand to fifty thousand dollars to invest, and who wanted some "action."

Value Line survey said on April 26 (they listed a seventy-five-dollar recent price) that "Shares of [Penn Central] are finally beginning to receive the investor attention they merit. . . . Even with the recent runup in price (10 percent in the past month, over 20 percent in a little over three months) [it] still has at least average appeal for potential price appreciation over the next three to five years."

Value Line said also that in view of the recent advance, little could be expected for the coming twelve months, that is, unless another acquisition could be made that would increase earnings. They also noted that insider transactions in December and January "showed no decisive trends."

The service noted that what the two companies did before the merger "will form a nice base from which to measure future progress," and "we doubt that earnings that low will be seen again." They concluded that an earnings recovery "will begin this year and our estimate of $4.30 a share may prove a minimum expectation." To add fuel to the public fervor, *Business Week* headlined a story eight days later, "The Big Merger Begins to Click." Though the projected savings of the merger had been expected to reach their goal in eight years, Wall Street analysts were now cutting the timetable to five, and the magazine echoed their hopes. After citing some problems, they said, "Still, the management of the combined system generally is satisfied." Saunders and Perlman were quoted as claiming that the merger "is going ahead of schedule." So a veritable chorus of voices were shouting to investors of the stock's bullishness, in effect—though none could directly be legally charged. Another lesson to investors from "contrary opinion": If everybody agrees, do a reverse on Norman Vincent Peale and think negatively. If this sounds heretical, so be it. Jesus Christ would hardly find solace at Willow Run.

Investors should ask themselves whether all this bullishness was overdone and whether it all amounted to "too much protesting" of the railroad's virtues.

As Senator Hartke later stated with reference to Swiss bank holdings in Great Southwest, "one of the things is that the people [management] do not know and investors do not know what really is going on." And, though the Street saw the Penn Central as an easy way to make money, the road's structure was so complicated, the involvements with Penphil and Executive Jet were so twisted, that Hartke was prompted to say to Bevan, "I guarantee you it is very difficult for me to weave a way through here. It is sort of like going down through the Notre Dame Four Horsemen and trying to find an open lane."

The Nitty Gritty

One of the things the financial institutions failed to do was to find out what was really happening at the scene—or perhaps, in delegating the research to others, they failed to judge the ability of those others (in some cases, stockbrokers who recommended PC) in making a balanced assessment.

As for what the merger really did to the railroad (as opposed to what the investors were led to believe about it), one veteran railroader said, "It was just a goddamned operating mess."[31] In order to effect the union of the roads, new train routing had to be rearranged or combined. The people who were responsible, the classifi-

[31] *Fortune*, August 1970.

cation clerks, were not taught the five thousand new combinations necessary. Perhaps management as well as Wall Street had its eyes on the new glory instead of bothering with such mundane details as teaching the staff which cars were to go where.

As one former Central worker at the Albany yard later said, "They'd get a car for Harrisburg, which wasn't on the old Central, and they'd say, 'Where the hell is Harrisburg? I know where Pittsburgh is. Shit! I'll send it to Pittsburgh.'"

Some cars were not provided with the papers (waybills) normally used to show their destination. Supervisors were thus sending out entire trains for which nobody knew their routing. When they arrived at the other yards, the pileups became fierce; so those trains were sent to other yards, just to get rid of them. Some areas became so jammed that later arriving trains, correctly routed, couldn't get in. "Many times crewmen had to leave entire trains on sidings along the mainlines, and the Penn Central suddenly began losing trains. In one case, at the close of 1968, a coal train of more than a hundred cars was lost for ten days outside Syracuse, *Fortune* later revealed.

Investors were for the most part oblivious (particularly those who did not read the SEC insider transactions, and kept buying the stock in May and June of 1968, bulling it up to $84 on June 7. June and July were most interesting months, for while the stock was making perhaps its most spectacular performance, there appeared to be an acceleration of informed minority selling. With the stock ranging in the $80 area during the period, and institutional buying increasing (a natural corollary), PC's Senior Vice President Guy W. Knight sold 1750 shares; Vice President for Coal and Ore Traffic A. Paul Funkhouser sold 1900; Executive Vice President Henry W. Large sold 1000; another executive vice president, Walter R. Grant, unloaded 3380; and John G. Patten, vice president for freight sales, got out of 2180. Executive Vice President David E. Smucker really rang the bell, with his sale of 9000 shares on June 8 in the $85 area, for a personal total of approximately $765,000, all according to the SEC. And who could blame them? They had seen the stock rise spectacularly in the past five years, and they had a substantial profit. Investors rarely bother to note how much a stock has already risen before they buy it. The public may have been influenced by the company's 1967 annual report, which pointed out that the road was "moving over 10 million tons [of coal] annually";

also that they were "handling about 21 per cent of total piggyback shipments, and approximately 20 per cent of the nation's automobile output."

Moving them they were, but to the right destinations?

Advice

As the insiders were selling, the institutions were buying. Indeed, one columnist-stockbroker wrote on Junc 15, 1968, that "last year the institutions made net purchases of (all) common stocks in the amount of $7.7 billion. This is more than twice the net purchases as recently as in 1964." It was a time when most analysts felt that the market could *never* go down because the institutions were buying so heavily. The Street's ebullience swelled to a fever pitch that coincided with the institutions' buying. Unfortunately, the informed minority's selling was the other side of the coin—and the resultant market crash and recession helped deflate many an expert—for a time.

One of the stocks many mutual funds, banks, investment counselors, and insurance companies were buying was Penn Central. The same columnist who noted over-all institutional buying and counted it bullish was highly optimistic on the new railroad combine, interestingly. He noted, "There is persistent buying in Penn Central (78)." This was mostly probably due to investor assessment of its real-estate holdings, he felt. There was also that tax-loss asset, "making the company's profits tax-free for several years." As it turned out, PC was having so many internal troubles that it would have little use for tax-loss provisions, for it was not to earn much money on which to use it. The analyst concluded: "I think those who buy Penn Central stock now will realize important appreciation in the future." He is still practicing at the same old stand.

Other brokers helped fuel the fires of greed. With the price at $81 a share, another on June 21, 1968 ticked off the positives (substantial benefits of the merger to come):

1. Savings amounting to $80 million annually after 8–10 years.
2. Probable worth of the companies' real-estate operations on a conservative "guesstimate" at $1 billion, or about $43 a Penn Central share, a fraction of present values carried on the books.

3. Potential tax shelter.
4. Expansion and diversification.
5. Creation of one of the country's leading "conglomerates."

The report concluded with a prediction of $5 per-share earnings, so at $81 a share, it was "conservatively valued."

A week later Penn Central made the headlines with an announcement that it planned to acquire an apparel firm, Kayser-Roth. PC stock went up $1.75 a share that day, though Kayser fell $1.62 on the news, which may have said something.

Value Line noted that (as of July 26) Penn Central had risen 31 points since the merger had been announced. However, in the four previous days' trading, it had fallen precipitously. Actually, it had fallen more sharply in the previous seven days—for a total of 10 points. Now at $73 a share, the stock was a "superior buy for 3 to 5 year capital appreciation potential," though still rated "average" for the coming 12 months. They also stated that insiders were "substantially on the buy side," according to recent reports. *Value Line* and I must have been reading different books. They also said that a normal average price for 1971–73 would be $98 a share. One cannot take away from them the excellent chart accompanying the write-up and the detailed financial data included.

Value Line were not the only people who felt the minor drop in PC's price constituted a buying opportunity. Another brokerage firm said "Penn Central is an attractive purchase for longer term capital gains and the present setback places the stock in a strong buying area." The issue was selling at $73, and the broker said, among other things, "Finances are strong." All in all, the report seemed to echo many of the points raised elsewhere. With so many agreeing so much about so little, who could fight the urge to join the multitude?

Then there was this business of the "finances." A professor of finance at Columbia's Graduate School of Business, Roger F. Murray, later criticized some rosy views of PC's cash situation. According to the March 4, 1971 issue of the New York *Times,* he felt, "Good hardnosed security analysis would have prevented the shock and some of the losses that attended the [stock's] wreck."

To show his heretical approach (and to indicate that business school types can't be all bad), he attacked the concept of cash flow as a determinus of available cash, since cash flow, a popular Wall Street (and B-school) term *sounds* like money, but is merely an accounting calculation. Whereas cash flow also includes earnings, some of PC's were made as sales of real estate—much of which, in actual dollars, was not paid in, but rather was *expected* over a period of time.

Other myths exposed were: "Concepts like diversification have no inherent virtues" and that the analyst should not be awed by sheer size in a company. Good lessons for the investor, too. But the most important caveat would be one he may not have uttered but implied: "Believe little of what you hear and less of what you read when judging a company."

And few of the bulls on the stock, some of whom were responsible for investing hundreds of millions of dollars, bothered to go out on the tracks to see what was really going on. Professor Murray criticized the analyst fraternity for not judging (or perhaps being able to judge) the quality of management. I have heard far too many trust people, investment advisers, and fund analysts decry that intangible necessity, management. As one Penn Central director said of *its* group:

"They didn't seem to have a clear idea of how much commercial paper [corporate loans] they had out. They had no control on cash; they didn't know if it was coming or going."

Another PC director, San Francisco businessman Robert S. Odell, told the Washington *Post* later (on June 26, 1970): "It was one of those incompatible situations you find in business from time to time where you have so much friction and lack of authority, it's just a mess."

Of President Saunders, Odell reportedly said, "[He] has a lot of talent as a lawyer, but he just didn't know how to run a railroad. He took the position that the Pennsylvania had purchased the Central, rather than merging with it, and there was continual conflict between the men from each road. On top of that, they had two men for every job—with the Pennsylvania man usually on top."

The conflict between Saunders and Perlman did not appear in brokerage reports, nor in the periodic write-ups institutional analysts turn in. Perhaps *they* were not being told the real story either. Perlman told the Washington *Post*, "The Pennsylvania wanted volume regardless of profitability," echoing what others reported. Perlman, who apparently did not have Saunders' panache, showed some candor when he said, "We wanted to put more money into the railroad, but they invested in real estate and developed it." Saunders denied money had been siphoned to other than railroad operations.

No Different from the Rest of Society

One year after the PC bankruptcy, a trust analyst told me, "I am not interested in management. I am interested in sales breakdowns." This analyst, and hundreds like him, remain. If the reader is incredulous at the naïveté of the analytical fraternity, let him ponder the innocence displayed by other groups toward the realities of the society.

While working on a political campaign some years ago, I had chanced to be faced with volunteers who wished to help the candidate's drive to political office. They extolled his virtues—on how he was different from other politicians, on how his motives were people-oriented rather than money-oriented. Actually, he was ego-oriented, and we all had a good laugh (especially the candidate) when the story got back to the staff.

Then there was the story on the first page of the New York *Times* on May 22, 1971, "60 Western Intellectuals Berate Castro" for his actions against a poet, Herberto Padilla. They were "disillusioned" with Castro. The dictator's treatment of Padilla (amounted) "to the negation of revolutionary legality and justice." If such signatories to the statement as Alberto Moravia, Simone de Beauvoir, Jean-Paul Sartre, and Susan Sontag, "intellectuals" and political philosophers all, could be so naïve about Castro, why not analysts about the stock market?

It is, then, a lack of understanding of the dynamics of the market that count most in security analysis: How do you examine stocks when you don't really know what the whole thing is all about, if you don't know what the real game is? An awareness by the reader should go a long way to improving his investment performance. And all the publicity, the corporate statements, the institutional fervor, the excited price rise should give him pause. Stay away, should be his conclusion. "They're not getting me into that sinking ship," should be his attitude, "even though they've painted up the cabins and polished up the halls." Of course, in this case it was a railroad, but it could have been a nursing home company, a fried chicken joint, a mobile home manufacturer, a "soft" lens producer, or whatever new fad comes along to tempt the greed-response brain areas of the Street.

Not Minding the Store?

The ostensible purpose of corporate directors is to safeguard the interests of the stockholders of that company. What were they doing while the Penn Central was barreling its way down the track to its inevitable end?

"It is not so much what they did, but what they did not do that helped cause the railroad's decline," said the House committee.

"Time and time again, the railroad's directors acted as a rubber stamp of approval for the irresponsible decisions and activities of top management."[32]

If the board fiddled while the railroad burned, the directors were not all Neros. Of the concerned minority, Robert S. Odell's voice was raised again and again in anguish over the way the road's assets were being squandered. It did not appear that he was listened to.

Robert S. Odell was president of Allied Properties in San Francisco, and he served on Central's board and then the Penn Central Transportation Company when it was formed as a result of the merger. Mr. Odell, according to his congressional testimony had made various suggestions as to the company's operations to Saunders and Bevan and had been ignored. "His attempts to discuss the issues at the board meetings were always sidetracked by Saunders and certain other board members."[33]

Thus Mr. Odell was driven to inviting the other board members who were not officers to a dinner to be held in Philadelphia the night before the following board meeting, feeling as he did that Saunders and Bevan had railroaded other possibly beneficial suggestions.

"Dear Mr. ——: I would like you to be my guest at a business dinner for members of the Penn Central Board of Directors without any management directors [Saunders, Bevan, et al.] present.

"The meeting would take place, [etc., etc.]."

[32] Staff report of the Banking and Currency Committee, Part six, Chapter 3, January 3, 1972.

[33] Ibid.

This letter was sent to the following directors: Louis W. Cabot of Cabot Corporation, William L. Day of the First Pennsylvania Banking and Trust Company, John T. Dorrance, Jr., of the Campbell Soup Company, Otto N. Frenzel of the Merchants National Bank and Trust Company, Dr. R. Walter Graham, Jr., Edward J. Hanley of the Allegheny Ludlum Steel Corporation, Gaylord P. Harnwell of the University of Pennsylvania, Fred M. Kirby of the Allegheny Corporation, Seymour H. Knox of Marine Midland Trust Company of Western New York, Franklin J. Lunding of Jewel Companies, Inc., Walter A. Marting of The Hanna Mining Company, Thomas L. Perkins of Perkins, Daniels and McCormack, R. Stewart Rauch, Jr., of the Philadelphia Saving Fund Society, R. George Rincliffe of the Philadelphia Electric Company, Carlos J. Routh of Pittston Company, John M. Seabrook of International Utilities Corporation, and Daniel E. Taylor.

Concerned as they were about events at the railroad that they were overseeing, only four said they could make it, and one other said he would try. One, Mr. Day, later declined.

Although most refused to attend, they responded with explanations for their refusals. John Dorrance, president of Campbell Soup, wrote to Odell, "It would seem that if the press or financial community became aware of this [meeting] it would be most unfortunate." Both he and Dr. Graham felt it should be held following the board meeting. Mr. Day felt much the same: "If news of this meeting leaks out, I am afraid it could be completely misunderstood," he wrote.

Other directors could not make it, they said, because of "other business." Thus the dinner meeting was called off.

Mr. Odell wrote to Mr. Cabot, informing him of the meeting's cancellation. Suspecting that management was behind the poor response, Mr. Odell said, further, that he intended the meeting to be secret, but most importantly he wrote:

"There is no doubt that the Penn Central is in critical financial condition with critical management problems. *If the present situation is not improved and corrected, receivership or bankruptcy is inevitable*" (emphasis is the House committee's).

Mr. Odell threw a barbed one next, when he wrote,

"Every director, as you well know, is in a fiduciary capacity to represent the stockholders to the best of his ability and to deal with the financial and management problems realistically, impartially and judiciously."

Mr. Odell did not want the meeting to be kept a secret from Mr. Saunders, as indeed it could not have been for long. Yet it was his contention that Saunders sabotaged the meeting, as revealed by the following from Mr. Day's reply to the dinner meeting invitation:

"After talking to Stuart Saunders (as you suggested I do), I have decided that it would be unwise for me to attend."

Later, at the regular board meeting on November 26, 1969, Mr. Odell listed some of his complaints against the PC's management:

". . . The New York Central was in excellent condition before the merger. It had $71,000,000 cash, $160,900,000 current assets, and investments and advances of $61,387,000. Roughly, quick assets of $294,000,000. Current liabilities and debt due in one year amounted to about $210,000,000. . . . To say that the merger of New York Central and Pennsylvania has been a tragic mistake to date is an understatement."

Of course, individually, the informed minority had been taking some of *their cash out,* but let us go on:

"As of November 18, Penn Central's cash was roughly $74,000,000. Current and long-term liabilities at December 13, 1968 were $1,919,447,000, and due in one year $76,716,000." He added Great Southwest's debts and liabilities of $184,000,000 and Arvida's $38,000,000.

After assailing poor money management and the increase in debts due to real-estate ventures, plus the nonutilization of the tax-loss advantages that the Street, incidentally, had used as a plus in judging the stock, he expressed amazement that the apparently capable Albert Perlman had been sidelined "and the presidency taken over by a sixty-one-year-old public-utility executive at $250,000 a year without any railroad experience."

Though he had good things to say about the incoming Paul Gorman, "it is my opinion he does not qualify to replace Al Perlman."

After commenting on Perlman's outstanding credentials for the job, Mr. Odell said, "I might truly say that if you have a sick horse, you don't go to the outstanding M.D., internist, or surgeon; instead, you go to a hell of a good veterinary."

Mr. Odell also mentioned that the Internal Revenue Service was making a study of expense accounts and personal use of airplanes, private cars, and automobiles, implying that he thought there was some hanky-panky going on. Further, he wished his resolution (which would eliminate Saunders' position and reinstate Perlman) be noted in the minutes if there were no seconding. Otherwise his resolution might not appear, and as a director he might be held culpable if the impending disaster he felt would strike the railroad occurred.

It was not the first time that Mr. Odell had expressed reservations about the Penn Central. In July of 1968, he wrote Saunders of what he considered to be questionable investments in real estate that the railroad was making. It should be noted that Odell was a real-estate man and Saunders wasn't. And whereas Odell felt that many of the investments were dubious, Wall Street was hailing them. Incidentally, in interviews with the House committee, Mr. Saunders said that Mr. Bevan had complete control over PC's real-estate activities.[34] However, in a letter Saunders wrote to Odell on July 15, 1968, he said,

"I might also say that I, of course, follow the activities of Macco [one of the real estate operations] closely as well as that of all of our other subsidiaries."

But, of course, Mr. Bevan was more directly involved.

Yet, according to the ICC (in a 1760-page report released on December 20, 1971), Bevan, in addition to his activities with the private investment group, Penphil, had "a further possible conflict of interest" involving him with a CBK Industries, Inc., so apparently Mr. Bevan had other things to think about, according to the ICC. By the way, the railroad's pension fund and contingent compensation fund (overseen by Bevan) were also investing in CBK, they said, "and suffered losses when CBK sustained financial reverses."

Saunders Helps Out

Penn Central Chairman Stuart T. Saunders addressed the New York Society of Security Analysts on September 5, 1968—and he added more coals to that speeding engine, now wildly out of control. Shipping customers were tearing their collective hair out as shipments were lost for months. Entire trains disappeared into the

[34] Ibid.

maze of tracks and yards seemingly run by guys with flypaper on their fingers.

"It is a great pleasure to address the New York Society of Security Analysts again," Mr. Saunders began. The last time had been in 1964, and Mr. Saunders indicated they had made great strides since.

"We have accomplished the largest corporate merger in the history of American business, we have become both the largest railroad and one of the largest real-estate companies in this country," he said, and in less than two years he was to watch the largest bankruptcy in American business, so one cannot say he didn't think big. Wall Street liked that.

"Some people apparently have gotten the impression that we are more interested in diversification than we are in the railroad. I can say flatly that this is not true." His interest in the road had not waned. Shippers were diverting business from the Penn Central to other lines and to trucks. One could understand his continued interest and concern.

"Another worthwhile benefit [of the merger] which is difficult to measure is the fine esprit de corps which has developed in our organization."

". . . We have a great team—one that is attacking our problems aggressively and cooperatively, one that is determined to make money and to improve our service." No doubt the pressure of time prevented him from mentioning the other team—the one that was fighting the first team. Senator John O. Pastore of Rhode Island later described the relations between Saunders and Perlman as a "feud."

If the investment community could be accused of dreaming instead of facing reality, what about Mr. Saunders? No one could accuse him of accentuating the negative. His optimism was in the best traditions of the American ideal. "We are ahead of our target in accomplishing the rail connection and consolidation of facilities which are required to merge the railroad operations completely," he said.

It would be difficult to charge Mr. Saunders with untruths about the conditions along the routes of the Penn Central, for he usually traveled by jet. This was in contrast to Saunders' predecessor at Norfolk & Western (from which he subsequently joined the Pennsy), Bob Smith, who earned the appellation "Race Horse" for his habit of using his lanky legs to traverse much of the trackage when not riding the rails.

As for internal conflicts, Perlman also was unhappy with the executive vice president for operations, David E. Smucker. The latter was a rough-and-tumble type, "who cursed with an eloquence that was awesome even to steam veterans," said *Fortune* later (in its August 1970 edition).

"Smucker ruled in the old autocratic Pennsy style, a leadership trait that won him his men's endearing appellation of 'Mother Smucker.'"

The magazine said that Mr. Smucker was not enthusiastic about Perlman's attempts to streamline operations. For his part, Smucker reportedly did not take kindly to Perlman's disdain for the Pennsy's alleged stodginess.

"You run a wooden-wheeled railroad," Perlman reportedly told Smucker, a phrase that did little to endear him to the Pennsy executive.

Perlman kept pressuring Saunders to get rid of Smucker so his marketing types could run full gallop. Saunders eventually gave in and "Mike" Flannery, a forty-five-year-old Central man, was lifted into the post. Flannery was the type who ran up and down the line, exhorting his men like a Civil War-type cavalry captain.

"Flannery can really chew you out, but he always has time to listen to you," one operations man said.

Perlman was not satisfied with this change and reportedly demanded more. Henry W. Large, executive vice president for marketing was another whom Perlman felt did not shape up. Though Saunders had given in to Perlman on Smucker, he balked on Large.

"You just don't like Henry Large," Saunders reportedly said to Perlman at lunch at the Sky Club in New York's Pan Am Building.

"I do like Henry Large. He's a great big lovable St. Bernard. No one can help but like him. But he's giving away the railroad," Perlman is reported to have answered. It was his philosophy against the Pennsy's again, with the reference to the volume business approach versus his high-markup one.

"But the shippers like him," said Saunders. A good point.

"Well, who doesn't like Santa Claus?" Perlman was supposed to have replied, and the conversation did not lead to radical changes in the road's operations.

Later, when Perlman was retired for "age," Saunders, at the suggestion of a board member, hired Paul A. Gorman as company president, and Gorman in turn replaced Large with Edward G. Kreyling, Jr.

"We're killing Santa Claus," Kreyling said. "They won't be giving things away any more around here." Either by that time it was too late, or maybe it was the Pennsy men who were right—but in any event, the Penn Central train kept highballing it wildly down the track toward the inevitable.

"Already we are getting good results in terms of faster train schedules, more efficient yarding and operational savings by use of the best routes," Saunders was telling Wall Street on September 5, 1968. It was this month that Vice President for Industrial Real Estate Samuel Hillenbrand sold thirty-five hundred shares of PC stock.

"On September 25, we formally open our new twenty-nine-million-dollar freight classification yard near Selkirk, New York. . . . It will be the major switching point for freight traffic moving between the East and New York City and New England," said Saunders.

A little over a year later, trains working their way out the yard gave solemn homage as they rolled past the wrecks of 108 Cadillacs that lay in mangled heaps caused by an earlier derailment. The tracks south of the yard heading for Weehawken saw trains going at forty miles per hour as opposed to the seventy they were originally meant to do there. A year after the wreck, "slow" orders due to unfinished repairs forced trains to drop down to thirty, and then to ten miles an hour.

If Mr. Saunders was not riding the rails, neither were the analysts who heard only good things about Penn Central, and whose bullish optimism would not have permitted them to listen to bearish tidings about the road in any event. The broker who told the investment counsel about Four Seasons Nursing Homes (he called it "Two Seasons") was shrugged off six months before it too went into bankruptcy.

Such is often the case. Many brokers have tried to poor-mouth stocks that were rising, rising as if never to stop. They have told their customers, large and small, up to a point. At some juncture, they realize that one doesn't make a living that way. Too often the holders refuse to hear anything bad about their stock. I recall the time I was physically threatened by a holder of SCM after writing in a market letter that it was a "short sale." This may be an extreme case, but how many commissions do brokers receive in reward for telling the fund that "their baby is ugly"?

Mr. Saunders went on, but this time in greater detail. If there is anything analysts like it is detail, just like the old Indian proverb about the blind old wise men who examined the elephant's trunk, tail, head, etc., individually—and proclaimed it a snake or a tree. Each described his part in detail but couldn't see the whole.

Mr. Saunders concluded with the claim that "We are a company with high aspirations," and that certainly was true. Mr. Saunders' optimism about his company's ability to match their aspirations with performance was something else.

A few days later the prestigious White, Weld & Co. brokerage house commented that "his speech *clarified* [emphasis mine] several matters of interest." Taking a cue from Mr. Saunders' exuberance, they concluded that "at its current price, the stock offers long-term appreciation potential based on," among other things, "a tentative estimate of $6.00 [earnings] for 1969," excluding the New Haven. Now that the stock had fallen almost back to where it had started when the merger took place, some analysts felt it was a bargain. Not mentioned was the fact that it was still more than 60 percent higher than what it had been before the furor began.

With its troubles with shippers multiplying, internal friction heating, and, by Saunders' own admission, at least one of its subsidiaries, Arvida, not doing as well as it might, not to mention the fatal engine trouble developing in Executive Jet, the Penn Central was painted more attractively to investors as its clay wheels began to crack.

"I am more and more impressed with the appreciation possibilities in Penn Central, selling at around 67½ as this is written," said the same columnist mentioned earlier, in his piece of October 15, 1968. He took about four hundred words to list the components of the giant combine and then said, "The stock offers a most interesting combination of huge assets and excellent management, and it involves no little leverage." It was the kind of company review bound to impress investors. One could not fault it for comprehensiveness if not for perspicacity.

Penn Central ended the year at $63.38 a share, with its holders including no less than 64 mutual funds,[35] among whom some of the largest were Chase Fund of Boston, Dreyfus, Fidelity, Investors Mutual, Investors Variable Payment (both part of Investors' Diversified Services), Keystone Growth Common, and Selected American Shares.

There were also 35 insurance companies holding the stock in *Vickers'* year-end review, current as of August 1968.

Meanwhile, at Altoona, Pennsylvania, graphic illustration of what was really going on—the condition of the cracking clay wheels—was quite vivid. So many "bad order" cars (those needing important repairs) were piling up that the rusted hulks took on the visage of a railroad grave yard. But many of the road executives were more intent on pursuing "diversification" (the Street liked that) that it would appear that the railroad was being abandoned.

"A look at the Penn Central's operations at Altoona illustrates how pinching pennies on maintenance can shortchange both the railroad and its customers," said the *Wall Street Journal* on September 8, 1970. The "bad order" cars had their sides stenciled as to the date they were so designated. Some remained unrepaired for at least three years. Meanwhile, Arvida kept on building apartments and golf courses. This fact did little to calm the nerves of shippers who awaited freight cars to pick up their cargoes of coal and plywood.

Penn Central—"The Treadmill to Oblivion"

The year 1969 began with the train tearing its way along the track, as far as Wall Street was concerned. Earnings for 1968 were to be announced at $3.91, versus $3.08 for 1967. Another brokerage firm said PC "is an appealing investment from three standpoints—as a railroad, as a real-estate holding company, and/or as an emerging conglomerate."

It might have been helpful for analysts to note the operating ratios, of the road, that is, the total operating expenses as a percent of their operating revenue. This figure appeared in PC's supplement to their annual reports, and were available upon request. They showed for 1964, over 80 percent; for 1965, 79 percent; for 1966, 78 percent; for 1967, 82 percent; and for 1968, over 83 percent. Thus

[35] Holders as tabulated by *Vickers' Investment Company Guide.*

one can see that for 1968 less than 20 percent of revenues were available for all purposes other than maintenance, transportation, and assorted other operating expenses. A pitiful amount—insufficient, actually—was available to pay its debts, both current and coming due. Long-term debt due after one year (from December 31, 1968) was just under $1.5 billion. Total fixed charges for the year were $95 million, whereas income available for such payments was only $92 million. All of this information was obtainable from the company, though I have never seen a research report that mentioned it. Investors can get such data from their broker, who will get it (if you're a good customer) from the SEC in forms called 10-K. Or you can get it yourself there. The SEC maintains regional offices, by the way.

An investment advisory firm, Equity Research, said at the beginning of 1969 that the stock had "explosive" potential. And *Value Line* service continued to recommend the stock for "above average appreciation" for the longer term, with the stock selling at $67 on January 24, 1969. The Kayser-Roth deal had been called off, and *Value Line* seemed to be feeling a bit uneasy about the situation. Not enough, however, to remove it from the recommended category.

The cracks in the clay wheels were not apparent to the investment community. In addition to the massive earning power the Street saw in the railroad, buying the stock had another important advantage: One received the fairly substantial advantage of a $2.40 per share dividend. In 1968, for example, the railroad paid out some $87.8 million in dividends. Of this action, Representative J. J. Pickel (D. Tex.) later said:

"It appears to me as an effort to beguile the public and put up a good front."

The lower the stock went, of course, the higher the percent return the investor got. At $67 a share, he received a 3.6 percent return on his money—not to mention the profit he would get if (or when) the stock went back to the high level it was allegedly worth.

The high dividend may have enabled the insiders to get a good price for their shares. The estimable David Bevan got around $66 each for the 3000 shares he sold on January 6, 1969. That little trade grossed him $198,000, less commissions. Had he waited to sell it after the bankruptcy he might have gotten as little as $27,000, which only goes to show how good an investment manager he was, justifying the faith the Penphilers had in him.

Mr. Fox, incidentally, also sold 1200 shares, and Mr. Gerstnecker 2000 the same month.

The second-largest broker of them all, Bache & Company, said on January 30, 1968: "Based on the base patterns' potential, a test of PC's all-time high could develop."

Some technicians would question how a "base" could be formed around $70, where the stock was selling at that time. Dissenters could argue that it would be like building a foundation on the twentieth floor. The SEC reports showed Mr. Gerstnecker selling another 2000 shares in February, while the stock was "basing."

Within one month, Penn Central stock had fallen through its base in a 10-point derailment.

A Bear on the PC?

Wall Street did not pay much attention to the interview between A. Scheffer Lang, a former federal railroad administrator in the Department of Transportation, and editors Luther Miller and Gus Welty in their trade publication, *Railway Age,* on February 10, 1969. Mr. Lang noted the difficulties Penn Central was having "in particular, with regard to service to shippers . . . .

"The Pennsylvania no longer enjoys the kind of technical and management pre-eminence it once enjoyed, on the industrial scene or even in the railroad industry," Mr. Lang said.

". . . In almost any technical or management area you want to name, you can find one or more roads that do a better job. I think you'd find general agreement, moreover, that there are some roads which do a better job in virtually every area. But these other roads don't have the same history of—or the capability for—self-perpetuation that the Pennsylvania does. So we have an organization which has fallen behind in its quest for pre-eminence," Mr. Lang said.

He felt that the railroad was "operating in a caretaker role" rather than moving forward. Mr. Lang drew an analogy with the bankrupt New Haven, "which has so much as said that its job was to take care of the railroad in its present form—and if this drove it into bankruptcy, so be it."

One would think that the analysts reading that piece would have gotten shivers down their spines at the thought. Some did, others didn't. Either they did not read it, or they were caught up in their own emotional blindness to negative thoughts, not an uncommon trait on the Street.

Still, stories were beginning to leak about what was happening at the front lines—and GHQ would appear to have issued a "quieting" statement in the form of an interview Mr. Saunders had with the New York *Times* on March 9. Mr. Saunders was asked about tales "circulating in recent weeks" of misrouted trains, lost freight cars, and mislayed waybills.

Mr. Saunders replied: "Undoubtedly we've had some service problems—some of them much more acute than we anticipated." He denied that any freight trains had been lost and wondered how those stories came about. He admitted that the worst service problems happened in December 1968 and January 1969. However, he said:

"I think that our service problems have bottomed out, that we have turned the corner. In fact, I know we have." He noted that in three of the worst ones, St. Louis, Avon (Indianapolis), and Seneca (Buffalo), "we've seen definite signs of improvement" in the past few weeks.

He said of the doubts being whispered about, "Apparently there is a lack of understanding." He described the troubled ones as "Cassandras in and outside the railroad industry." Some were merely "competitors." You couldn't expect to put together such a giant system without *some* trouble, you know, certainly not "overnight or in a matter of weeks or months."

One bit of evidence, by the way, of the doubts about the system had been the price drop—which said more than mere words could about what was going on.

The *Times* man, Robert Bedingfield, told of a story wherein, "Western meat packers shipping to the East Coast markets via piggyback [trailers that could be mounted on truck bodies and lifted off and transferred to trains or vice versa] have been instructing their Chicago people to take the trailers and containers off the trains at Chicago and use the highways from Chicago to New York rather than Penn Central."

Mr. Saunders said he didn't hear the story and doubted its veracity. It was true that they had lost some business, but, he said, "shippers are giving business back to us because of our improved service."

The reporter repeated stories of internal strife at the railroad. Mr. Saunders admitted some difficulties, but "Those wild stories that have been circulated by and large are not true."

He pointed out that Mr. Smucker had been replaced by Mr. Flannery and that other steps were being taken to improve performance.

When asked about possible dissension within the marketing department and some layoffs, Mr. Saunders indicated that some streamlining had been done—and indeed he had "checked on this just within the past few weeks and I am told that everything is moving along harmoniously there."

Mr. Saunders' reputation for optimism was unblemished.

One must understand the difficulties inherent in the combination, not all of which were out of the way, he said. And, he indicated, progress was being made.

As I noted, Saunders' interview appeared in the *Times* on March 9, 1969—a Sunday. PC stock on Monday did not appear to be affected either way, closing the day down $.62. Trading volume for the day was average, 24,000 shares. The next day, March 11, according to the SEC reports, Mr. Bevan sold another 3000 shares as the stock dropped from $57.25 to $55.75. Whether Mr. Bevan shared Mr. Saunders' optimism could not be ascertained. It was Ambrose Bierce who described an optimist as a "proponent of the doctrine that black is white." I cannot judge what was in Mr. Bevan's mind when he sold—and so cannot attribute to him the sentiments of an anonymous observer who said that an optimist is "one who doesn't care what happens as long as it happens to somebody else."

That somebody else would be the collective investment community that had bought or recommended the buying of PC in the $80s and $70s. As the PC annual report reached investors the third week or so of March, the stock sold in the $56 area, falling another $2 a share by month's end. That it did not fall farther can possibly be attributed to the rosy outlook propounded by Saunders and Perlman in their joint message to stockholders.

"The outlook for 1969 is brighter than it was for the past year, especially with regard to our railroad system," they said.

One would think that if the stock had been "cheap" in the $60s it was even cheaper in the $50s, since "We expect to have to have smoother and more efficient operations from the experience we have gained and the physical improvements we have made," they told the shareholders.

"We are projecting a gain of at least $65 million in gross revenues from the higher levels of freight rates, and we anticipate a substantial increase in traffic volume," Saunders and Perlman said. The report read like a politician's promise to the voters. It had been issued a week after Mr. Bevan sold another 3000 shares in the $54–$55 area, according to the SEC reports. In less than four months, he had taken some $515,000 in gross receipts from stock sales, despite the statement by Saunders and Perlman that they "have complete faith in the wisdom of our merger and in our ability to achieve, much quicker than originally anticipated, the projected merger economies and efficiencies."

The annual report also noted that Messrs. Fox, Jones, Grant, Cook, and Kenefick resigned in 1968 "to accept positions in other companies," which may help to explain why Fox and Grant sold stock. Bevan and Gerstnecker may have had other reasons. Mr. Butcher had resigned from the board, as did Walter Annenberg, who became ambassador to Great Britain. Mr. Annenberg's being so far removed may have cost him some money, but he surely could afford it. The investment community was just as far removed from the reality of corporate motivation—and some of them could afford it less than others.

Another brokerage firm recommended PC on March 26 with the stock at $55, possibly taking a cue from management's bullish statements.

"The sharp drop in the market for Penn Central common reflects disappointing operating results, but the shares could rebound sharply from this level on evidence of a material turnaround of railway operations," they said. In other words, if profits go up, the stock will too. It was the kind of no-nonsense stand that politicians take when they say, "No Comment." The analyst really put it on the line when he said, "The past year's enthusiasm for Penn Central was based on the earnings potential of the company's nonrailroad properties plus the added earnings leverage provided by a break-even operation on railway operations." However, he explained that the recent price decline of the stock reflected "a fading of optimism in the face of disappointing railway results." It was like watching a summary of yesterday's weather on TV, rather than a prediction of tomorrow's. You were bound to be right more often that way.

Standard & Poor's *Outlook* discussed "Stock's in the Limelight" and recorded that PC was selling at $52 on April 28, 1969. They explained that the stock had fallen since the first-quarter earnings had been announced as being lower. However, they said blithely, "The decline resulted from the East Coast dock strike, a coal miner's walkout, and costs arising from inclusion of the New Haven's operations on January 1." Things would be getting better, they said, seeming to echo Mr. Saunders' feelings.

Improved service, reduced charges, and merger benefits were cited. "Net for the full year could be around $5.00 a share, up from $3.81 last year," they said. The service is still very popular.

Moody's, considered by some to be S&P's rival for public favor, felt that "Penn Central common is worth holding for income, and gradual appreciation over the long pull," on April 28, with the stock at $52.

Meanwhile David C. Bevan was also in there pitching. When *Business Week* reported on May 10, 1969 on a reorganization plan for the road, Bevan was quoted as saying, "The new holding company will be a parent rather than a subsidiary, and its securities are expected to be *more highly regarded as an investment* [emphasis mine] than would those of a railroad subsidiary." Whether or not Mr. Bevan thought that way about his own stock was not discussed.

The Bank

Bankers are people who manage money, like the advertisements say. In addition to the basic function of "borrowing" money from depositors at, say, 5 percent and lending it to others at up to 15 percent is that of investing money from pension funds, trusts, and various collected funds of private investors. The banks of this country manage some tens of billions of dollars. How well do they do it? At least their *image* of ineptness was discussed with me by a leading trust department manager:

"As you know, Bill, we have not done too bad a job. We have consistently outperformed the Dow average, which cannot be said for some other banks. We compete for pension and profit-sharing corporate accounts with investment counselors, for whom I do not have too high a regard. You perhaps would be amazed, or perhaps you wouldn't, at the sort of stocks some of these guys bought during the 1967 to 1968 time . . . . you know, the National Student Marketing, Memorex, Leasco kind. But still we at the bank have an image problem. And so it looks as if we'll end up splitting away from the bank and forming a wholly owned subsidiary with a different name," he revealed.

There were bank investment advisers, though possibly not that one, who bought Penn Central in the $80s, $70s, and $60s. In one suit, a Chicago housewife invested in Continental Illinois National Bank's investment service account, according to a *Wall Street Journal* article on May 10, 1971. The plan was reportedly begun in 1968 and was aimed at the investor with at least $20,000 but with less than the typical trust account. The suit stated that about $7.5 million totally was invested under the plan. About $1 million of this was allegedly used to buy Penn Central stock—and in her case (she turned over her money on April 8, 1969 to the bank) they paid $54.77 per share on a proportionate basis with the other plan members.

Everything Is Gonna Be All Right

Bong! Bong! The old steam locomotive bell rang out to begin the annual meeting of the Penn Central railroad on May 13. Mr. Saunders and Mr. Perlman had rung the bell together, just as though they were the best of friends. They were pulling together (the bell cord), you see. Wilma Soss, corporate gadfly, was there, and so was Mr. Bevan, who apparently interrupted his sell orders to his broker long enough to attend.

"We are determined to show substantial gains in 1969 over 1968," Chairman Saunders told the 650 attending shareholders, as reported in the New York *Times* the next day. "We are confident that we will realize not only the economies of our railroad merger, but also its potential for greater profitability," he said. The bank and insurance company analysts present nodded approvingly as their confidence in PC stock was being affirmed.

Mr. Saunders figuratively took scalpel in hand as if to operate on Penn Central's sickest patient, the bankrupt New Haven Railroad.

He reportedly said that PC was spending $15 million to "recondition and to improve the paint and equipment [of it] . . . . We can make this property healthy and productive." The question that might have been pondered by analyst and investor alike was, "But is the patient already dead?"

David Bevan, "chairman of the company's powerful finance committee," revealed that plans were moving ahead for the sale of a small portion of Great Southwest Corporation stock.

Wilma Soss, president of the Federation of Women Shareholders in American Business, Inc. (which predated the women's liberation movement) really dug where it was at when she complained that credit cards were not being honored for ticket purchases. Mr. Saunders replied that the road would have to pay the card companies for the service. What he didn't say, as some railroad critics have argued, was that credit card purchases might attract more passengers, heaven forbid. In any event, the issue had as much relevance to what was really happening at the road as the exact pressure at which the boilers would be maintained before the stokers jumped off. The *Times* said that Mrs. Soss "acknowledges that she thoroughly enjoys asking embarrassing questions of corporate executives," but not having the meeting's transcript, I cannot say what *other* "embarrassing questions" she asked.

The picture Penn Central bigwigs gave to shareholders (and to the press inevitably, and through them to potential stock buyers) was, all in all, a rosy one. What followed over the months was that the institutions (the new public) and the little guy by and large continued buying and the informed minority continued selling, though we cannot say that there was any connection, can we?

There were a few outside sellers—chartists who saw "erosion" in the price pattern (some of whom were buyers at $70), a few mutual funds, some individuals who heard rumors (one of the few that turned out to be true) of troubles at the freight yards, and so the price slipped a bit more, closing May out at $54.

While Continental Illinois was holding Penn Central stock (and just possibly buying some), guess who was selling? Why, it was our little ol' friend, David Bevan again. During May of 1969, he sold another 3700 shares worth about $199,000, or a gross amount for the year of $714,000. The stock held up during May, and so Mr. Bevan fortunately got a good price. Investment counselors were buying with the rationale that if the stock was "cheap" at $60, it was cheaper at $50. Some mutual fund managements also felt this way, and their resultant buying power held the stock up as it closed the month at $54.60. Still the engine roared ahead like the mighty powerhouse of old. Who can forget the cowboy movies when the villains stoked the coals full blast into the engine just before they jumped over the side? In this movie there were more dupes than villains, and the former rode the parlor cars partaking of the wine of hope, oblivious and starry-eyed.

June was not the passengers' best month, as prices continued to slip—the clay wheels continued their cracking. Thus Mr. Bevan was only able to get some $48 for the 2300 shares he sold this month. This totaled for 1969 about $814,000, not the very best he could have gotten, but considerably more than some banks' investors. The road's vice president for purchasing, Malcolm P. Richards, just got under the May wire with his sale of 1000 shares, and corporate Secretary Bayard H. Richards sold 1700 shares in June. It, like Bevan's selling, was all quite legal and proper.

Foulups Continuing

On June 28, *Business Week* reported the frustration of Warren B. Buck, a traffic manager for a shipper of sugar syrup in Yonkers, New York:

"I shipped a car to Brighton, Mass., from Yonkers on Dec. 11. It arrived at Selkirk [the Penn Central's newest electronic classification yard] on the 14th. The next record I received on this car after two weeks of futile search was that it was still in Selkirk Dec. 31. It left there Jan. 2 and arrived in Brighton Jan. 7, a total of 26 days. The worst part was, the car was lost in Selkirk for two weeks and nobody could find it, computers or otherwise."

As to Mr. Saunders' sunny outlook on the road's "turning the corner," the traffic manager for Jennison-Wright Corporation said, "Penn Central service has improved a little, but it's still bad." He told the magazine that it took a month and a half to move his car from Toledo to Detroit. Still, Mr. Buck seemed to be crossing his fingers as he noted some improvement.

Business Week seemed to be sharing Mr. Saunders' optimism when they wrote, "After 17 months, the merger that confounded computers and gave shippers nightmares seems to be on the track." Mr. Saunders told the magazine, "Too many people are still mesmerized by negative thinking." The magazine could not be counted as one of them. Perhaps some doubtful holders of the stock held on as a result of the publication's judgment, perhaps not. Perhaps the article merely served to reinforce minds that had been made up and couldn't change.

Few analysts had anything good to say about the Penn Central's commuter operations. But most chose to ignore it, because they were like the sick patient who refused to see a doctor on the possible chance he may discover cancer. As the dreaded disease can often be cured by prompt treatment and usually proves fatal when ignored, so it is with investors.

"It's getting to the point at which something's about to blow," Barrie Vreeland, director of the Transportation Department of New York's Commerce and Industry Association told the New York *Times*. Ralph C. Gross, the association's president, said the rail situation was "detrimental to business expansion and economic growth." They had been flooded with complaints from corporate personnel officers whose people couldn't get to work on time.

Typical was Mr. Frederick A. Menes, a supervisor with the New York Telephone Company,[36] who was getting up at five-thirty in the morning so he could arrive at his desk at 8:00 A.M. Before leaving his house at Old Westbury, Long Island, he would tune breathlessly to radio reports to learn which train had been canceled. Sometimes he would catch a seven twenty-six out of East Williston that arrived at eight-twelve in Penn Station. It arrived—that is, providing there were no slipups. Even if this train were running, the cancellation of another would result in the seven twenty-six becoming a local and drawing into the terminal at eight-thirty or so. If the seven twenty-six was dropped (rarely would one find out why), he would have to dash for another train that presented its own problems. And fully one of two trains were being rerouted, repaired, or were otherwise out of action.

The situation on the Connecticut-to-New York City and Westchester County-to-New York trains was little better as the affluent riders on those lines organized petition campaigns and strikes to

[36] New York *Times*.

protest their travel agonies. When the Penn Central asked the Public Service Commission of New York State for a rate increase, it was met at the commission hearings by a storm of protest on July 31, 1969.

"I'm subjected to all sorts of discourtesies and loss of revenue because of the Penn Central. I and other people have been forced to cancel business appointments because we can't be sure we'll get to New York before 10:30 [A.M.] because the trains are late so often," groaned T. David Resnick of Larchmont, officer of a commuters group who testified at the hearing, his remarks punctuated by his slamming his hand on the witness stand.[37]

"My wife sits and sits, and she sits and she sits waiting for me at the station," he said. "I've told her not to pick me up any more. I'll be damned if I'll have marital trouble over the Penn Central."

Congressman Ogden R. Reid (R., N.Y.) said the Penn Central had a "public-be-damned attitude."

An assistant to the president of the New Haven Railroad in the 1950s and later a commuter himself, Herbert Askwirth, said that the rate increase proposal the road had requested was "based on false premises, misleading statements contradicted by its own figures, sweeping assumptions unsupported by proof [and] a cover-up of vital facts damaging to its case." No doubt the reader is shocked by such assertions.

Meanwhile, over the river in New Jersey, the agency comparable to the Public Service Commission, the New Jersey Commuter Operating Agency, was preparing a year-long report on the PC's operations in that state; the report was released on August 7.

"The basic conclusion of this investigation," they said, "is that Penn Central management is either unwilling or incapable of undertaking the type of supervision required to provide to a reasonably satisfactory passenger service."

As if to underscore that statement, less than two weeks later a crash outside Darien, Connecticut, killed four persons and injured thirty-one.

The big broker, Bache & Company (you know, the one that liked the stock somewhat higher) helped celebrate the month's end by again suggesting purchases of Penn Central, this time at $56 (on

[37] New York *Times*, July 31, 1969.

May 27). Since the stock had fallen during May to as low as $52, they said, "Penn Central has been showing some signs of buoyancy in this lackluster market as the company bounces back from a drab first quarter." That kind of buoyancy would cause the Coast Guard to disqualify the lowliest dinghy.

The report ticked off the usual stuff about "further economies" from the merger, the real-estate business "which continues to show great potential," their holdings in the Grand Central Terminal area, ad nauseam. A new fillip was added in their expectation that the Metroliner (a high-speed connection between Washington, D.C., and New York City) would help.

"In all," Bache continued, "we consider Penn Central a situation possessing enormous potential and would add to growth accounts." They were not talking about the sort of growth that precipitates a visit to the doctor, we might add.

A few days later, a federal judge loosened some ties on the roadbed when he ruled that the price PC had paid for the bankrupt New Haven had been too low.

As May ended with the price at $54, there was somewhat more selling—some more chartists, some mutual funds, varied individuals who heard rumors of troubles at the yards, and others who, in the parlance of the Street, "did their homework."

The Other Road

In June the stock cracked the $50 line, a fact that caused some psychological tremors. PC Vice President for Investments Robert Haslett sold some stock for his personal investment program (3000 in the $43 area), which followed another officer, a senior one at that, who sold 3910 shares as the stock hovered in the $50 range. Close by the latter's selling was that again of David E. Smucker, whose sale of 3600 shares did not do wonders for the stock. It could be argued that Mr. Smucker sold because he left his position with the road. It could also be stated that there is no law against holding his stock, if he believes it a good investment and can afford to do so.

The railroad had been expecting massive influxes of federal and state aid for some of its passenger lines. Meanwhile, it named a "coordinator," Charles A. Goodwin, for commuter service on the Hudson, Harlem, and New Haven Lines at the end of June. It was a new post—whether his appointment would do anything for the now-failing clay wheels was pure conjecture. The job was analogous to being made the only traffic cop at the entrance to the Brooklyn Battery Tunnel. Ironically, next to the newspaper announcement of his job was a story out of Chicago, in the New York *Times,* about how commuters on *their* line "sit placidly in clean vinyl seats reading about the Chicago Cubs on smooth-running double-decker coaches that whisk them back and forth—on time."

The Chicago & Northwestern, 13 years before, had been losing $2.5 million a year running turn-of-the-century cars with broken windows and doors and leaking roofs. Passengers "sat under their umbrellas in the rain." Train schedules were a mess, and engines broke down regularly. On April 16, 1956, after a stockholder revolt succeeded, Ben W. Heineman was made chairman of the board. Mr. Heineman found that the road was selling its rails for scrap in order to meet its payroll. Among other things, Mr. Heineman replaced steam engines with the diesels that were being used for switch engines. He installed his own management crew, and apparently found the right formula, for subsequently the Chicago & Northwestern was reporting profits of almost $2.5 million a year. Thus it was that, while the Penn Central was screaming for government aid and its passengers were just screaming, Chicago commuters were talking about the Cubs.

Some PC owners were talking about the stock, which by the end of August sold for $42 a share. This did not deter the vice president for freight sales, John G. Patten, who reportedly sold another 1400 shares.

Doubts

Questions were beginning to circulate about the viability of Penn Central as the weather turned cooler in September and some more investors cooled toward the stock. Whatever his reason, the vice president for accounting, J. K. Warner, Jr., sold 4000 shares.

In a sequel to the crash in the Darien, Connecticut area, the Penn Central announced on September 2 that, dear reader, the *Northbound and southbound trains here would no longer operate on a single track.* Whereas the railroad had blamed "human failure" for the accident, commuter groups had argued that there was no signal system for controlling two-way traffic on the single lane.

As for the railroad's statement when the change was announced, a spokesman said, "It really had nothing to do with the accident."[38]

Meanwhile, rumors swirled with the newspapers on Broad Street and Wall. Losses were showing up in the quarterly statements the road had been issuing, although Mr. Saunders reportedly[39] said, "We've turned the corner." Some observers said that Mr. Flannery had replaced Mr. Smucker at the insistence of the company's directors—a group that had not often challenged management. Meanwhile, shippers' cries of monumental delays grew louder. As Mr. Perlman reached retirement, offers were supposedly dangled to possible replacements who held high positions with other roads. Rumors had it that W. Thomas Rice of the Seaboard Coast Line, Louis W. Menk of the Northern Pacific, and John Fishwick of Erie-Lackawanna were all offered the PC presidency and refused. It would be difficult to confirm this, but the fact was that *some* railroad chiefs were asked and turned the offer down. You can guess why. Thus it was that 62-year-old Paul A. Gorman, who had been president of Western Electric Company, was named on September 22, 1969 as the new operating chief, replacing the 67-year-old Perlman.

It was no reflection on Mr. Gorman that the realization came to some on the Street that something was wrong at the Penn Central when railroad men turned down the job. Even the minisophistication of the investment community did not extend to all. There was a marked if belated reluctance of institutions to buy the stock—and with their support waning, it fell below $40 on September 19, just before (did somebody know something?) Mr. Gorman was named. In the week following it dropped some more, closing the month at $37.

Most of the banks that had bought higher still held on, as did Fidelity Trend Fund, with its 200,000 shares; Investors Mutual, with its 346,300 shares; Fidelity Capital, with its 231,100 shares; Shareholders Trust of Boston, with 55,000 shares; Axe-Houghton "B" Fund, with its 60,000 shares; and Commonwealth International Savings Fund Ltd. (a part of I.O.A.s Group in Canada). The insur-

[38] New York *Times*, September 3, 1969.
[39] New York *Times*, September 23, 1969.

ance companies remained sanguine, with Security Insurance of Hartford reportedly holding onto their 220,900 shares. Those who have worried about the economic domination of insurance companies may have had little to fear from this quarter.

Cheer, Cheer, for Old Déjà Vu

"How did you happen to get into Penn Central?" I asked a bank trust officer.

"Well, we were interested in the stock, and the word was passed down to our transportation analyst. He asked the transportation analyst for the broker who services the account. They were all bullish. We bought."

"Do you still use this broker?"

"You have to understand the way banks work," he said. "When we decide to try a broker's service, we give them a thorough testing period. It is hard to get on 'approved list of brokers' who are in for a regular commission payout. However, once on, it also takes a while to get off, sometimes a few years, since we're all set up. I think our system for keeping tabs on performance is a bit weak. Perhaps this broker has been wrong too often, I don't know."

"Wouldn't you say you are perhaps a bit too rigidly structured?" I asked him.

"Possibly."

This particular bank had bought PC in the $70s—and at least had the courage to sell in September, when the stock broke $40, which it did on September 19. Equity Research, the advisory service that became a broker, had recommended the stock on January 2, 1969 around $60,[40] and had continued to do so.

"I thought it was a good long-term buy and a good buy on weakness—and that's all we've had except for an early brief spurt to 71. It has gone down with the market ever since," Murray Harding, the Equity analyst said sadly.

Nearing the end of September, Equity said that the stock had "explosive potential." The month ended more with a "pop" than a "bang," with PC selling at $37. The bang was to come later. Equity finally withdrew their buy suggestion, saying that they had "given up for now," and they expected the dividend would be cut, prob-

[40] New York *Times*, October 2, 1969.

ably in the first quarter of 1970. Someday, however, it would realize its "explosive potential," they said. In the meantime, they noted, labor and other costs were rising, giving the road problems.

Readers can take note of Equity's cutting the cord and running. We all make mistakes, and at one point it behooves us to realize them and sell. Perhaps it should come sooner than it came to the service, but come it must.

October brought no release from the deadly monotony of the stock's fall, much like the clickety, clack of a car's wheels against the track. Down, down the stock went; it was $33 by October 3, rallied to $37 by midmonth, and went back to $33 by month's end. Hope for the line rose briefly among some with Gorman's appointment, and perhaps helped the mild rally. Analysts were voicing a dream that Gorman would turn the railroad around. And here, dear reader, is an interesting point. It is true that new management can and often does "turn things around." However, it can take anywhere from three to ten years to turn a large company to better things and restructure a corporation. Do look for stock buys among such changes—*but at least*, say, two years after the new team takes over.

In Mr. Gorman's case, the ride to destruction was a fait accompli. On October 7, the New Jersey Public Utility Commission blamed negligence by the railroad in two deaths a year and a half before. Commuters jammed the New York Public Service Commission hearings in October, crying that service on the Hudson and Harlem Divisions was "deplorable and deteriorating."

"You can't wear a light gray suit on the train—it's too filthy," Alfred McAvoy told the commission.[41] "When you finally find a rest room to wash up in Grand Central, you have to pay 25 cents for a towel. And then the towel's been used before," he said. Mr. McAvoy had been commuting for twenty years between Yonkers and New York, and it finally got to him. "Trains are continually late," he complained.

Several people criticized the commission "for not enforcing suits it has filed against the Penn Central to make the road improve its service."

"We've heard all this before," sighed PSC commissioner John Ryan.

[41] New York *Times*, October 9, 1969.

And so had we, and so had you seen stocks decline and decline as advisers told us to hold on. That's what many were telling the banks and insurance companies and mutual funds, or the stock would have fallen more precipitously. It is the steady price erosion that proves the more deadly.

On October 15, perhaps the final chapter on this segment of the Executive Jet story (it was later taken over by Sundlin) was written by the Civil Aeronautics Board when it ordered Penn Central to get out of EJA, and fined the road $65,000. The CAB charged that "Penn Central violated the Federal Aviation Act by acquiring control of Executive Jet without the Board's approval."[42]

Such approval was necessary under the law, and the CAB has consistently denied it as it seeks to separate the various competing transportation modes.

Wait a Little Bit

On October 20, the Penn Central turned in a third-quarter report that seemed to say that the "turnaround" had a way to go. Combined operations showed a $8.9 million loss, as opposed to the third-quarter profit of $15.2 million in 1968. On October 21, the *Wall Street Journal* reported that Mr. Saunders expects "much better results" for the fourth quarter.

"Traffic volume during the last two weeks in September and so far in October has been excellent, exceeding forecasts and setting postmerger records in several categories," Mr. Saunders said. "If this level of traffic is sustained we should be able to show much better results for the fourth quarter," he said. He must be admired as a man who does not discourage easily. As for the other executives, I couldn't say, except to note that they had been selling, remember? Perhaps it was just a fortuitous set of circumstances in Bevan's and the other cases.

A Mistake?

"Do you think the merger was a mistake?" Virginia Mae Brown, chairman of the Interstate Commerce Commission, asked a PC attorney during hearings in Washington on November 6, 1969.

"It would not be becoming for me to say the Penn Central merger

[42] *Wall Street Journal,* October 16, 1969.

was a mistake," Mr. Hugh B. Cox answered. "But if there is not an improvement soon, the consequences will not be pleasant to think about."

Mr. Cox was just a shade less optimistic than Mr. Saunders had been when Cox said, "We are not suggesting that the condition of the Penn Central will continue indefinitely to be as disastrous as it was in 1968 and has been in 1969. It is reasonable to hope and indeed to expect that there will be some improvement if Penn Central is to continue as a viable and vigorous rail system."

That word "continue" might have troubled some investors, as the stock fell to $32 that day, and the next day to $31, and on the twelfth to $29. On November 8, the New York *Times* reported on the fall to $31, "Its massive merger in 1967 was less than successful."

Moody's service said on November 10 that they expected the year to show "only $.50 a share," and at best improving to $3 in 1970. Also, it was possible that a dividend cut "is conceivable." Thus they concluded coyly, "buying at this time would be highly risky, in our opinion." What the investors who bought in the $60s and $70s on their recommendation should do at this juncture was not discussed in this issue.

On November 11, a 10-car train ran off the tracks north of Chappaqua in Westchester County, matching the stock, which had just broke $30. The clay wheel split was all too evident now. To others, it was a "buying opportunity." When the ICC granted a 6 percent freight rate increase, the stock rose three points on November 18, trading 154,000 shares. "It rose on good volume," they said at a bank—perhaps this would be the key to a return home and they would eventually get out even. It was a combination of hope mixed with pride—it was not easy for many to admit their whole system was overstratified, rigid, unimaginative. There was always the trust committee that had to approve changes on their trust investment list, and it was just as hard to get a stock off as on.

"Why do you keep buying?" I asked a trust officer.

He replied rather sheepishly, "It's on our list."

So have the few bright ones sprinkled around the country in trust and pension-fund managements been stifled again and again.

"Large organizations are sometimes victimized by their own size. Because their functions tend to be complex, simple techniques for handling such functions are overlooked in favor of massive structure, involved tables of organization and flow charts, until the structure itself becomes the ultimate reality," wrote a trust officer for a midwestern bank.[43] He had come from the money management section of a multibillion-dollar manufacturing establishment. The bureaucratic structure was so involved, he told me later, that a vital decision to invest or not in the market took two years to pass through the "process," and by that time the market had reversed and turned up after a major decline. They had been bullish two years early and just caught the bottom of an upturn, and so fate had lucked them into the genius status. They still congratulate themselves at their "shop" for their foresight.

"At this point," he wrote, "creativity dies, because a given idea no longer matters, but the passage of an idea through many hands, or its solemn consideration by proliferating committee alone sanctifies it."

The ICC On Guard

In expressing opposition to the ICC-granted increase, then Congressman Richard L. Ottinger (D., N.Y.) described the agency as a "toothless watchdog."[44] He claimed there was a "working economic relationship" between the ICC and the railroads. The *Times* reported that he said that a former ICC chairman, William H. Tucker, after leaving the agency, served nine months in his law firm, Maguire & Tucker, "which virtually shares offices with the Penn Central Railroad, then became vice president for New England operations of Penn Central."

Representative Ottinger also said that a former public-relations man for the ICC was fulfilling the same capacity for the PC in Washington. And the congressman charged that another lawyer for the government committee had gone to work for Maguire & Tucker.

If indeed it could be said that any conspiracy was going on, it could not be said that it particularly helped the Penn Central.

What Happened?

By November 26, a recent minor rally in the stock had brought

[43] *Trusts and Estates*, September 1970.
[44] New York *Times*, November 18, 1969.

it to $32 a share. What crossed the Dow Jones news tickers in board rooms across the country that day did not exactly cause recent buyers to jump with joy. The directors of Penn Central announced that the dividend payment for the fourth quarter had been omitted. After dropping to $30 on the news, it closed at $31.25. One could guess that the insiders who had been selling must have been relieved that they had earlier taken some of their money home. Mr. Saunders said the dividend action was prompted by "business conditions." He also warned that the industry faced a possible strike next month and that "inflationary wage demands . . . . will again increase operating costs."[45] Was Mr. Saunders now turning pessimistic? Would investors take his words and translate them into the action of selling the stock? Possibly. But Mr. Saunders *also* said that "railroad operating results will show a favorable trend in the fourth quarter." Hold on, folks. And one broker said, "There was some disappointment among investors that Penn Central did not declare a small stock dividend, even though it omitted the cash payment." All the dreamers in America were not on Fifty-second Street, it would seem.

Sherlock Holmes, We Should Call

What about that dividend? What part do dividends play in the investment scene? Some small holders retain or buy stocks purely on the basis of the cash dividend the stock pays. Some financial institutions buy only stocks paying dividends—and some, notably funds, have it written into their prospectus—"income funds," they are called. The payment of cash periodically helps other funds declare their own payout, often to the satisfaction of their holders. The broker who hasn't heard the plaint of the investor, "If it doesn't work out, at least I'll have the dividend," hasn't been around much.

While the dividend money was going out of the company's coffers, the company was in a cash bind. "As of June 30, 1969 applicant's [PC's] current liabilities of $500,391,914 exceed its current assets of $452,023,797 by $48,368,117," revealed the ICC.[46] It was as late as September 29, 1969, that Penn Central paid out a quarterly divi-

[45] New York *Times*, November 27, 1969.

[46] ICC Finance Docket No. 25854, authority granted by the ICC for the PC to issue notes, decided October 29, 1969.

dend of $14,465,273. "Apparently when they knew they were in financial difficulties, they still paid a cash dividend," said Warren G. Magnuson, chairman of the Senate Commerce Committee.[47]

Supposing the dividend had not been paid in 1968 to 1969? What then?

Well, the money could have gone to paying off some of the short-term debt that continually plagued the road—and was the immediate cause of its eventual bankruptcy. Penn Central had been going into the money market replacing maturing debt with short-term notes, a procedure the ICC had found objectionable, though they went along. As money rates went up, the road had to pay higher and higher interest rates, a factor even Mr. Saunders ascribes to be one of the causes of the bankruptcy. It was Mr. Bevan who was responsible for the fiscal policy—and I found no record of his having suggested omitting the dividend (at least before the final one in 1969), despite his difficulty in raising money during the squeeze. As rates went higher, the railroad became obliged to pay out more and more in interest, which, as it happened, became an intolerable burden.

"[In 1969, you showed an actual] $4,388,000 of profit," Senator Hartke later pointed out to Chairman Saunders.[48]

Mr. Saunders said to the senator: "That is correct."

Hartke: "And you declared a $43 million dividend."

Saunders: "That is correct."

Hartke: "And you already knew you were short of cash?"

Saunders: "We have been short of cash for ten years I guess. I have never known the Pennsylvania Railroad when it didn't have . . ." At this point Hartke interrupted and mentioned the outstanding loans. Saunders replied they felt at the time "this was manageable."

Hartke: "In 1969 you didn't think you had much trouble, right?"

Saunders: "We didn't think we were going to have trouble such as we did or we wouldn't have done it." He pointed out that they did omit the last dividend in 1969. "In retrospect, maybe

[47] U. S. Senate Commerce Committee hearings, Part 1, Serial No. 91-90, June 25, 1970.

[48] Senate Commerce Committee hearings, quoted earlier.

the third dividend that we declared last year of $14 million, maybe that is debatable. We may have made an error of judgment." It was, he said, "an exercise of what we regarded as business judgment."

Senator Hartke pointed out that an ICC commissioner's report on the Pennsy's financial condition mentioned in 1966:

"It is plain that these carriers had been operating from a working capital position generally considered to be too short of normal requirements."

"Why," the senator asked Mr. Saunders, "in the face of that would you declare $43 million worth of dividends in 1969? I mean your situation—even your annual reports showed deficits and deteriorating working capital position since 1967 . . . . the deficit ran an incredible rate of $27 million in 1966; $75 million in 1967; $376 million in 1968; $526 million—I don't think you can plead that lack of information or lack of warning in this regard existed."

Mr. Saunders answered that the deficit was on the basis of consolidated earnings (including real estate and other holdings) and not merely for the railroad operations. He claimed the dividends were justified on the basis of the over-all corporate results.

Later, the senator again pressed Mr. Saunders: "You knew you had a shortage of cash. You knew this all in—"

Mr. Saunders cut in: "We always had a shortage of cash."

Hartke kept repeating the figure, "$43 million in cash." He seemed not to be able to believe it.

On July 29, 1970, Alfred E. Perlman was queried by the Senate Commerce Committee about the 1969 cash situation. He said, "I have with me the 1969 improvement budget which was not even submitted to the board of directors by the chairman because of lack of cash."

What would some extra cash mean to the railroad operation—some of which was not available, since it was being paid out in dividends? Mr. Perlman continued:

"And yet this contains many items which would permit over 200 percent return on the investment if we had the money to do the work." He described three categories of work money could have been used for. The first was for safety—bridges, rebuilding of tracks.

"The second category," he said, "is the items that have to be done for holding the business we have or getting new business. Like new spur tracks for new industry coming in, or certain kinds of freight cars for the automobile industry, or the steel industry.

"The third category is made up of what savings could be made through technology, if we had the money to do the work."

"When was that submitted?" Senator Hartke asked.

Mr. Perlman said that it was presented in the fall of 1968 to the chairman of the board for implementation the following year.

It would be giving Mr. Saunders and company the benefit of the doubt to say, as Mr. Perlman believed: "[that] Mr. Saunders came from one of the wealthiest railroads in the country and his outlook on these railroads' problems may be entirely different from mine . . . . a man that comes from one side of the tracks may have a different philosophy than the other."

But one investor who admitted he was "bagged" in PC stock had his own theory: "I think they retained the dividend so long in an attempt to keep the stock up. Possibly the stock would have collapsed a year sooner had the dividend been omitted then. Of course, had they done so, possibly the money could have saved them from eventual bankruptcy. Of course, that is pure conjecture on my part," he added.

It was just one man's opinion. Most just chalked it up to the "breaks," and continued to pursue their uncertain way. However, if that cynical investor was right, one might also venture to say that the stock had been held up so the insiders could get good prices for their stock. It is something to think about, *n'est-ce pas?*

So finally, on November 27, the dividend was omitted. There had been rumors to that effect in the week preceding the action. Yet one week before the dividend omission, "Mr. Saunders told reporters that such talk was based 'purely on thin air,'" according to the *Wall Street Journal* of November 28. An interesting oddity was the fact that Penn Central had, thus far in the year, paid out more dividends than they had earned. Saunders kept a stiff upper lip in announcing the act.

"Current indications are that railroad operating losses will show a favorable trend in the fourth quarter," Mr. Saunders was reported as saying.

Standard & Poor's *Outlook* took note of the dividend loss—and said that "despite the possibility of a turnaround in rail operating results and large potential earnings from non-rail areas, the stock (31, NYSE) may remain on the defensive under the pressure of tax loss selling." Their analyst could not be faulted for not reading the newspapers, since Saunders' comments regarding a turnaround were repeated as S&P's view, too. The advisory service apparently had not completely soured on the stock as an investment. "It would just be tax-loss selling that would hold it down," they seemed to be saying. As for the "defensive" comment, investors who had bought the stock at least partly on the strength of S&P's writeups also felt somewhat "on the defensive."

As many investment advisers were still buying the stock on the way down, so the services remained bullish, if less enthusiastically. *Value Line* felt, on December 5, 1969, that the road probably would not turn around in 1970. But they projected a turnaround two to four years after that, with significant earnings from real estate operations and acquisitions. Penn Central ranked in their "highest category" for 3-to-5-year appreciation potential. Those who had paid eighty dollars for the stock could continue their price averaging, no doubt. All they needed was a little patience—and a lot of money.

Troubles?

During the first week in December, the new president, Paul Gorman, took over the job, telling reporters, "This job is certainly going to be a real challenge."[49] How much of an understatement that was, was illustrated by a remark about the Pennsy made by an old Central man at the time: "We competed for a hundred years. We still do."

Equity Research, to their credit, had recently told customers to take their losses. More in a wistful vein was the comment by a former marketing man from the Central: "We almost had it in our hands," he said of the new ideas the Central had been instituting before the merger, "we almost had a helluva marketing department that would have revolutionized railroading and maybe even made the Penn Central profitable."

Money, cash, was still the problem and was getting no better. A coal shipper said of the road, "They say they have no money to give

[49] *Newsweek*, December 8, 1969.

us cars. But they always seem to have enough cash to swing a real-estate deal. Damn! It's time they got back into the railroading business!"[50]

Saunders was not the only one who voiced pride at the real-estate operations. While one ICC man reportedly felt the line could go bankrupt, others, notably in the investment business, voiced the opinion of which the following was typical: "They have assets up to their ears. The question, I guess, is how fast they can liquidate assets into quick cash. Hell, they are the largest real-estate holding company in the country!"

Yet even Moody's was beginning to give up the ghost as they advised on December 15: "[It] now might as well be held, but we would sell it on any near-term strength, even though a cash dividend could be re-instated in 1970." The stock was selling at $29.

Still, some banks were holding on (waiting for the rally?) and some investment counselors were buying. How could you sell the road short when it owned such as Arvida, Great Southwest, and realty hotels? Even Mr. Saunders said in a year-end report that these three subsidiaries "will make greater contributions to profit this year than in 1968." He also reportedly[51] claimed that Penn Central's pending acquisition of an oil refiner and Great Southwest's pickup of a mobile-home producer "will boost consolidated Penn Central revenue by more than $100 million in 1970."

So if things had not gone exactly right—and the stock closed out the year at 28¼—one can understand how billions of dollars' worth of the stock were still being held by insurance companies, banks, and mutual funds. Some investment counselors had sold. They tried to move faster, though not smarter. There were other "bag jobs" around—Four Seasons Nursing Homes, National Video, et al., that also went bankrupt. Thus I know of one chap who interviewed a nationally prominent counselor before giving up his money to him, or rather to his salesman. The counselor showed him around the place, pointing out that he had some thirty analysts. In the course of the pitch, he was told that Penn Central was sold out long before the end. The firm had its own "baddies," as the consumer was to find out later, though to the firm's credit they were lesser known —their customers later went down with the ship with such as Mo-

[50] Ibid.
[51] *Wall Street Journal,* December 26, 1969.

hawk Data, Memorex, and Damon. None of these went bankrupt, and so the customer only lost some 75 percent on his money in the next two years.

At the end of 1969, the wheels were showing large cracks, though to listen to Saunders, 1970 would be better. Thus Fidelity Trend Fund still held 200,000 shares, Investors Mutual clutched 391,000, Hamilton Fund was caught with 36,000, and Fidelity Capital Fund held 290,000. The fund that had gotten more publicity than any other, Shareholders (remember Fred Carr?), still retained 55,000. Reliance Insurance owned 16,700, Great American had 10,000, Participating Annuity (B) retained 20,000, and Security Insurance of Hartford stuck to the whopping total of 220,900.[52]

1970–The Year of the Fool

"Even during poor times, it is relatively seldom that investors have the opportunity to purchase the stock of a company which is a major factor in two leading industries, at a price which is less than 25% of book value," the analytical report said. It came out of the Penn Central's home town, Philadelphia, and was produced by the firm that had a director on PC's board. And it was convincingly done. Never mind that it was a "follow-up" report, and the outfit (Butcher & Sherrerd) had recommended the stock way higher.

"Add to this that per-share earnings could well pass $10 in the next four to five years, the company has an excellent record of profitable acquisitions, and the recent appointment of an unusually competent businessman as the new president," the report continued. Investors would read reports of other stocks later that sounded as glowing, and had read others in the past that sounded as good. I recall the broker who wrote up National Video with the claim that it too would earn ten dollars. How many little people plunked down their hard-earned on that one and lost? How many would do so again? How many institutions would eventually realize what their functions in the scheme of things really were? How many brokers would realize?

Speaking of brokers, investors might check out past recommendations of the firms they choose by a simple expedient. The *Wall Street Transcript* reprints retail broker reports. Try looking back at

52 *Vickers Insurance Company Guide,* Section 2, August 1970.

your firm's work by studying two- and three-year-old *Transcripts* to see what they said then. If your library hasn't any back copies, your broker might, or try the publication at 54 Wall Street for help.

Butcher and Sherrerd was following their original recommendation at much higher prices—and admitting that "Since June of 1969, Penn Central stock has turned in one of the worst performances on the Big Board." They noted that it had fallen more than 60 percent in total since June of 1968, "a decline which even the weak market of the past twelve months cannot fully justify. The size of the decline reflects a number of problems which, although serious, have in our opinion been somewhat overrated," they said.

In Saunders-like fashion, they admitted that earnings had been disappointing, "culminating in the generally unanticipated loss of the third quarter of 1969."

"Nevertheless," the Philadelphia broker wrote, "we believe that the final quarter of last year will mark at least a moderate reversal in this trend."

A second reason for the "poor stock performance" was the economy. After all, since much of the road's business was with the auto and steel industries, what could you expect? Another reason "may be the company's tight cash position." This was caused, they said, by capital requirements of the merger, you see. And some investors got an "unpleasant surprise" when their dividend was cut since they had "originally purchased the stock for the income it provided." Whether any of these were customers of the brokerage firm was not indicated.

Another reason was the company's labor troubles. Faced with higher costs, however, the railroad could get another rate increase from the ICC, so that was okay. Also, there was the appointment of a nonrailroad man, Paul A. Gorman, to the presidency of the road. It was felt on the Street that perhaps it would take a year or so to make any real impact on the Penn Central's real problems.

"Considering all these factors, we believe," Butcher and Sherrerd wrote, "that Penn Central stock had been unduly depressed and that it represents an attractive long-term investment at current levels." In some sixteen hundred more words, the broker pointed out the positives: "Enormous Assets per Share," "Attractive Price of the Stock," "Excellent Outlook for the Company's Real Estate Operations," "The Company's Profitable Acquisition Record," "Improved Competitiveness of Railroad Operations," "Expectation of Significant Merger Savings," "Increased Government Assistance," etc., etc.

Thus, there was the "Exciting Long-Term Earnings Potential," they said. "We believe that a conservative earnings projection for Penn Central as of mid-1970's is $8 to $10 after taxes; on this basis, we expect the common stock to at least sell at $100." There was no mention of the internecine squabbling. There was no objective judgment of management capability in my view, and there was no discussion of any possible hanky-panky. There was only unbridled optimism.

How did Mr. Butcher himself feel about this report? Was it snuck out without his knowledge? After all, Howard Butcher III's great-great-grandfather served on the Pennsy's board in 1849, three years after the line's formation. The Butcher family, according to the New York *Times* of January 9, 1971, owned 1.5 million PC shares. In a telephone interview, he told *Times* man Robert Metz that Penn Central had the greatest prospects of "'any stock I know about.'"

"'I don't know of any other stock that could go to five times what it is selling at now,'" he said. "'Oddly enough, you are talking to a broker who knows what he is talking about,'" he said. Perhaps one might detect a note of skepticism in Metz's writings, for he ended with, "Time will tell whether Mr. Butcher's parting shot was justified."

Whether Mr. Butcher would turn out to be right would of course have to be seen. Whether he was in a position to know what he was talking about may to some extent be judged by the following testimony of Mr. Perlman before the Senate Commerce Committee on July 29, 1970:

Senator Hartke: "Did you know Mr. Butcher?"

Mr. Perlman: "Yes, sir."

Senator Hartke: "What was his relationship to the company?"

Mr. Perlman: "Mr. Butcher was one of the most ardent advocates of merger of the Pennsylvania and New York Central. When I broke off with the Pennsylvania, he sent envoys to try to patch it up again."

Senator Hartke: "That was back in 1959?"

Mr. Perlman: "Yes, sir; and he was a very ardent promoter of the merger."

Of course, Mr. Butcher was no longer a director, so perhaps his intelligence on the road was weaker than previously.

Butcher and Sherrerd were not the only bulls on the PC. Even a director, the president of the Security Insurance Company of Hartford, E. Clayton Gengras, had bought two thousand shares shortly before the brokerage report. Soon after both these events, the Connecticut Commissioner of Transportation, George J. Conkling, wrote a letter to PC's vice president for New England operations, William H. Tucker, complaining that the railroad had failed to notify them of recent schedule changes, that passengers had difficulty getting train information over the phone, and that the road had allegedly delayed printing the new schedules.

In Washington, New York Representative Richard L. Ottinger asked the National Transportation Safety Board to investigate conditions on the PC's commuter lines.

The chairman of the Transportation Action Committee, a commuter group, wrote that Governor Rockefeller "should declare a state of emergency and the Penn Central should be listed as a disaster area."[53]

He complained that "thousands of passengers are made to wait for hours on subfreezing station platforms for trains that did not appear, or if they did come, broke down or were stalled on their way in."

Mr. Milton A. Harth, leader of the commuter group, had met with Penn Central management and reported their "disdainful attitude toward passengers, their incorrigible lack of public responsibility, and their arrogant flouting of public service standards and government orders [that] are not only anachronistic but most frightening."

The stock, meanwhile, was rising, phoenix-like, perhaps partly due to an ICC authorization on January 20 for the New Haven subsidiary to raise commutation fares, perhaps partly due to brokerage recommendations. PC stock rose from $28 to $33 in the middle of

[53] New York *Times*, January 19, 1971.

January. Perhaps the railroad had indeed turned the corner. Perhaps it really had been a "bargain" after its 60 percent drop. Ten-trip tickets between New York and Stanford, Connecticut would now go up from $12.45 to $23—and maybe this would rescue the road and make it the big winner its backers had hoped for. Perhaps Mr. Bevan would now buy stock in PC in anticipation of the turnaround Mr. Saunders had foreseen. *Value Line,* certainly, had not given up. With the stock at $34 on January 23, they continued to say that Penn Central shares could prove richly rewarding for the 3-to-5-year pull.

They thought the combination of a turnaround in railroad operating results, important acquisitions, and a tax shelter estimated at $500 million would produce a Normal Average Price of close to 100 by 1972–74, almost 200 percent above current levels. Though less sanguine about near-term action, who could resist a 200 percent profit? And if one heard about the Butcher and Sherrerd report that also looked for a $100 price, how could you go wrong?

Further, it now appeared possible that the states of New York and Connecticut would take over commuter lines. "Assuming that a state takeover will occur near midyear, the deal could produce net favorable swing in Penn Central profits of $2.5–$3.5 million for 1970 and about $7 million for 1971," the advisory service said. Some investment counselors stepped up their purchasing. Analysts saw the changes coming. As did *Value Line,* they could envisage a $2.50 a share result for 1970 profits for PC. Were the wheels cracking so wide they could be heard around the PC's jammed freight yards? "Nonsense!" The government was going to step in and help.

Back in the (Down) Groove

The ebullience that had sucked investors in at the $30-and-up level was not to last. Within two weeks the stock resumed its normal pattern, and slipped to the $26 area. On January 26, a commuters' strike led them to refuse to give up their tickets. Maxwell J. Lillienstein, a lawyer, wrote to the New York *Times* (January 30, 1970) with reference to the Butcher report, saying that "negatives could come from several fronts."

He felt that the railroad could suffer financial losses if things did not go as well as Mr. Butcher had predicted. "A bill has been introduced in the State Legislature which would remove the railroad's right to tax abatement in Westchester County and New York City," he wrote. "If successful, [it] would cost the railroad approximately $6 million a year.

"In addition," he noted, "I am aware of several actions, one a class action, which either have been or are about to be instituted against the railroad on behalf of commuters who have suffered literally millions of dollars of damages in the form of lost man hours of time."

Willard L. Bleyer also wrote to the *Times*. In the same issue of the paper Mr. Bleyer said: "The shocking condition of the road shows the company has no pride, no efficiency and no money to spend on rail service." Could there be better reasons for not investing in a railroad company?

Another commuter quoted an exchange of letters he had with the PC, in which he said that in two years of commuting from Stamford, Connecticut, he had not gotten a seat. He ventured to say that travel was better two thousand years ago. A PC man replied by saying that two thousand years ago, man could only travel on foot. Mr. Brooks answered that various animals were used, and that "Aaron had ridden into town on his ass."

On January 30, the Butcher and Sherrerd partner, Howard Butcher III, was censured by the Securities and Exchange Commission on another matter in connection with Plant Industries stock. Mr. Butcher and his firm consented to a five-day suspension without admitting guilt on charges that they violated certain securities laws. White-collar crimes, you see, get rather lighter punishments than blue-collar ones.

As for PC stock, it was flat on its posterior as it cracked the twenty-three-dollar area for the first time in April. A PC public-relations man, William Lashley, sold one thousand shares that month and his wife a thousand the month after, the SEC reported. Mr. Perlman had only nineteen hundred left, and he sold five hundred of these on April 1.

There were other bulls on Penn Central. A. Oakley Brooks, president of de Vegh Mutual Fund, a no-load outfit, was interviewed in the February 1 issue of *Forbes* magazine, comparing PC to IBM.

"Do you realize that for ten years the rate of gain in labor productivity in railroads has been double that of industry?" In other words, the rails were carrying more freight with fewer employees. "They were using these gains to cut rates to stop losing their share of traffic. They've stopped losing traffic." His particular favorite, it should be noted, was Seaboard Coast Line. He also favored cement stocks, which "are down 40% to 50% from where they were at the end of 1968," he noted.

Still Turning Around?

The apparent reason for the Penn Central stock's fall from its recent $34 level to $28 came out on February 4, 1970. The PC appeared to be some way from turnaround as yet, as they announced a $13.2 million loss for the fourth period of 1969. The final period of 1968 showed earnings of $36.9 million, so the turnaround was, at least for a time, going the other way. Mr. Saunders blamed the bad showing on passenger operations, whereas PC's nonrailroad operations, Arvida, Great Southwest, and Buckeye Pipe Line were doing fine. The latter three, he noted, increased their contribution to earnings by 21 percent. PC stock fell 2½ points on the heels of the loss announcement.

Value Line took the loss news calmly. They ranked the stock poorly for year-ahead performance, but still in their highest for the longer term. The service lowered their estimate for 1970's earnings, but perhaps not lower enough, from $2.50 to $1.75 per share. It continued to fall, but inexorably so. Most banks still held on—some continued to buy. They may have had more faith in PC management than Mr. Anthony Haswell.

Mr. Haswell was chairman of the National Association of Railroad Passengers, an organization of train buffs, and he made the rather startling charge that the Penn Central was playing fast and loose with its accounting procedures in letters to the ICC and the SEC on February 15. The railroad had written off $126 million of its investment in equipment for long-haul passenger service west of Harrisburg, Pennsylvania and Albany, New York. He claimed that the road could not do that since it did not have the power to discontinue trains without ICC approval. Further, he charged that the railroads were using a method of accounting that overstated their passenger losses.

The nonprofit association had five thousand members, according to Mr. Haswell.

Mr. Haswell was not exactly writing to a friendly source at the ICC. He had earlier attacked the agency for allowing railroad officials to use figures that the agency allegedly agreed were "grossly and inaccurately" overstating losses on passenger operations, and that the ICC "refused to put a stop to their [railroad men's] propaganda campaign to end the passenger train."[54] Railroads like the Penn Central would presumably like to get out of the passenger business, so their use of supposedly "inflated" loss figures might help to dampen rider opposition. If this were true, however, they might do another thing. The allegedly inflated figures might excuse management for its poor profit performance if it could be shown that passenger service could not possibly be profitable. The popular formula, Mr. Haswell said, did not accurately estimate the savings that would accrue if trains were dropped. And it was not the formula the ICC required in reports from the railroad companies. He said that:

"In June 1955, former [ICC] Commissioner Richard F. Mitchell indicated his belief that the actual loss on passenger service was only 60% of that shown by the [publicly utilized] formula. In the same year, John W. Barringer, now president of the Missouri-Kansas-Texas Railroad, stated that 'elimination of all passenger trains would probably shrink revenues more than it would reduce expenses'; and W. W. Patchell, then vice president of the Pennsylvania Railroad said that 'we cannot even consider the possibility of going out of the passenger business because we would lose more than we would save.'"[55]

Mr. Haswell also claimed that "In 1956, John Budd, then president of the Great Northern Railway, estimated that the available loss for 1954 was much closer to $100 million than to the $670 million [popular] formula deficit." Mr. William H. Tucker, in October 1966 a vice chairman of the ICC and later Penn Central vice president, "stated that the formula does not measure the costs that would be eliminated by ending passenger service." Mr. Haswell quoted also from a 1968 prospectus of the Santa Fe Railway: "The passenger train deficit for 1967 for all railway's passenger trains was

[54] Senate Commerce Committee hearings, March 16, 1970.
[55] Ibid.

$47,978,875 as reported under the accounting formula prescribed by the Interstate Commerce Commission which charges passenger service with a proportion of costs for overhead, maintenance, taxes, and other items. *It does not represent what would be savable if there were no passenger trains at all*" (emphasis mine).

Mr. Haswell said that "In 1966 I wrote the Commission asking that it take action with regard to a specific instance of misuse of the passenger deficit statistics by Stuart Saunders, then chairman of the Pennsylvania Railroad. The Commission replied that it was about to undertake a further study of the entire matter and that the points I raised would be considered," Mr. Haswell said. "However, no further action was taken by the Commission."

The Game

Mr. Haswell's basic complaint was that passenger losses were being overstated in order to influence the ICC and the public to accept the discontinuance of service. But it could also theoretically be argued that, in the Penn Central case, the following were true:

1. The investment community was led to believe that passenger losses were greater than they really were (or might be figured by other accounting means) as a device to hide earnings deterioration on their other businesses.
2. If the Street believed that passenger losses were so great, and focused on them to a greater degree, the alleviation of these losses would yield significant profit advantages over-all. In other words, "Just wait to see what will happen when we cut out the problem and forge ahead!"
3. If earnings progress was not being made—even losses were then being sustained—it would tend to absolve management, since one could say that passenger losses were inevitable—and nobody could do any better. The analogy here is excusing the poor performance of a mayor by observing that "the city is unmanageable."

From Mr. Haswell's testimony, the following are statements by PC officials about the passenger problem:[56]

[56] It should be pointed out that Mr. Haswell quoted executives of other roads in his testimony.

March 21, 1966:

Pennsylvania Railroad press release reporting by David E. Smucker, vice president, operations, of company's intention to discontinue the *Spirit of St. Louis* passenger trains:

"We must take drastic action to reduce our staggering passenger deficit," said Mr. Smucker, adding that over-all passenger operations on the PRR in 1965 resulted in a $41.8 million net loss compared with $34.9 million for the previous year.

May 9, 1966:

Pennsylvania Railroad annual shareholders meeting, as reported in the Philadelphia *Inquirer* of May 10:

"[Chairman Stuart T. Saunders] said that in 1965 about 48 cents of every dollar of net freight operating income was consumed by the passenger deficit of $41.8 million."

October 16, 1967:

Statement of Alfred E. Perlman, President, New York Central System:

"From World War II through 1958 alone, the Central spent more than $250 million in new passenger train equipment and facilities, and more than $14 million to advertise and promote passenger service. Yet during the period, the Central lost $500 million in passenger operations—or half a billion dollars that could have been utilized to upgrade freight service and give local communities an economic shot-in-the-arm."

And on November 1, 1967, Mr. Perlman in announcing various train discontinuances said in a press release: "the Central lost more than $16 million in passenger train operations last year" and that deficits are "sharply increasing."

On May 7, 1968, Mr. Saunders reportedly told shareholders at the Penn Central annual meeting, "One of our most persistent and most difficult problems is our passenger deficit. This service produced a staggering loss of $85 million last year. We simply cannot live with this burden, and we have launched a vigorous campaign to reduce it."

The same tack was being taken later that year as Mr. Saunders was reported as telling security analysts, "Another *promising area for sizable savings* [emphasis mine] is our passenger service."

Persons even more cynical than I could argue that a vital factor in a profit-and-loss situation is that of costs. An important ingredient here is that of labor. And it was Mr. Saunders who agreed to a staggering labor settlement that became a condition of the merger. Was Mr. Saunders the unwitting architect of his own downfall?

Of course, the other side could argue that even if it could be said that such figures were bloated (a debatable point), it was a fact of train life that passenger losses were knotty problems. Further, it was pure conjecture that these were "used" by management to feather its own nest. Well, there are two sides to most questions.

But it did not end there. Mr. Perlman on January 28, 1969 was reportedly complaining in an address to the Federal Bar Association, "In 1968 [the passenger deficit] rose to approximately $100 million. Obviously, even the Penn Central cannot long carry a burden of this magnitude." It was just possible that Mr. Perlman figured that the alleviation of these deficits would cause the PC to put more money into his more beloved freight operations, just as critics of the Vietnam war expected its end to result in the transfer of billions into "social benefit" projects. In the latter case, these hopeful ones may be disregarding the nationwide revulsion against periodic tax increases, and the expected pressure to see the war money go into tax reduction (or at least holding down increases) rather than "projects." In Mr. Perlman's case, perhaps it too was wishful thinking.

The passenger deficit issue was kept alive and boiling by PC management—and as late as February 3, 1970, the railroad was taking out ads on the subject in local newspapers. The following day Mr. Saunders held a press conference, during which the *Wall Street Journal* reported that he said, "The railroad's passenger deficit of more than $100 million for 1969 wiped out every dollar of freight profit."

Incidentally, the ICC in July 1969 released a report entitled "Investigation of Costs of Intercity Rail Passenger Service," in which they found that the *actual* or *avoidable* losses on passenger train service were only 55 percent of the totals the railroads had been using in their calculations under the "fully allocated deficit" accounting method. Further, Mr. Haswell pointed out[57] that even the lower figure makes no provision for such noncash items as de-

[57] In a letter to George M. Stafford, acting chairman of the ICC, on February 10, 1970.

preciation nor for the increase in federal income taxes that would result from a reduction in expenses. Upon making these adjustments, he claimed, only 30 percent of the "fully allocated basis" losses could actually be saved by the elimination of passenger services. One would have to assume that the road's accountants could do the same calculating as Mr. Haswell.

The ICC further stated in its report:

"The ICC [using the fully allocated deficit method] was never designed to show either what the railroads could save by eliminating passenger service or the extent to which revenues from freight service were being used to pay for operation of passenger trains. Nevertheless, there has been a natural, though not universal, tendency [for the railroads] to use the ICC full deficit to *portray* [emphasis mine] the burden of the passenger operations."

The report also cited its decision of 1959 in which it determined that the fully allocated method is "not intended to determine the expenses which would be avoided if all passenger services were discontinued; and [it is] not intended to measure the elusive 'out-of-pocket' costs."

Mr. Haswell argued in effect that though the ICC in its own papers pointed out the discrepancy between the two accounting methods, it did little to implement its findings in restraining possibly misleading promotion by the railroads. For its part, the commission, in the form of a letter from the acting commissioner to Mr. Haswell,[58] said that the government agency is "wholly without authority to control the public pronouncements of railroad officials in this regard." Nevertheless, the ICC had indicated its feeling in its decisions and "they can best be left to speak for themselves," he wrote.

Back at the Loser's Corner (*the stock market*)

On February 25, 1970, PC stock was selling at twenty-five dollars a share, somewhat below the eighty-dollar area when it was most recommended. Investment counselors were selling. "We know how to take a loss," one remarked. In haste to make up their losses, many bought such as National Student Marketing and Kentucky Fried

[58] This letter, dated February 18, 1970, was sent in response to Mr. Haswell's letter to George M. Stafford, acting chairman of the ICC.

Chicken. They lost on those too, but one could not say they weren't trying.

"Why are so many investment analysts so bad?" I asked a *Barron's* editor.

"Well, the counselors are often overworked," he answered. I know of three fellows who manage half a million. The head watches the market, one spends his time placating clients, and the third attends to paperwork and such.

"I am also surprised," he said, "by their lack of questioning research. I don't know how many have told me of new plants opening and new territories envisioned. But few ask the question that a businessman would ask, 'Who do I sell the stuff to?' Few analysts bother to go out into the field and question customers and competitors. They are too busy adding up columns of figures about projected earnings and sales breakdowns."

"Too few," I said to the editor, "are really business-oriented rather than academically oriented. They have too little sense of a stock being too high and ripe for selling or too low and ripe for long-term buying."

"I think we agree on that," he remarked.

To return to the Penn Central specifically, the other shoe was dropped on February 25, when the road omitted its dividend for the second time. It combined this announcement with some minor shaking of staff, as if to say that things were being straightened out now. Kreyling and Flannery were officially installed, but Bevan, Saunders, and company remained. It was still their show, apparently. The stock fell only a point the next day, as investors, along with Saunders, kept hoping for better days. On March 2 it fell below twenty-six dollars. Their hopes were fueled by an announcement that three other roads were seeking freight rate rises of 6 percent before the ICC, which presumably would spill over to the Penn Central. Thus PC's price decline was a gentle one, like the settling of snow on an early November day—not disabling in itself, but portending of weightier things to come. It wasn't until March 12 that the stock glided down under twenty-five dollars.

Meanwhile, if investors were not being ignored by PC bigwigs in their public-relations efforts, Mr. David Goldrich of Harrison, New York, contended that he had been. Mr. Goldrich, a commuter and lawyer, had taken the railroad to court for breach of contract, the breach occurring, he maintained, in his not being provided satisfactory service. No railroad attorney appeared in court to contest his suit.

"They have completely ignored me—the utter disdain to which the commuter is daily treated," he said. "It is right in character."[59] Mr. Goldrich had instituted the suit after arriving eighty-eight minutes after leaving his suburban Westchester County home for New York City.

But Mr. Goldrich displayed the same kind of optimism that caused Napoleon to march on to Moscow that frigid winter and Mr. Saunders to issue his "turnaround" statements when Mr. Goldrich was quoted as saying "that he hoped his action would impel the railroad and government officials to try 'to provide the type of service to which the commuter is entitled.'"

On March 4, the PC announced that it would ask the ICC to allow it to discontinue forty-eight passenger trains, which though it gave no solace to riders, gave some to investors, who saw it as another move in the rebirth operation Mr. Saunders had implied. Included was the famed *Broadway Limited,* a Chicago-bound sleeper. Mr. Haswell had something to say about this too. "Management is seeking a scapegoat for its postmerger blunders." The reader could imagine how that sat in the executive halls of the railroad. "That one stung," one could imagine them saying in Philadelphia. Other trains to go were the *Spirit of St. Louis* and trains to Pittsburgh, Cincinnati, Cleveland, Dayton, Detroit, Indianapolis, and Louisville, the *Wall Street Journal* reported on March 5.

Further complicating things was an impending strike among such railroad workers as machinists and sheet metal workers, and as the old Wall Street adage goes, "Don't sell on strike news," most didn't. The news on March 4 that Congress had voted a thirty-seven-day moratorium on strikes against the railroads caused the price of PC stock to drop half a dollar. It had pretty much been anticipated. The stock dawdled for a week—and dropped below twenty-five dollars for the first time on March 12, trading only fifty-eight hundred shares that day. "Bullish!" some technicians shouted, for it had been trading around twenty-five thousand shares daily the prior week. A drop on reduced volume is often considered to be bullish, despite the lack of statistical evidence to support this opin-

[59] New York *Times,* March 4, 1970.

ion. In fact, serious studies have shown just the opposite. But the Street refused to be swayed by such facts, preferring analysts' prejudices and inspirations.

Why?

"I love trains," said Miss Katherine Hamil, a retired magazine writer who had been riding the *Broadway Limited* for some forty years. "This is comfortable, pleasant, and nostalgic. I sleep well aboard, and the service and food are still really quite fine. I'm in no great hurry—but even if I were I'd go by train," she told the *Wall Street Journal* in its March 10 issue. The *Broadway Limited* was one of the forty-eight trains the Penn Central had petitioned the ICC to let it drop. The line contended that this train had lost $102,000 during the prior year, as against a $531,000 profit in 1968. Perhaps the *Broadway* case was symbolic of others, as buffs shed tears over the passing of an era.

"The *Broadway* was for stars and executives. We served all the department store buyers and people like Joan Crawford, Donald O'Connor, and Lauren Bacall. It was pretty exciting back then. The steward was lucky to close the dining car by 1:00 A.M.," recalled Orville Kresi, the last steward in charge of the still-opulent dining car.

It would be easy to blame the popularity of airline travel for the decline of such passenger cars—and to do so would not be entirely wrong. But there were other reasons. If one tried to dial railroad timetable information, he would often have to wait some thirty or forty rings before the phone would be picked up. There were scattered offices the PC maintained where one could buy tickets, but this too involved long waits and discourteous and inefficient service. And one could not cancel without a serious penalty. The airlines prospered and have grown largely because of their speed. But the true breakout in their success was in their payment of commissions to travel agents to promote ticket sales and handle customer arrangements. The Penn Central refused to do this—as well as pay fees to credit card companies to make it more convenient for the customer to pay his bill. In short, the airlines were oriented to serve the customer, the railroads merely self-serving. It should be obvious to the reader that one builds business by better serving the consumer—but this axiom was lost on most railroad executives. Perhaps intercity passenger trains would go anyway—but it would be nice if they were given a chance.

"Going by train used to give me the time to do paperwork on board—and the train was my traveling hotel. It was as relaxing as trying to buy a ticket was unsettling," a high-powered entrepreneur who used both modes to carry on his business said. "They have their place and I'll be sorry to see them go."

In line with its policy of keeping investors informed about developments in recommended issues, *Value Line* noted in its March 13 issue that the PC had announced its intention of dropping the forty-eight trains. Commenting that it would take some time before the ICC would grant the authority, the service said, "On the basis of this timetable of projected passenger train discontinuances, we estimate Penn Central results could be favorably affected by about 10¢ a share this year and an additional 25¢ a share in both 1970 and 1971." "Chin up, investors," they seemed to be saying.

Commuters versus Stockholders

Business Week in its issue of March 14 devoted over seven pages to the commuter crisis. The riders had been focusing their wrath on Chairman Saunders, who had reportedly answered a question as to why the railroad had not invested more in its commuter operations, with, "You wouldn't do it. I won't do it. I'd be crazy to do a thing like that. The stockholders would never get a penny back." It was nice to know that the road's management was concerned with the welfare of its stockholders—and that it was putting its money where the stockholders *would* be getting it back.

"But a fundamental question has arisen over the position of the privately owned railroad: How does it balance its duty to the public against its responsibility to make profits for stockholders?" was the question posed by the magazine. Implicit, of course, was the assumption that two goals were mutually exclusive. One might question whether the road's management was capable of turning it around no matter what they put emphasis on. Another question might have been posed: "Did the railroad's management care about neither their passengers nor stockholders other than themselves?" But these last two questions were not posed by the magazine in an otherwise comprehensive article. The piece asked, in effect, "Couldn't the road make the commuter service profitable if it had invested more money in it?" The publication pointed out that both in Chicago and on the San Francisco peninsula, commuters were getting reasonably good service. The Chicago & Northwestern had netted two million dollars in 1969, for example. The PC, it was pointed out, had not made a comprehensive effort to improve passenger service because it did not have the money.

"This is why Penn Central's Saunders has chosen to concentrate nearly all the road's capital investment in freight," the magazine said. Neither they (possibly because this was not the subject of the article) nor the majority of security analysts had noted that with all their effort going into freight, why hadn't freight service gotten better? Indeed, it could be said to be getting worse. Quality of management is still a subject most analysts shun because it is difficult to judge, rather than accept the challenge to do the extra work involved.

The Experts

Who was it who said, "War is too important to be left to the generals"? Of course, it may also be too important to be left to politicians, who presumably were being substituted for the generals in the mind of the questioner. In Wall Street, that highly structured house of canards, there are food analysts, chemical analysts, conglomerate analysts (a vanishing breed), oil analysts and rail analysts, some of whom are quite intelligent. The problem is that their ability to analyze is not measured by any objective yardsticks. Most get out of business school (where they are taught very little about real business) and go straight into bank trust departments, mutual funds, or brokerage houses. They are asked at the start which field they wish to specialize in, and provided that particular area isn't too heavily covered, they are given it. After two or three years "following" their specialty, they are qualified as "experts." Few if any ever worked in the field of their expertise, except that food analysts may know how to cook. Indeed, few ever worked in any fields. A few do, however, to emerge from the structure to shine. Just a few.

The rail analyst fraternity is by and large, as hidebound as the industry they follow. Indeed, as it is said of pet owners that they begin to resemble their pets, and vice versa, so do rail analysts sometimes begin to resemble their rather moribund industry.

And so it was that few rail analysts foresaw the destruction of Penn Central. It is also true that few were particularly bullish after the stock had fallen some 60 percent from its high. The *Wall Street Transcript* held a roundtable of rail analysts, which appeared in their publication on March 16, 1970.

Karl Ziebarth of Hayden, Stone said: "Well, I think we all agree that the Penn Central had faced a serious financial squeeze for the last eighteen months . . . . But I do think that they have made some very important and exciting management changes which will ultimately bear fruit. I think that a number of the internal physical changes, such as building new yards and completing connections will be wrapped up this summer, which will give some light at the end of the tunnel.

"Now, let me emphasize," he said, "I wouldn't at this stage recommend Penn Central. It's altogether conceivable that the stock will go lower. However, I think you would be wrong to paint their problem in too dim colors."

W. Glenn Cameron, an analyst with William D. Witter, said at this point, "I think that the inherent potentials in Penn Central are among the most exciting in the industry. It's a question of when and where—what and at what price do you buy the stock." Mr. Cameron indicated that he didn't think this was the time.

Mary De Sapio, a Bache & Company rail analyst, observed: "The exciting changes that Karl refers to are Penn Central's nonrailroad operations. Penn Central's a perfect example of diversification in the right direction. . . ."

The discussion continued with a cool but hopeful air toward the stock.

One should not be too harsh on these rail experts. There were others who were still calling the stock a "buy."

The inability to analyze individual situations unhampered by prejudice or personal bent was typified by a remark of a food analyst who I introduced to a stock listed on the New York Stock Exchange: "I can't buy it. You should see what happened to me in Green Giant." That kind of scientific approach would have kept Edison from discovering the electric light until 1978.

The Report

With Penn Central stock selling at twenty-four dollars on March 16, an envelope measuring eight by ten inches was arriving at the mail boxes of investors, the desks of brokerage analysts, and the tabletops of beleaguered money managers and their analytical staffs amid the piles of broker recommendations, press releases, and other company handouts. It was the railroad's annual report, and it would presumably tell all—about the financial condition and results of PC—that land-owning, passenger-passing, pipeline, coal-mine-investment, terminal-controlling, hotel-holding colossus. It would show the investment community how the company had done the previous year (1969), though the actual results had been announced months before. This would be a summing up. And it would indicate what management thought of prospects for the developing year (1970). And how corporate officials assessed their results and what they felt were the company's strong and weak points. It would reveal financial details, breaking down earnings for their various and far-flung subsidiaries. It would indicate what management intended to spend on improvements for the year, and break down the source and application of funds. It would be *the* source book for analysts (perhaps combined with its statistical and financial supplement, which some, but not all, would read).

Was the Penn Central still a good investment? Or perhaps it was just a "hold" to await better developments down the line. The report would reveal strengths not apparent in the recently poor operating results that would make the stock a buy later, if not immediately. It, along with other data assembled by the analyst, would surely have an impact on the price of the stock, something corporate managements have known for some time—witness the attention to awards for excellence in annual reporting by *Financial World* magazine, which announces its judgments with all the hoopla of a Miss America contest (well, almost all the hoopla).

This was the place to get the facts—or was it? There appears to have been some difference of opinion as to the materiality of annual reports, or, let us say, *some* annual reports. There is, some analysts point out, a certain latitude in how financial results are "managed" in corporate reports. Even the accounting profession has been going through something of a soul-searching as to how (or whether) the C.P.A. firm justifies its fiduciary capacity to the shareholder. Accounting firms of late have even been sued where individual stockholders felt their interests were damaged by false or misleading statements allegedly made by or certified by the accounting firm hired by the corporation. Leonard Savoi of the C.P.A. trade association has made statements indicating his concern for the image that may result when C.P.A. firms do not mind their p's and I's. In Penn Central's case, there has been more than a little controversy over the way in which certain financial items were handled.

First, let us see how Penn Central described the results of one of their subsidiaries, Great Southwest Corporation, in PC's annual report:

"Great Southwest Corporation, in which Penn Central owns 90 per cent of the voting stock, now includes the California-based Macco Corporation, which became a wholly owned Great Southwest subsidiary in March, 1969," the PC management proudly began.

"Since launching its initial enterprise of a 2,400-acre industrial park between Dallas and Fort Worth in 1956, Great Southwest has become one of the nation's largest land developments, with interests in Texas, Georgia, California and Hawaii." One could figuratively hear the sighs of admiration of the analysts who were proud of the PC's diversification program, not to mention that of Mr. Saunders, who had beamed to analysts about it.

"Net earnings for Great Southwest Corporation last year set another new high of $34,364,000 after taxes, an increase of 25.3 per cent over 1968 earnings of $27,425,000." PC even did the arithmetic for you.

The praise went on—it talked about Great Southwest entering the mobile-home business through an acquisition of its own, a modular housing (all the rage) division being created; Great Southwest picking up another company, a home builder, a deal with a Hawaii-based builder "for development of 285,000 [wow!] acres of resort, residential and agricultural properties," and purchase (for two million dollars) of 50 percent of a manufacturer of computer hardware. The rundown on Great Southwest concluded with the note that:

"Six Flags, Inc., GSC's [the same] recreation park subsidiary, currently operates Six Flags over Texas and Six Flags over Georgia and will complete construction in May, 1971 of Six Flags over Mid-America at St. Louis."

That was it. In this section, it was not mentioned what that $34 million profit was comprised of. Nor were any details furnished separately of Great, etc.'s financial results.

So what? Well, there appeared to be dispute over that. *Forbes* magazine, which, to its credit, sometimes goes in for muckraking, went to the trouble of examining the annual report of the subsidiary, Great Southwest, in its October 1, 1970 issue. It noted that "In financial reporting today, what the balance sheet giveth, the footnote frequently taketh away."

"Fully half of last year's profit," the magazine said, "[$17.5 million] was not cash but a paper gain from the sale of GSC's Six Flags over Texas amusement park near Fort Worth. The park was sold for $40 million, but only $1.7 million of that was in cash, the balance is due in annual installments through the end of the century."

Charity would ascribe the discrepancy about the date of sale to a chronological happenstance, which was possible. But why would (if it in fact did) PC have Great Southwest take into earnings that which was only paper—and not mention the fact that the $34 million was *nonrecurring earnings,* that is, that they couldn't sell the same amusement park every year?

In any event, why should PC, as some might say, "beef up" the earnings of the Great Southwest subsidiary? *Forbes* had an explanation:

"It was partly because of G.S.C.'s reported profits that PC was able to report ordinary income of $4 million last year even though it lost $193 million on its basic transportation operations." Oh, yes —it should be noted that Great Southwest did note the true nature of its earnings in a footnote to *its* report, though this was not so in PC's report. As for the accounting firm (Peat, Marwick, Mitchell & Company) and its certification of Great Southwest's annual report, a partner there reportedly told *Forbes,* "The statements are within the parameter of both SEC regulations and opinions of the Accounting Principles Board." And another Peat, Marwick partner, George Shepherd, reportedly said, "We certify the figures. It's not our job to interpret them." True, true.

"The impressive performance of our real estate subsidiaries is described in this report," wrote Mr. Saunders in the annual document.

"These assets have proved valuable to us and we are confident of their continued success. Their health and strength will enable us to use them in our financing program for 1970," Mr. Saunders continued.

If investors were dismayed by noting that for all of 1969, Penn Central showed per-share earnings of $.18 from their operations against 1968's $3.80, they could take heart from the report, which read: "We are well ahead of our original timetable of eight years for completing the [merger] but we still have a long way to go." There was "a favorable trend of reduction in heavy per diem costs [charges for use of cars owned by other railroads] . . . ." Management ticked off its progress:

"In our operating department, we eliminated one region, reducing the number to eight. Further reorganization is planned in 1970 to cut costs and increase efficiency.

"We abandoned 422 miles of line during the year. This, however, is only the start of streamlining our rail network into a more productive system.

"Since merger, 33 key terminals have been combined and virtually all important rail connections have been made.

"Service had been improved and simplified in the movement of freight shipments through the major gateways of the road."

The report went on to indicate how things were going to get better. Subsidiaries were going great guns, diversification was growing apace (as recently as February, the PC had purchased the stock of an oil refiner).

The report seemed to indicate that all was under control. Yet later, the trustees chosen to carry on the railroad's affairs after bankruptcy said, "any comparison [between their report and earlier ones] is misleading since the prior figures appear to have reflected a corporate policy at that time of putting the best conceivable face on the facts."[60] They termed figures for periods before 1970's, "dubious allies of the truth."

One trustee reportedly charged that "We know at least three dif-

[60] *Business Week*, May 29, 1971.

ferent ways they [the road's management] were trying desperately to put their best foot forward."

For one, they allegedly failed to charge off abandoned track as an operating expense against earnings. ICC testimony allegedly developed evidence (said *Business Week*) that Mr. Saunders "ordered that such charges be minimized." For another, "the previous management [that prior to May 1970] made loans to subsidiaries that were in turn returned to PC in the form of dividends." Some accountants feel this was justified to reduce taxes. "Conglomerates do it every day," they argued. It would also have the effect of making corporate results appear better than otherwise, others could say.

If the 1969 report was not exactly cheering, it was at least soothing. And thus it could be said that subsequent price performance of the stock was calm. On March 17, PC closed at 24⅜ (most had not received the report yet); on the eighteenth it was 24⅛, and only dropped to 23¼ on the nineteenth. It was not until the twentieth that the stock fell below $23 a share. Indeed, it closed out the month still just $0.25 under $23; so if indeed the compilers of the annual report had the stock in mind when they wrote it, they could be said to have been successful.

Hidden inside the figures—according to a later *Fortune* magazine piece (in August 1970)—were some other fancy accounting practices. "Some bills for freight charges, which reportedly are uncollectable, were credited to income," thus increasing profits in more than one annual statement. Wages were reportedly not taken out of capital rather than income. Profits from sales of securities, obviously nonrecurring, were allegedly taken into income, the magazine charged. This is a partial list and, as the magazine said, many practices were what the C.P.A. profession calls "accepted principles of accounting." An accusing finger was pointed at Peat, Marwick, Mitchell & Company, which, it was noted, received $600,000 from the road for its yearly customary services.

As *Fortune* reported, "Thanks to some unique bookkeeping, the parent Penn Central Co. was able to report remarkable profits, happy figures that lulled creditors, shareholders, directors, and managers." Yet other observers would say that Peat, Marwick did absolutely nothing wrong. It really was not their job to interpret.

In any event, what protection was there to the investor? Or to put it another way: Were there any clues in the 1969 report that investors could have used to indicate future disaster? Though it was not easy, the investor (and one might assume incorrectly that the institutional investor would have done so) could have read the footnotes at the end of the report. He would have found that, on page 24, note (4), "During 1969 the Commission [ICC] ordered the transportation company to reclassify a $21,000,000 gain on security sales originally included in 1968 earnings from ordinary operations to an extraordinary gain in reports to the Commission." Again, there was the nonrecurring gain treated as a recurring one. It might have made one suspicious. And even *Fortune*'s accusing finger was later withdrawn.

Still, it was not easy. At least, according to *Fortune,* the railroad did not help to make it easy; for a great deal of 1969 income was actually dividends from subsidiaries. Okay? Yes, but this too could be considered suspect. The railroad reportedly showed a $14,500,000 dividend from one, the New York Central Transport Company, a truck line. Yet the over-all profit of the subsidiary was only $4,200,000, a neat trick, though a legal one. "To get the dividend, Penn Central virtually cleaned out all Transport's equity, leaving a sparse $225,632. Another wholly owned trucking line, Merchants Dispatch, was said to show a $2,800,000 profit for 1969, while it was padding PC's offers with a $4,700,000 dividend. And Manor Real Estate Company allegedly showed a loss for the year of $714,000, yet paid parent Penn Central over $2,000,000 in dividends. And Despatch Shops, Inc., was said to pay its owner a $1,000,000 dividend while earning only $252,000.

Critics could say that the aforementioned was nothing new. The $3.80 per-share earnings PC showed for 1968 had allegedly been inflated by a $54,000,000 gain from security sales (nonrecurring) which it listed as ordinary (recurring) income. Let us put this matter another way for those not sophisticated in financial matters. Suppose you owned a restaurant. Your profit would consist of income less expenses, which include salaries. One year, as a promotion, you sell meal tickets to patrons for $500, which entitles them to three years of eating without further charge. Then someone approaches you to buy the restaurant. You show him how much you made for the year, including the $500 as income and not informing the potential buyer that you have sold these tickets. Your income is inflated, but future income would be (for the next two years) proportionately less. The buyer is not getting a true picture of the restaurant's earnings.

Another interesting ploy the PC used in 1968 was to include in its profits a $11,700,000 "hope" dividend. It seemed that Washington, D.C.'s Union Terminal was owned by the Washington Terminal Company, which was in turn owned by Penn Central and the Baltimore & Ohio Railroad. The Washington Terminal Company transferred its ownership directly to the two roads—and the dividend was reportedly paid to the PC *in expectation* of monies it would receive when the terminal would be bought by the Interior Department, which supposedly had intentions of converting it to a visitors' center. One would have to give high marks to PC management for its creativity.

Mr. Charles Woodruff, executive vice president of Manufacturers Hanover Trust Company, which had loaned vast sums of money to the railroad, said, "We were awed by its size. We should have had more information about the company. But I've heard that Penn Central financial people were adroit in avoiding giving information."[61] One wonders whether the blue-collar worker trying to borrow $3,000 for a new car would have gotten the same cavalier credit investigation.

And a government official later was quoted as saying that the PC's financial data was "fabricated, and bank credit groups just didn't pick it up until too late."

So investors could be excused if they guessed wrong, for the financial establishment (which one would assume knew better) were said to have been bamboozled. Yet there were clues lying all over the place that a drunken, blindfolded Sherlock Holmes could have found in his sleep. In addition to all those we've mentioned (and not the least of which was the actual condition of the road, which could have been ascertained by consulting with the line's customers), there was another item in the 1969 annual report: "interest on debt." The total for 1968 was also given for comparison, and 1968 showed $68 million. However, 1969 showed that interest had soared to $96 million! And there was all that insider selling. I have never been able to convince the banking fraternity what it means. When I pointed out to a money manager for a large eastern

[61] *Business Week*, June 26, 1971.

trust bank that August Busch was selling large amounts of his Budweiser stock (in addition to four other revealing parameters), he told me, "He [Busch] probably needs the money."

Holding Up

As March rumbled on, PC stock managed a mild recovery, perhaps prompted by the annual report, which, to some investors, large and small, seemed to give hope. George Herbert, in his *Outlandish Proverbs,* said of hope, "He that lives in hope dances without music." And it was Samuel Johnson who said in Boswell's *Life,* as long ago as 1762, that "Hope is itself a species of happiness, and perhaps, the chief happiness which this world affords; but, like all other pleasures improperly indulged must end in disappointment." Yet it was Cicero who said, "While there's life, there's hope." Hope is an uplifting sentiment, which, needless to say, has its place in our lives—yet there is one place where it is misplaced, and that, I fear, is the stock market.

And so it was that the mutual funds held on to Penn Central, and one big-name investment counsel bought after reading the 1969 annual report, as did many small investors. The railroad was making an effort, one could say. Didn't Mr. Saunders say in his annual report that they were eliminating 5800 miles of track? And didn't this mean, he said, that this would result in savings of $9 million a year? The stock rose to $23 on March 19, and to $24 on the twenty-fourth. As the month came to a close, however, the stock oozed back toward its natural direction and closed at $22.

At the Station

If one could say that the road's annual reports "covered up" the true financial condition from investors and bankers (just as do those of most other corporations), what would one say if he heard about the comment from the PC executive who described the newly built Pennsylvania Station at Thirty-third Street and Seventh Avenue in New York City as a "joy now for people to come and board a train here." Yet inside the station there were not enough seats for those awaiting long-distance trains, nor ticket windows, nor redcaps.

"I can't believe what's happening to me," Mrs. Theodore Maline told a reporter.[62] "In this big modern station there's still no place to sit down and no redcap to help me. How are we ever going to reach the train?" she cried. She and her four children were sitting on the floor with their suitcases, awaiting the train for Spartanburg, South Carolina.

"We planned it for the future and it's turned out perfectly," the terminal manager, Kenneth Simpson, said. He was referring to the commuter facilities, noting that long-distance travelers constituted only 5 percent of their passenger traffic. But as the railroad thumbed its nose at one class of riders, the other class, the commuters, were screaming bloody murder at their plight. "Nobody seems to like the railroad who uses it—and that includes the freight shippers," one broker said, "except possibly those who read its annual reports."

Easy Does It

As the crippled railroad creaked its way around the April bend, its stock held fast around the $22 area. Average daily trading volume was about 11,000 shares. On April 10 the road ordered some boxcars to be built—not enough to satisfy indignant shippers or, apparently, fearful investors. On the fifteenth, the stock dropped to $21 for the first time. Facing the oncoming train now was a twenty-foot-thick wall. Inside, the engineers (management) were fuming, fidgeting, and fussing. It seemed that somebody had sold the brakes for money to buy fuel to drive the railroad down the track toward the wall. The wall would be less ominous were it made of cement. Rather, it was made of the paper PC had been writing in recognition of loans obtained to pay off other loans, which, in turn, etc. Penn Central had not made a special point of it in their annual report, for they were too busy extolling the virtues of various acquisitions—but there it was on page 14. Under the heading, "Penn Central Consolidated Source & Application of Funds/Year 1969," it listed under "Source," $635 million in financing (new debt) and listed under "Application," $302 in reduction of long-term debt. Thus the railroad was incurring new debts at twice the rate it was paying others off. Still, the stock was widely held by mutual funds, banks,

[62] New York *Times*, April 6, 1970.

insurance companies, and investment counselors. They hadn't panicked—yet. Perhaps they were mesmerized by the value of all that real estate. After all, in the view of some bullish analysts, "If the railroad got into any real trouble, they could sell off their property," as one remarked.

As the story goes about the "speculator" who bought 10 million cans of sardines in hopes of making a quick killing (and getting killed in the process), "Sell—but to whom?"

Banks, in addition to holding umpteen shares for their trust customers, had also been lending money to the Penn Central. Smaller banks were also victimized. Charles Woodruff of Manufacturers Hanover Trust recalled one banker who told him he had loaned the railroad $1.5 million "on the recommendation of the big fellows from New York."

Yet some government investigators said the banks were more sinned against than sinning. Or perhaps "bamboozled" might be a better word. "Penn Central's financial data were fabricated, and bank credit groups just didn't pick it up until too late," said a government man.

Worse than Money

But if charges could ever be leveled against Pennsy financial officers, they would be paltry indeed compared to what was happening out on the tracks. On April 8, 1970, a twelve-year-old boy named Charles Rodriguez suffered burns over 85 percent of his body, electrocuted when he grabbed overhead wires while playing on top of a boxcar in a freight yard at Garrison Avenue and 156th Street in the Bronx.

In the prior five years, eight children had died and thirteen limbs were lost by others in the Penn Central's Bronx yards alone, according to a report in the New York *Post* on April 17, 1970.

"Everything was burned but his brain. He was sitting there and talking, 'God, this looks terrible.' If he'd only have shut up. But he kept looking at his arm and talking," said Dr. Lewis Fraad on the death of young Rodriguez.

The Penn Central did, they said, conduct an investigation. It might be questioned how deep or thorough it was, however. Or perhaps management was too busy to attend to the matter quickly.

A week and a half after the accident, the railroad said it had "not been determined how he [Rodriguez] entered the property," according to the *Post.* A reporter visiting the site a week after the accident saw a large hole in the chain-link fence surrounding the railroad yard. Half a block away, another hole yawned invitingly. Or just one block away, one could descend an unguarded stairway leading to the yards.

As Dr. Fraad spoke to the reporter, an eleven-year-old boy, Jeffrey Brown, maneuvered his wheelchair into the office. It was a difficult task for the lad, for he had only one arm. He had lost both the arm and a leg the past December 19 when he too had been burned playing near the Penn Central tracks at East 174th Street and Bronx River Parkway.

"Nobody never told me to get out or chased me," Jeffrey said.

Oh, Oh

One could not really blame PC executives for negligence, for they had more important things to worry about—like the earnings report released two weeks after the last incident. The stock closed at 21⅝ on April 21, but this was just a whisker before it was due to hit the wall. The next day, PC announced a first-quarter deficit of $17.2 million, which I'm sure was a surprise to Pennsy insiders. True, most of the drop (in the comparable quarter in 1969 the company showed a $4.6 million profit) was due to railroad operations. However, even their vaunted subsidiaries, Great Southwest Corporation, Arvida, Buckeye Pipe Line, etc., contributed only $6.8 million to profit, down from $7.7 million the year before.

One might feel almost as sorry for Pennsy management as for the children's parents. Even their much-heralded Metroliner run from New York to Washington, D.C., had so many "bugs inside the bugs," reported *Business Week* on May 2, 1970, that it was taking forty-eight cars to keep twenty-four in daily operation.

The earnings (or rather, lack of earnings) report did not sit well with the investors who had held onto the stock expecting the turnaround to materialize. The news hit the Street with the force of a wildly careening train hitting a brick wall, which in essence it was doing. *Bam!* Sell orders were telephoned frantically to nervous brokers. "*Sell!*" The stock closed at $20. Still, the selling had not reached a crescendo. On the twenty-third, it closed at $19. "*Sell!*" The disappointed bankers, investment counselors, and mutual fund managers ringed the ears of their brokers. "*Sell!*" The following Monday PC broke $18 and then $17. Conferences were held by investing groups around the country. The decisions were not unanimous. Boards had to be consulted in some cases. Some could not move as fast as individual investors, who fretted when their broker couldn't answer the phone because he was in the bathroom. One could imagine the expression on Howard Butcher III's face. Or on the columnists' who promoted it at $80, or the brokers whose research staff churned out the "buy" recommendations in the $70s, or the "oversold" comments in the $50s. Still, as one broker said of the stock, "At least we'll go down with the commish."

Calmly, Calmly

One could not say that the panic had set in as yet. Average volume was running around 30,000 shares, possibly lulling those who believe that going down on light volume was bullish. It was on April 24 that Robert Metz of the New York *Times* took the time to aim some barbs at Howard Butcher III. Mr. Butcher had told a reporter (presumably the same Mr. Metz) that he "didn't know of any other stock that could go to five times its then current price [$29 in January]." Mr. Metz reminded Mr. Butcher of that statement in his column. But not being able to reach Mr. Butcher this time, Metz spoke to his brother, King Butcher (King Butcher?). The latter Butcher said that he thought PC had "been through the worst of it." Asked whether he thought the stock could still go to five times $29, he said, "Some day it could happen." Asked further whether the family still owned 1.5 million shares, Mr. Butcher replied, "Probably not quite that much. We sold some." He was asked how much —"200,000?" Probably not that much, he replied, and, "I'm not going to say any more." He did admit that the shares were sold at higher prices. All of which may have surprised some investors, no doubt.

Value Line advisory service was virtually unflappable. Written a few days earlier, with the stock at $22, its April 24 report said that PC still had excellent potential for 1972–74 despite earnings deficits in recent quarters. Perhaps the analyst or analysts who wrote this report had some difficult times as the stock broke $19 only a week later. The service was not getting off the train—even if it meant (to some) certain destruction as the wall loomed near. Or perhaps they did not see the wall, as so many others hadn't.

Value Line actually said the railroad deficits would allow the possibility of a turnaround of some magnitude. To which no comment is required.

There had been some institutional selling during the first quarter of 1970, as the service noted. However, "indications that a significant proportion of the remaining shares (in fund portfolios) may have been sold in the first quarter of 1970, suggest that the pressure from Fund sales on Penn Central's market price could well be easing." Thus one could not say that the service could not see a silver lining in every cloud. To their credit, it should be added, *Value Line* did not think the stock would do well in the near future.

Bevan and Saunders did not sit idly by during the financial troubles that afflicted the railroad, no sirree! There were some $106 million in bond payments due the holders (a sinking fund) during 1970, and management did their best to raise the dough. Bevan reportedly was in New York with hat in hand in February, and Saunders and Bevan's assistant, Jonathan O'Herron, went to the Interstate Commerce Commission in an attempt to get freight rate increases in the same month; the latter two also saw Secretary of Transportation John A. Volpe in March. At least that's what *Fortune* claimed in August 1970; Volpe said he didn't know about Pennsy's plight until early summer. In April and May, Saunders and Volpe reportedly were trying to get government help in the form of loan guarantees. Meanwhile, Bevan was trying to put together a $100 million bond offering. While PC biggies were scurrying about, another officer and his wife, William Lashley, each sold 1000 shares. And on June 22, G. P. Harnwell sold 1650 shares, SEC records show. Mr. Perlman only sold 500 in April, but he had only 1400 left after that.

The Clean-up

On May 11, photographs appeared in newspapers showing a maintenance crew cleaning up car interiors in the Harlem Division commuter trains. The photos had been distributed by the railroad, but the real clean-out occurred a day later on the floor of the New

York Stock Exchange. The technical analysts who had been waiting for big volume in the stock before acting, now got their chance. The stock traded 171,000 shares that day, dropping 2½ to a new low of $15. The caption on the picture had read, "Whitewash Is the Name of the Game," and investors could grunt knowingly at the thought.

Now the panic had set in. The immediate cause probably was a statement by Mr. Saunders at the company's annual meeting in Philadelphia. He said that the Penn Central Company would have to reduce its capital expenditures from $268 million to $166 million during 1970. Investors recoil at this sort of thing, for to them it means that (1) things are not going too well and (2) growth may not be possible when companies cut their budgets, since presumably expenditures would be used on improvements, new plants, etc., that eventually could yield profits. Saunders blamed "declining industrial activity and unprecedented inflation," as well as the high cost of borrowing money as contributing factors to the PC's problems.

With some problems at the meeting being admitted publicly by management, even including new President Gorman, those corporate gadflys, Wilma Soss and John Gilbert, complained about the $250,000 management contract PC directors gave Mr. Gorman; this was followed by rounds of applause (for Soss and Gilbert, not Gorman).

"How, in view of our stringent financial affairs, can the board give this 62-year-old man over $200,000 a year, a fairly long-term employment contract, and a stock option?" asked Mrs. Soss. If naïveté was showing at this point, few of the 590 attendees noticed it. Mr. Saunders was getting $236,972 yearly for his efforts, which up to this point had not been overly successful.

That the stock did not fall even farther that day may have been due to the hope expressed by Mr. Saunders that passenger losses could be unloaded on the federal government, a ploy that the May 13 *Wall Street Journal* described as being "dangled" before the crowd. Elsewhere in the paper, "analysts" were quoted as "noting hopes that the railroad might announce some improvement over a big deficit for the first quarter, there was disappointment that the company could only report an 'austerity' plan at its annual meeting yesterday." Some analysts were still hoping—they had not heard the crash. The stock even stayed level through the May 15 Friday closing. This day also *Forbes* indicated they were not among the "hopers," when they said, "If there were a prize for the annual report that goes furthest in trying to put a good face on a bad situation, the prize would go to Penn Central. The company had a simply disastrous year in 1969. Nevertheless, it managed to report a small ($4 million) net profit before an extraordinary loss of $125 million. It did so by imaginative bookkeeping and tax offsets." Others were hoping, too. There was *some* reason to hope, in fact, which made the hope all the more pitiful. The Senate had just passed a bill providing for a quasipublic corporation (which later evolved into Amtrak) to run passenger service in this country. Republican Hugh Scott of Pennsylvania, then minority leader, said, "With this legislation, I believe we have provided the necessary framework that will enable America's railroads to meet the challenge of a new era." Others dubbed the bill "new and innovative." There were few doubts raised on the Senate floor, but the May 18 *Wall Street Journal* said that "What's needed most, from management, the unions, the public and the Government, is hard-headed realism. The new corporation then might have a chance to make some progress toward its aims. Otherwise it's only too likely to be an exercise in futility." Or an exercise in rhetoric.

It was May 18, and the stock was selling at $15, so investors knew all about exercises in futility. The next day the Penn Central carried on as if it were still viable. The line asked the ICC to allow it to cancel 17 Boston-to-Providence trains, making 67 runs in all under application for discontinuance. Investors were cutting and running too, as the stock closed at $14 on the nineteenth, trading 124,000 shares, a big day. The following day, some investment advisory organizations (the kind that manage pension funds) awoke from their daze and sold. The stock closed at $13 that day and next—with volume running 82,000 and 134,000, respectively. They were screaming in the streets the next day, Friday, May 22, as the stock was split asunder, dropping below $12 and trading 306,000 shares. Those who had been in the crash were coming out of their comas and calling for their brokers rather than their doctors in this symbolic conflagration.

There Are Mergers and There Are Mergers

Robert E. Bedingfield of the New York *Times* was questioning

Mr. Graham Claytor, Jr., president of Southern Railway on Sunday, May 24 about mergers in the industry, possibly with a thought cocked to the PC deal.

"So far the Southern Railway has not become involved in a major merger proceeding. Why is this?"

"The reason we haven't had any major merger is that there hasn't been any that I thought would be profitable to our stockholders. It's as simple as that," Mr. Claytor replied.

"I'm not interested in enlarging the size of this railroad merely for the purpose of having more railroad under my or my associates' supervision unless we are going to produce better and cheaper transportation and more profits for the stockholders I represent."

This was something of a contrast with that other merger up North.

"Standard & Poor's Couldn't Be Wrong, Could They?"

Standard & Poor's, that paragon of investment advice, had recently dropped PC's credit rating (used for bond interest rates) from Bbb to Bb, which, according to the *Business Week Letter* of May 25, classified it as a speculative security. It was nice to know that S&P wasn't altogether asleep, although some market observers might question any rating for the road above Z.

Since young Rodriguez had died, there was no diminution in the accident rate out at the tracks in the Bronx. While most eyes were focused on the PC's price, a ten-year-old boy named Tucker lay in a hospital with his leg crushed. Rocco Riccardi, a fifteen-year-old, had died under a train, and fourteen-year-old Bruce Aluisa struggled for his life with electrical burns over 75 percent of his body. Asked for comment on the Aluisa accident, a Penn Central spokesman reportedly said that he "should have been able to read." Earlier the Public Service Commission quoted the railroad as saying that "a large portion of the fencing along the tracks is the responsibility of the city, the cost of police protection . . . . would be a burden upon the company." Not like Executive Jet, right?

Saying It Like It Is—For Once

On May 28 the ICC ordered the railroad to keep two Chicago-to-Cincinnati trains for at least six months. The PC had requested it drop the trains among other Western runs. The railroad had contended it was losing money on these trains, but the ICC said that evidence showed that passenger patronage had been deterred "by erratic and declining service." Losses were due to "a failure on the part of carrier management rather than a failure on the part of the public to support this service," said the bureau. "The carrier does not have the right to claim that the losses it has helped to create are an undue burden upon it," they said. Incidentally, there appeared to be no mention of a railroad request for a raise in fares anywhere to repair the fencing in the Bronx or to hire more guards to patrol the area.

On May 26 the stock traded 104,000 shares, closing just under $13. The next day 338,000 shares changed hands, with the stock rising almost a point. Some technicians considered this rise bullish, since it was accomplished on "good volume." The following day, Thursday the twenty-eighth, PC closed down an eighth on 188,000. And Friday 191,000 shares crossed the tape as the stock dropped below $13 again, at 12⅝. The apparent reason for the weakness was that the $100 million bond offering was withdrawn. It couldn't be sold to institutional investors, who had by this time become somewhat wary. The bonds had been offered to yield 10½ percent, a pretty fancy figure indeed, though one that would not have been rewarded had the railroad gone under, which at this point seemed possible. One thing institutions do that the public often does not is to read the prospectuses of the companies requesting money. Not doing so resulted in punishment to some when their "new issues" went bust and their stocks went from $10 to $0.10 after the 1968–69 new-issue craze subsided. As an object lesson in doing so, let us examine the prospectus the PC issued in connection with its attempt to raise the $100 million:

One should ask: What will the company do with the money? This prospectus tells you. In Pennsy's case, it was going to help retire $106 million in long-term debt falling due in 1970 and to help finance $100 million in capital spending. Fine. Should they have waited so long (so close to debt's maturity) to pay off long-term debt? This is not unusual but bears considering.

The PC stated that it had $75 million in commercial paper (a form of short-term loan) maturing before June 30, and that since April 21, more paper was coming due for payment than the amount of new paper they were issuing. How long could that go on?

June Squeaks Out

The first week of June saw volume in the stock run 99,000, 136,000, 111,000, 106,000, and 91,000 shares. The stock's price, however, did not change this week. Where was all the frantic activity coming from? Was the smart money selling? Or were they buying? Were the banks coming back in the stock because of what they knew—that the railroad, with all its troubles, would turn around next year, if not this one? Did the mutual funds reverse their selling policy or merely intensify it? What new brokers would recommend the stock as being "oversold"? Was *Value Line* changing its opinion? Was Standard & Poor's going to name it "Stock of the Month"? Were the gnomes of Zurich (canny fellows) now buying in? Had somebody discovered the crash? One recalls Al Capp's "Fearless Fosdick" character, his chest riddled with three-inch holes, telling his sergeant, "They didn't hit me in a vital spot."

Unfortunately, few investors are in a position to learn what really goes on inside giant corporations and why stocks are really going up or down. It is better for them not to guess. Utilizing some of the methods discussed in this book may help. But in the case of Penn Central, more of the facts have been illuminated than is usually the case. For example, in the period of May 19 through May 27, while trading was unusually heavy, "the corporation was publicly silent about its financial condition and its future plans, the House of Representatives Committee on Banking and Currency noted. Little known to the public, too, was the fact that "On or about May 19, Stuart Saunders, chairman of the board of Penn Central, discussed the possibility of a government-guaranteed loan with Secretary of the Treasury David Kennedy" (remember that subsequently the bond offering had to be dropped for lack of takers).

On May 21, David Bevan met with banking representatives to discuss the cancellation of the offering and the possibility of government support. The bankers would be more receptive to lending money if the government would remove the risk, no doubt. On May 27, Pennsy's board of directors met at 11:00 A.M. and were informed of the decision to postpone the offer.

During the period of May 19 through May 27, Chase Manhattan Bank unloaded 262,300 shares of PC stock, according to the results of the Banking and Currency Committee's investigation. On May 19, the House report said, 77 percent of all the sales recorded, over 142,000 shares, were made by just 9 financial institutions. On May 27, these groups apparently accounted for virtually all of the sales, 372,400 shares. No announcement was made, the committee said, of the PC's private board meeting until 26 hours later, at 1:20 P.M. on May 28. It was also pointed out that Chase Manhattan was a major creditor of Penn Central, holding $50 million of its debt at the time. Further, Stuart Saunders, while president of the PC, was also a member of the board of the Chase. "It appears then, that Chase Manhattan 'had friends at Penn Central,'" the report remarked.

Morgan Guaranty Trust Company, like Chase, had some "interlocks" with the Penn Central. They were in on the discussions of loan guarantees, held $35 million of PC's debt, and had some $6 million in deposits from the railroad. Morgan and Chase were among the sellers during the volume deluge. Another seller was Continental Illinois Bank, according to the House committee. The bank held more than $23 million of PC's debt and was in on the loan guarantee discussions, though it did not have the board ties that Morgan and Chase had. Conill, as the bank is now called, was to be an important participant in the drama, as we shall see later. The committee also raised questions about trading by the Provident National Bank of Philadelphia, Alleghany Corporation, and Investors Diversified Services. But the question I have is whether the emphasis the committee took was misplaced. The attitude the committee staff took is expressed in the statement, "Much of this public [those who bought the stock sold by the nine institutions] today holds Penn Central stock which is worth only a small fraction of its selling price in the spring of 1970. The purchasers of this stock can rightfully feel that they were victims of a massive shell-game carried on by financial entities in a position to know the innermost financial secrets of the Penn Central organization."

The "shell-game" involved others, as we shall see. But I would question whether the pejorative is apt. If it truly were a massive "plot" to unload PC stock on an unsuspecting public, why didn't the participants do so when the stock was some six times higher? Or even twice as high? It was a little late in the game for plots. If indeed there were any plots, they occurred when the stock sold in the

$80s or $70s. And it appears that the financial institutions were not in on the real action at that time. If it could be said that there was any duping, it was the banks who were duped. By the time most of their selling occurred, the railroad company had already shown two disastrous quarters with massive losses. The train had already crashed. The signs of impending doom were there long ago for the sophisticated to see, but these banks apparently did not see them. Yet they continue to manage billions of dollars in pension fund and trust money, the real tragedy.

Rockefeller Answers

As for the House committee staff, David Rockefeller, chairman of the Chase Bank's board, accused them of "incorrect and unjustifiable assumptions."[63] Committee chairman Representative Wright Patman of Texas said the bank apparently had acted "on the basis of either great clairvoyance or inside information" in making massive sales of Pennsy stock in late May, just before the financing fell through. Rockfeller said a Chase analyst had been keeping track of PC developments since early 1970. "'On May 13,'" the *Times* reported Mr. Rockefeller said, "'after a leading brokerage house changed its recommendation on Penn Central stock from "buy" to "switch," the [bank] analyst sent a cautionary "flash report" to the bank's investment department and began a detailed projection of the prospects, which was completed May 21.'"

Subsequent selling by the bank, Rockefeller said, "'were definitely triggered by the conclusions which resulted from the detailed analysts conducted by the investment department's railroad analyst on the basis of public information.'" John M. Meyer, Jr., chairman of the Morgan Guaranty Bank, also indicated in testimony that his bank had no inside information on PC, nor did it consult with other banks on its selling.

What did Mr. Rockefeller's testimony say about the "leading brokerage houses," which up to that time had been recommending PC as a "buy"? What did it say about those who oversee the department that manages pension trust funds and individual investment accounts? What did it say about Mr. Rockefeller?

[63] New York *Times*, May 3, 1971.

The Last Thrash

There was a three-ringed drama going on at the Penn Central. In one ring, commuters were being treated somewhat less than courteously. A report released on June 3 by James McGirr Kelly of the Pennsylvania Public Utilities Commission said, "Sometimes Americans are considered by other nations as being soft. It is suggested to such critics that they ride the Penn Central commuter lines." Mr. Kelly said that "A cursory review of the testimony [to the Commission] regarding the trains and station facilities disclose a pattern of neglect bordering on contempt for the public." Customers on the line were forced to wait hours for trains that never arrived and about which no notice was given. Internally, Penn Central could be said to have somewhat inadequate maintenance procedures. When the line got its new fleet of cars (dubbed Silverliners) in 1958, it did not bother, according to the Kelly report, to provide any instructions at the site or by manual to its maintenance personnel. This was done twelve years later only after government prodding.

The Rescue Mission

Another drama was taking place in Washington, D.C., that told a lot about the workings of politics and politicians in high places. It had its heros and villains, plot and subplot, intrigue and climax, but whether it was a comedy or tragedy was for history to decide. It began, curiously enough, with a funeral.

The event was the burial of Richard K. Mellon; it was one of the Mellons, I believe, who said that depressions are caused to return wealth to its rightful owners. Just who the rightful owners of the Penn Central were was open to question, but the directors of the railroad were assembled at the site in Pittsburgh on June 5. As Robert Sherrill, writing in *The Nation* on June 29, put it, "Not wanting to spend all their time frivolously, they used the graveside get-together to plan how they might persuade the federal government to bail the nation's largest railroad out of its present financial difficulties."

Senator Hugh Scott, the Republican minority leader, was also there, and they agreed to meet at his Washington office four days later at 9:30 A.M. Scott called the power figures of Congress to the meeting. There were Senator Mike Mansfield, Representative Wright Patman, and Senator John Sparkman of the House and Senate Banking and Currency Committees; the chairmen of the Commerce Committees, Senator Warren G. Magnuson and Representative Harley O. Staggers; Transportation Secretary John A. Volpe and his assistant, James M. Beggs; and Treasury Under Secretary Paul A. Volcker.

Now, who would you guess ran the show (at least, according to Sherrill)? Was it Scott, since they met in his office? No—try again. Senator Sparkman, chairman of the Senate Banking and Currency Committee? It had to do with loans, didn't it? No, another guess. . . . Sorry, it was Volcker. For those of you who guessed right, we award a thousand-dollar bill and the chance to open an account with Howard Butcher III.

Why Volcker? I certainly would not want to imply any sinister motive, but it was a fact that he had been a vice president of the Chase Manhattan (they do keep cropping up, don't they?) before joining the Treasury. Chase, it may be noted coincidentally, was the second-largest holder of Penn Central stock after Morgan Guaranty.

Armed with flip cards supplied by Penn Central (who else?), Volcker reportedly wove through a loom of statistics to show how badly off the railroad company was. One participant at the meeting said later, "I noticed that Volcker seldom had to look at the flip cards. He seemed to know the Penn Central data by heart"—which, of course, should only be ascribed to good preparation, right?

Volcker implied that the free enterprise system was at stake—and unless the gentlemen present agreed to the government's help (read that "taxpayers' help"), the system might fall. What kind of help and how? Either it was Mr. Volcker's idea or the Administration hierarchy's (Mr. Volcker would hardly have presented the case without White House direction in any event); the establishment had apparently decided to help bail out the road, one might say, for the road's own profit. The device to be used was the obscure Defense Production Act, normally used to help small businesses fulfill their defense contracts. Thus Barry Shillito, Assistant Secretary of Defense, spoke next on the essential nature of the PC to the maintenance of national security. At that point a spoilsport of a senator, Warren Magnuson, interrupted with a question about the extent of

Penn Central's defense business. Shillito admitted that the road got about $100 million from the Pentagon, which was about 5 percent of the PC's $2 billion income.

The plan ostensibly was to have the government guarantee to the banks repayment of loans they would make to the railroad. How would you like to own a bank and lend money at a profit with the risk underwritten by the taxpayers? Incidentally, no less than thirteen of the Pennsy's directors were also bank directors, including Saunders, Perlman, Bevan, and Gorman, with such banks represented as the aforementioned Chase, Morgan, and Provident National of Philadelphia, not to mention Girard Trust, Wells Fargo, and Philadelphia National.

As Representative William A. Barrett of Pennsylvania later said, "The very fact that the big banks were beginning to cut Penn Central off from credit [the bond issue was being dropped] should have given the Nixon Administration reason to doubt the advisability of backing new loans for the corporation. When banks wouldn't lend to a $7-billion corporation, then something is drastically wrong and I question whether it is proper for the federal government to become involved in an apparently open-ended guarantee of credit in such a situation." By the way, the deal as proposed would allow the banks to charge 8 percent interest. One would think that the rate would be considerably lower with the taxpayers eliminating the bankers' risk.

The government action would "officially" prevent the road from turning bankrupt, with Volcker reportedly warning that if this happened, "no coal would be delivered to utility companies in critical areas, and needed chemicals would not be delivered to industry in critical areas." The existence of the New Haven for so many years in bankruptcy might place some doubt on that statement.

Mr. Saunders' Optimism Stilled

On June 8, the Pennsy board met and relieved Mr. Saunders of his post. Saunders took his dismissal "like a general who has just lost a major battle," in the words of one director. "He was a gentleman about it," said another. Apparently this action showed the Administration that the road would present a new face to the nation (when it got the money). Nonetheless, Mr. Saunders would get $144,155 annually in retirement pay, which made one observer wonder why his taxes would, at least indirectly, go to "reward" the ex-chairman.

On June 9, Senator Scott issued a statement that congressional leadership and committee heads had agreed to the Administration plan to guarantee bank loans to the railroad. He said that the road moved about $2 billion in Defense Department purchases a year.

It was Carlyle who once said, "You might prove anything by figures," and indeed Scott and Magnuson injected a bit of subjectivity into theirs. Scott was trying to make the Administration look right in propounding the loan, so he used the *value of the shipments*, rather than the revenue the PC would receive for the shipping. Magnuson was interested in embarrassing the other party (he's a Democrat), so he used the latter approach.

The Nixon Administration formula now proposed legislation to provide $750 million to PC and other roads that might have financial difficulties. Though the statement didn't indicate whether direct loans or guarantees were involved, some checking revealed that only guarantees were being considered.

Some observers felt that the Administration was worried lest a "domino effect" would occur if the PC went into bankruptcy; this might also seriously damage the stock market, which lately had not been doing too well anyway. Others later observed that "it was a bailout for the banks who had lent Penn Central money and would be paid off at ten cents on the dollar if it [PC] went under." Few thought that the most obvious reason, that of keeping the trains running, was the real one. Perhaps it was a combination of all these factors that moved Wright Patman, chairman of the House Banking and Currency Committee, to observe, "It is too bad that the human misery of people without adequate homes does not move the Administration as much as the difficulties of a $7 billion corporation." Senator Vance Hartke later said[64] that he thought the government should lend the money directly; for one thing, he felt that the government could offer a lower rate of interest than the banks. This saving would help the railroad, which presumably was the Administration's primary intention. It would not help the banks, however.

Under the Administration's plan, $100 million would be allo-

[64] *The Nation*, June 29, 1970.

cated right away, presumably because short-term paper was coming due before June 30. Those holding the paper would be hurt, of course, if the plan were not adopted, since they could then insist on immediate payment, which would probably result in the railroad's seeking relief from its creditors by going the bankruptcy route. Creditors, including the banks, would be restrained from collection pending court action.

In a news conference the same day, Paul A. Gorman, who had been given Saunders' chairmanship post to go with his presidency, said he would use some of the money to improve commuter and Metroliner service. He would continue, however, to press for the elimination of all long-distance passenger trains. Yet Mr. Gorman was having his own troubles behind the scenes. Some directors had set up a special committee to watchdog his day-to-day activities.

"Mr. Gorman won't need to be given more than three days' instructions at one time," said one clearly disgruntled director, according to the June 10 *Wall Street Journal*. The board's reshuffling of authority also resulted in the quitting (or ousting) of three of its members.

The Broker

The third ring in the Penn Central circus saw some strange goings on. They featured the activities of Howard Butcher III, senior partner of the brokerage firm of Butcher and Sherrerd, a Philadelphia member firm and principal investment adviser to the University of Pennsylvania, chairman of its investment committee, and a trustee. Others in the cast were his wife, Elizabeth Butcher, W. W. Keen Butcher and Edward P. Bromley, Jr., the firm's research partner.

You may recall what Howard Butcher III had been saying about PC in early January 1970: "I don't know of any other stock that could go to five times what it is selling at now." The stock was then selling around $30 a share. His firm had also recommended it much higher. He evidently believed what he was saying at the time (particularly in January), for according to the Philadelphia *Bulletin* of December 9, 1970, Mr. Butcher bought 10,000 shares for himself at $28 and on January 29, 1970, also reportedly purchased 5500 shares for himself at roughly the same price. He had thought the stock was oversold and expected a trading rally.

However, according to W. W. Keen Butcher, the brokerage firm was having some financial difficulties in March and Howard supposedly sold some Pennsy stock to contribute funds to the Butcher and Sherrerd organization. Howard put up $900,000 in cash on March 31 and another $1 million on June 11.

"Although much of the cash was raised by selling municipal bonds, he also liquidated his heavy position in Penn Central starting in mid-February and continuing into May," Keen Butcher said.

Two conclusions might be drawn from this. Either the firm's awareness of its financial plight came rather late, so Howard had to do an "about face" in his financial dealings, or he knew something was going wrong at the Pennsy and decided to sell. Of course, it is possible that the cash requirements of the B and S firm came on rather rapidly, between the time Howard bought stock on February 2 and the time he sold some two weeks later!

There was another way Howard could have helped the firm and still retained the shares, that is, if he still felt that they would go up in price eventually. That was to pledge his stock as security for loans at a bank (he presumably knew one) or to use the stock in contributing to the firm's net capital position. This is perfectly legal and proper. The exchange, however, reduces the value calculation of brokerage firm stock used for this purpose by 30 percent. Since Mrs. Butcher (who helped out too) reportedly did not own her stock outright, the equity value might have been somewhat lessened. Still, one cannot say that there were no other options open to them. Mr. & Mrs. Butcher also could have sold another stock they owned, International Utilities, in which they had a profit, but of course they then would have to pay taxes on the capital gain. Still, if you thought your stock could go up by 500 percent, you might think twice before selling. Withal, it was their personal decision, and who could fault them for their judgment?

On February 13, 26, and 27, according to the *Bulletin*, Butcher sold 3000 shares of PC stock at an average price of $26.22.

On March 2 the University of Pennsylvania investment committee told Howard to sell its shares "preferably on a scale up to obtain the best price." Penn Central had omitted its dividend, and the committee decided to switch to an income-yielding security.

Howard Butcher III continued to sell his, his wife's, and the university's Pennsy stock as follows, as the *Bulletin* outlined:

Date	*Howard Butcher*	*Elizabeth Butcher*	*Univ. of Penn.*	*Price (rounded off)*
Mar. 3	500			$25.88
Mar. 4	22,000	3000		$25.75
Mar. 5			2500	$25.88
Mar. 6	500			$25.00
Mar. 13			2000	$25.00
Mar. 23			1000	$23.00
Mar. 24			1000	$23.63
Mar. 25			2000	$24.75
Mar. 31		600		$23.50
Apr. 1			10,000	$22.75
Apr. 1		300		$22.63

While not wishing to imply any impropriety on Howard's part, it should be noted that the average price the Butchers got was $25.65 versus the average for the University of $23.69. Not too great a difference, one could say. Generally speaking, the New York Stock Exchange does not like to see brokers getting higher prices for their stock than for that of their customers, however. There is some confusion on this point, since it was allowable that the Butchers' decision to sell could be said to have been made before the university's. Most brokers would rather avoid the hint of impropriety and therefore show better prices for their customers. "The public is supposed to come first," they would say, and the function of the broker is to serve the public, not his own account.

On April 6, with no selling being done since April 2, the university had to repeat its direction to Howard to continue selling. Either he hoped to get them higher prices, or he was trying to hold the stock up. PC was selling between $22 and $23. Butcher reportedly protested that the stock should not be sold at that price. Some of the university's committee members "went along with him. Maybe the stock was low enough to warrant holding."

On May 4, the wife of another B and S partner sold 500 shares. On May 5, 7, and 8, Howard reportedly sold a total of 10,000 shares for a value of $184,300. Later, the *Wall Street Journal* (on October 22, 1970) remarked that Butcher had "access to crucial information ahead of the general public." I don't know where they got that idea. Their attitude disturbed Mr. Butcher, who said,

"I was reducing Betty's debit balance to provide capital for the firm. If I'd been really worried, I'd have sold in a hurry, not dribs and drabs."

On May 11, Edward P. Bromley, Jr., B and S's research chief, wrote a bearish memo on the PC. Butcher later noted that the memo was based on public information only: the annual report, ICC data, first-quarter earnings, stuff like that, just as Mr. Rockefeller's bank analysts had done. No one could say they were sleeping; slow, perhaps, but not asleep. Penn Central had sold as high as $86, but better late than never, right? The stock was selling just over $17 on "memo day."

Howard told his customers' men of Bromley's advice the next morning at their regular meeting. The salesmen had been sitting uneasily with the stock anyway, and they seized the opportunity to sell.

B and S men pushed the firm's volume in the stock to 76,000 shares from a typical 10,000 the previous week. On Wednesday, May 13, the firm sold 24,000 shares. Butcher and his wife sold a bit over 8,000 shares, though he later regretted this action:

"It would have been better public relations if partners had delayed selling for a week after the Bromley memo," he admitted.

Doing the Continental

Let us take a peek again at the doings in the middle ring of the circus:

"Continental Illinois National Bank did not have interlocking directorates with the railroad, but it had other close ties," read the staff report of the House Banking and Currency Committee.

"The bank had more than $23 million of the outstanding debt of the railroad and was a member of the bank steering committee which participated in critical meetings with Penn Central directors and high officials of the Treasury Department during the period June 10 to June 13. In the midst of these secret meetings involving banks, Administration officials, and the hierarchy of Penn Central,

Continental Illinois suddenly decided on June 12 to get rid of 108,950 shares of the railroad's stock. The sales apparently were based on an 'in-house' memorandum of the trust investment division, marked 'Flash' and warning 'Recent events indicate that the likelihood of returning to a profitable basis appears quite distant. . . .'

"The report also cites stock sales by the trust department of the Provident National Bank of Philadelphia, a bank which served through the years as more or less an 'in-house' financial institution for the railroad. David Bevan, the chief financial officer of Penn Central until June 8, 1970, was a director of Provident. John Seabrook, chairman of the International Utilities Corporation, was a director of both Penn Central and Provident National Bank. In addition, William Gerstnecker, a former Penn Central official, was vice-chairman of the board of Provident until his resignation in January 1971."

So reads the staff report, seeming to point the finger of insider information at the Continental Bank's action in selling their stock in the PC. If bankers need inside information to sell stocks two years after they hit their highs, let them have their inside information. Actually, dear reader, banks rarely do have inside information. As a general procedure (I'm not saying it never happens), bank trust departments that make decisions about investments for their clients usually do not get their dope from the finance section. The larger banks, National City, Chase, Morgan, U. S. Trust, Bankers Trust, etc., maintain vast research staffs to dig into stocks and follow them. What would be the point of retaining all that overhead if they could just ask the loan section? Many smaller banks also have research sections, United Virginia Bank/State Planters and City National of Kansas City, Missouri come into mind, and do a lot of good research work. Other banks subscribe to the information supplied to them by the larger New York banks. The research is there; the question is: Is it any good? My answer is: Not very.

I suggest following some of the rules in this book and trying the market yourself, rather than entrusting your money to bank trust departments.

Down There

Now let us leave the circus and join the farm. On June 10, with

PC stock selling at around $13, Paul A. Gorman expressed the hope that "within the next few days" he would have the money it needed. When asked exactly how much was needed immediately, he answered, "We have enough cash to cover our current bills, if that's what you are asking."

A spokesman for Senator Hugh Scott said that it was his understanding that $50 million in cash "would be made available to the railroads fairly soon so that it can meet its payroll." He said the road's creditors had been assured of the government guarantee of $50 million.

It was optimism time again. Not so on Wall Street, however, for whereas the stock had closed at $14 on June 9, it slid to $12 by June 11. *Business Week*, in its issue of June 13, echoed the ebullience of the non-Wall Street contingent with its lead to a story on the PC.

"Like the U.S. cavalry sweeping over the hill at the last minute, the federal government came to the aid of the Penn Central Co. this week with programs to guarantee loans." Transportation Secretary Volpe had asked the Defense Department to issue the short-term guarantee "for the common good and integrity of the transportation system," the magazine reported. Mr. Volpe was used to that kind of talk, having been a governor of Massachusetts. And one PC board member was said to have felt about the new chief executive, Paul A. Gorman, "I don't think he can run it. I don't think he thinks he can run it."

What, My Money?

Although there seemed to be some confusion about how much money would eventually be loaned the Penn Central and when, one of the figures being bandied about was $750 million. Using taxpayer money to help a failing company, whose difficulties could at least partially be attributed to mismanagement (not to mention the aid and comfort it would give the banks) did not sit well with some of those who would have to foot the bill. It caused the *Times*' Russell Baker, writing on June 14, to put tongue in cheek before putting hand into wallet.

"Before okaying the use of one cent of my money I want assurances that standards will be maintained," he wrote derisively.

"How do I know, that with the government looking over your

shoulder," he said to an apocryphal PC official, "the next time I go to buy a ticket, you will not sell it to me right away?" He was assured that he would still have to wait in line at least half an hour.

"Promises are cheap. The fact is, your standards are slipping. When I telephoned you just now, the phone was answered on the twenty-third ring. Before you came to the government for help, the railroad never answered a telephone unless it was one of the directors calling in to get an unlisted number.

"'That only applied to calls for passenger information,'" the PC man answered, "'and it still hasn't changed. If you call the number for Washington passenger information right now I'll bet my stock option it will ring for the next seven days without anyone answering.'"

Being assured that these and other standards such as train cleanliness would not be disturbed made Mr. Baker feel better about the use of his money.

Downtown

Things were not changing much on Wall Street either, and the stock closed the week ending June 12 at $11. Railroad men all over the country were wondering whether the massive size of the railroad stood in the way of its viability, regardless of the loan. Those questions should have been discussed when the stock was at $86 a share by the investment analysts who recommended its purchase.

A question investors should ask when merger news is announced is: Is it a good merger? Too often mergers are accepted at face value. One could also say that, during the conglomerate craze, some mergers were made with too many eyes on the stocks involved rather than the benefits to the respective entities. That is, I would not be too surprised to find that some mergers were made merely to "hipe" the stocks up, to fan public fervor rather than on the basis of the economics involved. When confronted a merger situation, investors should ask:

1. Was the deal made to trade on the "glamor" of one of the partners to the merger?
2. How would the combination benefit the joiners? Or how could it hurt?

3. Did the price runup prior to the announcement (of the deal) discount any potential benefits the merger might create? This is often the case.

Standard & Poor's (remember?) commented on recent PC developments in their *Outlook* service on June 15, "A major Penn Central management shakeup was followed quickly last week by Government action to provide guarantees for bank loans of up to $200 million." (Still some confusion extant on that number. But in that stratospheric area what's $500 million, more or less?) "These will carry the company through its immediate financial crisis," they said. The service commented that although these measures, including the possible sale of PC real estate, might alleviate current financial problems, there were other serious problems, including labor and interest costs.

The service did not appear to be too sanguine about PC's prospects as an investment, which prompted one broker to lament, "Now they tell me!"

Moody's Investors Service, in its *Stock Survey,* also commented on recent PC developments and also wrote with an unhappy countenance.

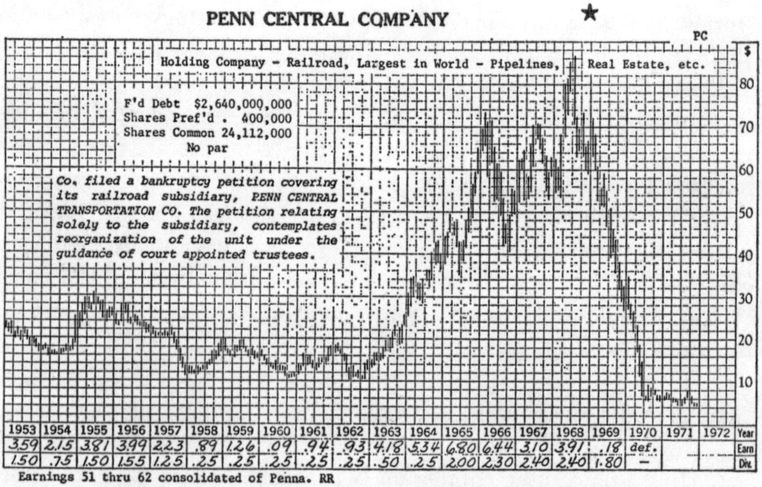

Chart courtesy M. C. Horsey & Co., Inc., Salisbury, Maryland 21801

"The stock lacks appeal, in our opinion," Moody's said, "and we recommend holding it only on a long-term basis for possible price recovery." (May as well cover all eventualities, it may go up someday, and then how would we look?)

The Directors

Monday, June 15 also saw the *Wall Street Journal* announcement of the resignation of three directors. They were Louis W. Cabot (of the Boston Cabots, Lowells, and Lodges), John T. Dorrance, Jr., chairman of Campbell Soup, and Thomas L. Perkins of the New York law firm of Perkins, Daniels, and McCormack and chairman of the trustees of the Duke Endowment. Would Dorrance's directorship mean a conflict of interest, since Penn Central was also in the soup? No, Perkins and Dorrance were also directors of Morgan Guaranty, one of the banks expected to qualify for government-backed loans to the Pennsy. The Penn Central also, it turned out, was into Morgan for almost $84 million of commercial paper, according to the *Wall Street Journal,* "the largest single item on the list of [the PC's] 'current liability accounts.'" A Morgan spokesman had recently claimed that the bank was merely an "agent" for the paper and not the owner. In any event, a possible conflict-of-interest situation may have prompted Perkins' and Dorrance's resignations. Yet one wonders whether this conflict had *developed* suddenly or had been recognized suddenly.

Mr. Cabot's secretary told the New York *Times* (as reported in its issue of June 13) that Cabot had submitted his resignation more than a month ago and that it "had nothing to do with the present situation."

Saunders to Bevan to Perlman

For whatever reason, there was no announcement Friday of the resignation of three Penn Central big guns, Stuart T. Saunders, David C. Bevan, and Alfred E. Perlman, but that fact seeped into the papers on Monday.

It was rather a quiet time for them, but a frenzied one for the analysts who had taken Mr. Saunders literally, even reading into his word thoughts that had not been there during the brighter times for railroad analysts when the stock was much higher, say at the security analysts meeting in New York in September 1968 at $67 a share. Their enthusiasm would easily be kindled by future corporate managements and stockbrokers, a fact that is not lost on the informed minority.

Yet one analyst had written a memo in 1968 saying, "Management's recent presentation at the New York Society of Security Analysts was generally disappointing. While many of the known profit potentials were discussed, there was an abundance of vague, unsure or contradictory answers. It was stated that 'non-rail' earnings are expected to advance in the second half at a rate comparable with the first half, but it appears that the swing in 'rail' earnings may be largely offsetting . . . . At 19 times estimated 1968 earnings, which are largely tax free and of debatable quality, the shares appear to be somewhat overpriced."

He had been one of a distinct minority. Most analysts sounded like this one in November 1969:

"Penn Central, the largest railroad and one of the largest real estate companies in the world, is a giant learning to walk. This year we expect it to struggle to its feet, and by 1970 to be moving forward. We recommend accumulation for investment accounts at current levels [$60]."

Now that the railroad was in deep trouble, brokers and analysts at investment companies felt somewhat bitter about the road getting government help. Whether they would have felt differently if they had profits in the stock was another question. Although there was considerable optimism in Washington for tax-money support, the provinces began to rumble. *Barron's,* in its issue of June 15, was one of the naysayers.

"The government is on the wrong track. By rushing to the rescue, it willy-nilly tends to perpetuate a board of directors which has amply demonstrated a lack of capacity."

The somewhat conservatively oriented publication said,

"It sets a dangerous precedent; what's good for Penn Central, after all, is equally good for the other Class 1 carriers (not to mention airlines) reputed in equally bad shape. Finally, by softening the penalty for failure and cushioning commercial risk, the White House weakens its own campaign to discourage inflationary excesses and restore a dash of prudence to the business scene."

Supporters of the measure argued that since there was (at the time) a shortage of cars due to Federal Reserve Board tightening (overtightening) of the financial purse strings, the Penn Central money problem might lead to a pattern of corporate collapse, since banks would be less eager to lend money to companies needing it.

On Tuesday, June 16, the loan program took shape, with the Administration sending Congress its formal proposal. The Department of Transportation, under the plan, would administer the government's guarantee on loans made to the PC and other railroads for up to $750 million. But there were stirrings.

Representative Henry S. Reuss, a Democrat from Wisconsin, sent a letter to Attorney General John N. Mitchell asking the Justice Department to decide whether the Administration was acting legally in using the Defense Department to guarantee $200 million of borrowing, the facet of the deal that was to be its emergency provision.

"It appears to be a clear abuse of the law," Representative Reuss said.

Apparently waiting to see the outcome of the legislation, the stock hesitated at $11 a share through the week.

For his part, Mr. Bevan did not hesitate, selling another 4900 shares on June 19.

He Doesn't Go Along

Meanwhile, Mr. Patman, hardly a banker's friend, was bristling at the thought of the PC's being helped out of their predicament and aided anew.

Patman asked the Defense Department to provide him with "all relevant documents" before the government guarantees any loans to Penn Central Company, the Pennsy's parent. The Department did not rush to reply. As the *Wall Street Journal* observed on June 19,

"Officials working out the arrangements have been trying to maintain total secrecy about the plan." That is, of the immediate guarantee for at least $50 million of the $200 million part of the deal. Pentagon officials were tight-lipped, refusing to answer reporters' questions. Patman set up hearings before his Banking and Currency Committee to begin the following week, and Treasury officials tried unsuccessfully to have the hearings closed to the public. Some of them would have to testify at the hearings, incidentally.

Among the documents Patman requested were a copy of the New York Federal Reserve Bank's recommendation in favor of the guarantee, based on their investigation of the railroad company's credit-worthiness.

Representative Patman's letter was hand-delivered to David Packard, Deputy Defense Secretary. Upon getting it, Packard called Patman in an effort to get the congressman to go along. Having spoken to Mr. Patman myself in connection with this book, I can understand Packard's problem. I wish there were more like the Texas congressman.

Other congressmen began to rail against the Administration's secrecy about the loan arrangements. Some officials said secrecy was necessary to prevent shocks on Wall Street. Congressional opponents felt that it was more because the Administration felt itself on shaky legal aid and political grounds, the *Wall Street Journal* said on June 19.

Meanwhile, a law firm was retained by the Pennsy as counsel for the loan agreement. Interestingly enough, it turned out to be Mudge, Rose, Guthrie & Alexander, Messrs. Nixon's and Mitchell's former firm. The banks wanted the Attorney General to sign the government's legal opinion okaying the $200 million loan guarantee. Mr. Mitchell loosened his collar at that one. The Justice Department reportedly suggested that another official there sign.

Not Our Fault

"The railroad is killing our children," a woman said softly over and over, while hearings were being held before the Public Service Commission during the week ending June 19. David Katsky, an assistant in the New York State Attorney General's office, testified that "The Penn Central has responded to criticism of its safety precautions [in the Bronx] in what we consider to be the most cavalier manner," which should not have surprised him, considering the road's record.

The PSC had been rather slow to act on the safety problem, and at least eighteen deaths and forty-four injuries had occurred in the prior five years. Witnesses described what they felt were unprotected fences and inadequate warning devices and signs.

Joseph Aluisa watched the proceedings in the hearing room at 199 Church Street in New York City with some bitterness. It was only a month since his son had suffered burns over 75 percent of his body from touching the PC's high-voltage wires. Mr. Aluisa was quoted by the New York *Times* on June 18 as saying, "There are no signs at the spot where my boy was hurt. Maybe if there had been one, he wouldn't be lying in the hospital now."

"It is clear," said William P. Jones, assistant counsel for the railroad, "that unfortunate as the accidents to intruders have been, they are the result of trespass, often with criminal intent." Newspaper reports of the hearings made no impact on the stock, since the accidents did not affect the railroad's loan prospects, thus the stock dallied through the week around $11 a share.

The Nixon Administration was cognizant of congressional criticism of the loan program—and could see the matter becoming an election issue two years hence. There were heated discussions within the Administration about the problem, and support was beginning to wane. Meanwhile, Paul Gorman and other Pennsy bigwigs met for an hour and forty-five minutes with Representative Patman on Saturday, June 20 in an effort to convince him to endorse the loan. Patman issued a statement afterward saying that he appreciated the "frank and open" discussion and the information the road was now supplying him. However, he added,

"As I have in the past, I expressed my deep concern that the government's interest be fully protected and that the taxpayers not be made liable for any financial losses resulting from a guarantee to this huge corporation." He also felt that using the Defense Production Act was not proper in this instance.

Bankruptcy

The Administration could see that the jig was up, and it dropped the plan. That was it; after the Patman meeting, the PC officials returned to Philadelphia to draft the bankruptcy petition.

"According to one insider one of the frightening developments that hastened the directors' decision to prepare the bankruptcy petition came last Friday when the railroad learned that the First

National City Bank of New York, a major creditor, suddenly stopped honoring Penn Central Transportation checks," the *Wall Street Journal* reported on June 22.

One Penn Central man reportedly said after the Patman meeting, "Patman and his staff absolutely licked their chops. It was a complete farce. Nobody lost their temper, but Patman's staff was especially provocative. They kept saying over and over that all this was a result of the Administration's failure to lower the cost of money."

Technically the reorganization was for the railroad subsidiary of the parent Penn Central Company. It was filed with United States District Court Judge C. William Craft on June 20 at 5:45 P.M. in his home, after a day of meetings among company officials that had begun at 11:00 A.M. that morning. It was a special kind of bankruptcy, Section 77 of the Bankruptcy Law. Unlike ordinary proceedings in which a corporation's property and assets are turned into cash, which is then distributed among the creditors, this section provided for a trusteeship to retain possession of and continue operation of the railroad. It had originally been signed into law by President Herbert Hoover on March 3, 1933 and had been amended the following year. The railroad would continue to run just as before. The bankruptcy scare had been boogymanned. The stockholders were hurt, but they were being hurt all along. The creditors might suffer—but the riders and freight shippers were no worse off than before—though that is not saying much.

"It is possible," said the *Times* on June 22, "that the Penn Central's 100,000 commuters and thousands of shippers will find service of the system in reorganization superior to what it has been since the Pennsylvania Railroad on Feb. 1, 1968, absorbed the New York Central Railroad through merger."

Most of the railroad community opinion seemed divided as to what caused the bankruptcy between bad management and skullduggery. John W. Barringer, head of the executive committee of the Missouri-Kansas-Texas Railroad and chief of the Reconstruction Finance Corporation's rail section during the '30s, told *Forbes* on August 15, 1970:

"I don't know which it was. But whether it was chicanery or bad judgment, I always felt that in view of the unsatisfactory condition of maintenance and their obsolete equipment, all their cash reserves should be husbanded for the railroad. Instead, they went the other way. All the money that came from selling the Norfolk & Western and Wabash stock and so forth should have helped the railroad. That was Perlman's idea, but he was overruled. They were bleeding the maintenance to keep up financial appearances while they diversified."

"If the Pennsy didn't file for bankruptcy, one of its creditors would have," one large stockholder said. By this action, loans coming due this month and succeeding ones would be held off and the railroad would be given some breathing time to try to work itself out. As for the stockholders, the issue was hit with the force of an atomic bomb. It traded on Monday, June 22 (when the news hit the papers) at just one price, $6.50, down from $11 the previous Friday, with turnover its largest ever, 455,000 shares. This was a price it basically retained for more than a year.

"I wish I were out of this market," said one financial analyst before the bell opened trading on the floor that day, as he expected the whole market to collapse on the news. Just as one's fondest hopes are rarely realized (especially on Wall Street), so are one's worst fears. The Dow closed down just four points.

On June 23, Judge John P. Fullam was chosen by lot among the available judges in the Eastern District of Pennsylvania to oversee the railroad's reorganization. When asked whether he was a student of Section 77 of the Federal Bankruptcy Act, he was quoted in the *Times* the next day as saying,

"No, but I expect to be by tomorrow."

The Winners

Few mutual funds, few investment counselors, few banks, and few insurance companies were among the winners in the Penn Central race to destruction. And probably fewer individual investors were. But if you consider the insiders who sold holdings considerably before the crash to have been winners, you also certainly should include in the winners' circle another entity among the so-called smart money. This was the Allegheny Corporation.

Clifford H. Ramsdell, vice president for corporate relations (sometimes called public relations) at the Allegheny Corporation, told the New York *Times*, as reported in its June 24 issue, that he recalled his company's decision to dispose of its position in the New York Central.

"We controlled the New York Central with 960,000 shares. The merger would have left us with less than a 6 per cent interest in the merged corporation. We didn't think we ought to have a third of our assets in a company we didn't control. We offered, therefore, to exchange the Central shares for Allegheny shares in public hands.

"About 85 per cent of our Central stock went out [was traded]. Our cost was roughly $25 a Central share and we received Allegheny stock which had a value of approximately $80."

This was his explanation for getting out of Central stock when it was "high." Others might just consider it good business practice to take your profit and run, good "smart money" thinking.

And there were congressional hearings after the fact. During one group of them, the Senate's Commerce Committee met on June 25 and 26, and July 8, 22, and 29. At the opening of the session on the twenty-ninth, Vance Hartke, who presided, said,

"The Commerce Committee is in charge of communications and can't get the microphones to work. I am not too sure we can get the railroads running either."

Their hearings took 624 pages in two volumes.

But the lessons for unsuccessful investing will not be found among them. They are, in my view:

1. When insiders sell, should you be buying? Remember that no insider really knows the "top" price to which the stock eventually will go. Nor should you try to guess it.
2. Mergers, as indicated, are not necessarily good. Do not buy a stock because of a merger. Rather think pessimistically about them, which may cause you to examine the case more closely.
3. When corporate officials make extravagant claims about their company, they may be telling the truth as they see it. But they may not be, or they may be carried away, just as you or I. Too much corporate talk should scare you away.
4. When corporate officials talk to security analysts, it just could be that they have ulterior motives. Of course, I'm not saying that Penn Central's did. But they could have.
5. When brokerage firms spout fantastic projections about earn-

ing power, they may be "dreaming." And you know what dreams sometimes turn into.

6. When a plethora of advisory services boost a stock, it is usually too late to buy, but plenty early enough to sell.

7. Check on the financial stability of any corporation that you consider investing in. Annual reports show debts maturing (coming due). You may have to scan the footnotes, but there is more truth in small type than in a thousand pictures.

8. Stocks are not created to make you rich. Some would say just the opposite.

9. Corporations do not exist to make you rich. But they may sometimes make those who run them so.

10. As to who really owns corporations, it is not usually the little old ladies in Keokuk.

In a postscript to this story, on January 5, 1972, warrants were issued for the arrest of Bevan, Hodge, and Lassiter. Philadelphia District Attorney Arlen Spector said in a fifty-seven-page document that the three "conspired in their corporate activities to divert in excess of $21 million from the treasury of the Penn Central for themselves and others."

They should, of course, be presumed innocent until proven guilty. And yet, in a conversation I had with a fellow who had worked at Glore, Forgan during Hodge's tenure, he said, "They'll never catch the big ones."

This man also told me of a conversation he had with another Glore, Forgan employee who was operating at a higher level than he:

"We all thought the thievery going on by certain people there was so blatant as to be almost funny, and I'm talking about stuff long before the Penn Central mess. One man who was closer to the action than I asked me if he could turn some people in by going through the Internal Revenue and if he would be paid by them. I said he could—and he could also find himself dead as a result. You see, the stealing going on by members of the Main Line aristocracy in Philadelphia was so deep they could not afford to let it get out."

I asked him his conclusions about his observations of the Penn Central and other deals.

"Corporations are portrayed as organizations working for the benefit of the stockholders. They actually exist to feather the nest of those who really run them. It's all a sham," he said.

"Would you like to name some names?" I asked him.

"Are you kidding?"

Perhaps the most important lesson for investors may be a paraphrase of a Hemingway line.

Ask not for whom public pronouncements by corporate management are aimed—they are aimed for thee.

nine

What Makes Stocks Hot-and Cold

LET'S SAY your name is Andrew Quicknerves (or did this happen to you, too?) and you bought Fairchild at $200. It was "hot" at $200, wasn't it? (Wall Street's term for this figure is "double par.")

At $200, the chances are that advisory services were recommending it—and "the news" about the company was good. (Remember when integrated circuitry was the rage? And who was the leader in integrated but Fairchild?) Pay no attention to the fact that Fairchild's president (a Mr. Carter, I believe) just sold a batch "on the way up." Why should you pay attention? Hardly anybody did. Probably needed the money, right?

Anyway, there it goes—the stock, I mean. Wow, isn't it exciting? The stock is going up four, five points a day, day after day. How could you lose? What growth, what exciting products, what great management, what potential—*what a growth stock!* Everybody knows you can't go wrong with a growth stock, right?

So, Andrew, you bought it. And the very next day you had a profit! And the next. Buy more on the way up, right? *Buy the strong stocks, right?* So you bought another hundred at $212.

"It was acting well," as they say on the Street.

Time passed (shown by flipping pages on wall calendar), and six months later you were not so ebullient. Neither was the stock, for it had fallen to $172. So what? *It's a good company!*

At $165, Andrew, you "averaged down" and bought another 100 shares. It's real cheap, now. Lowers your average cost. That way, when it goes back to $200, you can get out with a profit—right?

At $142, you were less concerned with profit than with "just getting even."

At $136, sleep did not come easily. "What should I do?" you yelled at your broker. But he's as frightened as you. Now that you yelled at him, he's more frightened.

"When will it end? I can't stand it." You lied to your wife, Andrew, about selling out earlier with a profit. But she knows.

Despair, desperation, sorrow. Andrew's reaction multiplied by the terror of thousands of others "locked in." And when the stock broke $100, you and all the other Andrews sold. They sold with a panic followed by sadness matched only by Ralph Branca's, Mickey Owen's, Alf Landon's, Tom Dewey's, and Lyndon Johnson's.

And who do you suppose bought? Calmly, dispassionately, objectively. You tell me. Were they the same ones who sold to Andrew at $200? Possibly.

The Climax Method

As if you didn't know, "smart money" normally buys on the way down (at what we may assume are wholesale prices) and sells on the way up (at retail). But, of course, the question is: "How can I, the average investor (or trader) put this apparently pat generalization into practice? *How* can I know when to start buying and complete a profitable transaction by selling?" I cannot assure you there is a quick and easy way. What I can do, for those of you who still care to get technical, is explain a method of charting.

First, let us do some studying. We can assume that money, "big" money, is identified in the market by the number of shares bought and sold. Thus trading in, say, hundreds of thousands of shares would represent the exchange of considerably more dollars than, say, three or four thousand shares. Thus we look to volume—the number of shares traded in a stock—for clues to the actions of "big money."

Let us take a year—for this example, 1963 (but it could have been any year)—and virtually any stock.

What, one may ask, were the high-volume leaders of 1963, for example? Not high volume throughout the year, but over short periods of time—thus eliminating normally popular issues with large capitalization, such as GM and AT&T. Any such list for 1963 would have to include Curtiss-Wright, Parke Davis, and Sunray DX Oil.

Curtiss-Wright "painted the tape" in the first two weeks of May, trading *over 200,000 shares in each week.* The high price attained in the second week of May was $23 a share, the following week, $24. It proved to be retail distribution by informed investors. The stock sunk to under $18 later in the year and did not surpass $20 until April of '64 (and then only briefly). Adjusting for a five-for-four split in 1969, the $24 price becomes $19. After touching a low of just over $10 in 1971 on this adjusted price, it made its high for this year at just under $16.

We will not bore the reader with the sordid (and for some painful) details of the Parke Davis episode ($36 at the height of its popularity in 1963 and a $38 high in 1964), and Sunray DX, at its peak of $39 in 1963, making its subsequent high in 1968 (at $51), before merging into Sun Oil Company on October 25 of that year. How widely the rumors flew at those exorbitant levels! They all look good at the top.

One thing to note when studying these phenomena: *The volume came in on the way up!* One might say this is bullish—big volume on the rise. *But the inescapable fact is that the volume came in after a great deal of the price rise had already taken place!* If, for the sake of discussion, we assume that the large volume represents "smart money," would they be buying *after* a rise or *before?* Perhaps we should be looking for volume at the "bottom" (frequently on the way down) for our buying signals. One big winner in 1964 was Westinghouse.

Westinghouse made the "most-active" list (most heavily traded) on the way down, at 29¾. The following day, June 25, it made the most-active list again, closing unchanged. Soon after, it rose (on light volume) to $31, after which huge volume came in on a "breakaway move," and the stock rose in steps to $45 in four months.

If volume is studied in terms of supply and demand, one can see that (other factors taken into account) a stock's rising on *moderate* volume can theoretically retain its movement indefinitely, since it may not be "meeting supply." However, if substantially higher volume comes in *after* a rise, we might assume either that the "smart money" or intelligent traders bought low and are taking profits, or that the stock is now meeting supply. If that supply stops the stock, *even though the stock may continue a bit higher,* the rise may be short-lived. If, on the other hand, a stock falls on light volume, it may mean that interest in the stock is dying out. When significantly higher volume comes in *after* a drop, it may indicate that the stock is "finding support" or heavy buyers. And, of course, one should always be on the lookout for a "climax bottom," which we shall now examine.

A Closer Look

Now let us put a microscope upon volume and study another issue—the "high-flyer," Fairchild Camera and Instrument Corporation. Here we are looking for a "climax bottom," or where apparently "smart money" takes a position in a stock, at a *low point*—at "wholesale prices." The stock had fallen from over $200, and as we focus on it, it is selling at $116 on October 17, 1966. The volume on this date was 48,000. This, as a study of the stock's history will show, is "normal" volume. On the next day, Tuesday, the stock traded 57,000 shares, closing at $124; no significance. On Wednesday 56,000 shares changed hands, the stock finishing at 118¼. Now look at Thursday, October 20: *143,000* was the volume, and the price was 116¾. It can be seen that *this* is money—lots of it. But is this the bottom? Alas, no, for the stock drifted lower. What happened? *The money coming in was not yet sufficient to "support" the stock and end its fall.* Or to put it another way, demand was still weaker than supply. And it is supply and demand that set prices on Wall Street, just as it does on Carnaby Street, Fifth Avenue, Fourteenth Street, and Main Street.

When did the bottom actually come? Let's look at Monday, October 31. The volume was 225,000. Was this the bottom? *The way the "real bottom" can be determined* (it appears to this writer after studying thousands of such situations) *is by the subsequent action after the "suspected bottom."* Volume tells you that "big money" is coming in; now we will attempt to determine *at what point* the power of that "big money" (demand) is sufficient to overcome the "supply" of the sellers.

The intraday high of October 31 (100¾) and the intraday low (96⅞). In this method we disregard the closing price. When we look to the following day and note *its* intraday high and low, to see if they are *both exceeded.* The high of Tuesday, November

1 was 102¼, thus beating the 100¾ of Monday. And the low of 97¼ likewise trumps the previous day's low of 96⅞! Since both highs and lows were beaten, we now have three of the four requisites for a "climax bottom." The fourth is that the volume on the day following the "suspected climax" day *must be significantly less than on the "suspected" day.* This is so since we must establish that the battle between the buyers and sellers is truly over, and that the march upward is really under way. To put it another way, the stock was "churning" there Monday—and the "churning" has now ended. The stock rose to as high as 126½ only two weeks later, at which point tremendous volume came in (on the upside) and "blew the stock off." Don't you suppose that the informed minority was selling there? It would seem so. And note too that the stock plummeted to under 100 *the very next day* (Monday, November 21) and another "trade" was afforded the nimble. The stock subsequently rose to a closing high of 172 on February 10, 1967! We know of nobody who caught *all* of the moves (certainly not us), but one could have made a few dollars on the action.

The Rules

First, we are looking for a significant drop from a high price (if we are seeking a bottom) and a significant rise from a low point (if we are looking for the "top").

Then, qualification No. 1: Look for extraordinary volume relative to *that stock's* normal pattern. Thus if the issue trades an average of 2000 shares, 4000 is not enough. However, 20,000 might be. Want a hard-and-fast rule? No got! This is an *art,* not a science.

Qualification No. 2: Look for a significant dropoff in volume the following day. This dropoff might be yet high in total volume for the stock, so long as it is much lower than the "suspected" day.

Qualification No. 3: Note the intraday high on the big-volume, or "suspected" day. This must be exceeded for a true bottom, even if only by an eighth. Why only an eighth? I don't know, but it's so.

Qualification No. 4: Note the intraday low. This must be exceeded for a true bottom, on the day following the "suspected" day.

For a "top," just reverse the procedure of qualifications Nos. 3 and 4.

Qualifications Nos. 1 and 2 must prevail, however. For a "top," qualifications Nos. 3 and 4 must prevail, that is, the day following the "suspected" day, the stock must go lower on an intraday basis in its high point and its low point. A tie is bearish, please note. A tie when looking for a bottom may not be good enough. *And a note of caution:* Stocks do not *HAVE* to give "signals" at the bottom or the top, but when it happens, it makes it easier, *n'est-ce pas?*

Back at the Lab

Here's another little "swinger," perhaps less known, but not less profitable to trade: Dennison Manufacturing, on the New York Stock Exchange. The stock sold for 73⅝ on January 9, 1968. That day it traded 22,800 shares, significantly large *for this issue.* Intraday high was 74; intraday low, 73⅝. Qualification No. 1, big volume, was met. The day following this "suspected climax day," the stock traded only 7400 shares—qualification No. 2, appreciably low volume relative to the "suspected climax day."

Now, the intraday high for the day following the "suspected" day was 74, thus failing qualification No. 3, that it should be bullish and exceed the "suspected" day. One may note (though superfluously) that qualification No. 4, the intraday low, also was not exceeded. The stock should be sold, particularly since this "failure" happened at a high-price area for the stock. Now we have a "climax sell signal." And the stock fell to as low as $46 only eight weeks later. What a short sale!

The stock made no reliable "buy signal" on this method, though heavy volume (on the downside) the days of February 21 (56,000 shares) at 48⅞ and 67,000 on February 28 at 49⅞ indicated the stock was *near* bottom. When a stock has fallen precipitously, heavy volume on the downside, even when not accompanied by a clear signal, shows it is apparently being picked up by "smart money." "Smart money" buys when the public is panicking, and heavy volume indicates the stock is finding "support." Incidentally, the stock rose again soon, to 75 on May 8. And on May 8 the stock traded 22,000 shares, another significant day. Was this a "sell signal"? No, because the stock again traded 20,000 shares the following day, thus not meeting qualification No. 2, low volume on the day following the "suspected" day. Since on May 10 the stock traded only 2800 shares, May 9 becomes the "suspected" day. The rule comes into effect only when the volume drops. Now back to the "suspected" day, May 9. What was the intraday high? 75. *Boom! Sell!* And yet note that the intraday low of 72 on May 9 was exceeded on the tenth by five-eighths. No matter: Qualification No. 3, the high, was not exceeded.

Ultimately the rationale behind all this apparent mumbo-jumbo is: What actually took place in the minds and hearts of those who bought and sold to cause these wild gyrations? What took place then, by the way, has taken place before—and since—and will continue to take place, and to make money for those who care to take the trouble to study it. Realize that this method is not foolproof, nor is any other. We use many tools in trading, and this is but one. But an analysis and consequent understanding of the process will go a long way significantly to improve one's results.

on foot too, tho' since sunk to nothing; such as the *Hudson*'s-Bay Company; the Linnen Manufacture Stock, Paper Stock, Salt-Petre Stock and others, all at this Day worse than nothing, tho' some of them then Jobb'd up to 350 *per Cent.* as the two first in particular.

But the *East-India* Stock was the main Point, every Man's Eye, when he came to Market, was upon the Brokers, who acted for Sir *Josiah*; Does Sir *Josiah* Sell or Buy? If Sir *Josiah* had a Mind to buy, the first thing he did was to Commission his Brokers to look sower, shake their Heads, suggest bad News from *India*; and at the Bottom it follow'd, I have Commission from Sir *Josiah* to sell out whatever I can, and perhaps thy would actually sell Ten, perhaps Twenty Thousand Pound; immediately the *Exchange* (for they were not then come to the *Alley*) was full of Sellers; no Body would buy a Shilling, 'till perhaps the Stock would fall Six, Seven, Eight, Ten *per Cent.* sometimes more; then the Cunning Jobber had another Sett of Men employ'd on purpose to buy, but with Privacy and Caution, all the Stock they could lay their Hands on, 'till by selling Ten Thousand Pound, at Four or Five *per Cent.* lost, he would buy a Hundred Thousand Pound Stock, at Ten or Twelve *per Cent.* under Price; and

Daniel Defoe, *Anatomy of Exchange Alley*, 1719
Rare Book Division, The New York Public Library

and in a few Weeks by just the contrary Method, set them all a buying, and then sell them their own Stock again at ten or twelve *per Cent.* Profit.

These honest Methods laid the Foundation, we will not say of a fine great Stone House, on a certain Forest, but it certainly laid the Foundation of an Opulent Family, and initiated the Croud of Jobbers into that dexterity in tricking and cheating one another, which to this day they are the greatest Proficients in, that this part of the World ever saw.

To come a little nearer home, We had another Gentleman, who, from a small Beginning, came to leave, *as they say who speak of the least*, 250000 *l.* behind him, and yet did not die an old Man neither. This Knight, to avoid as much as possible, Reflections upon the Ashes of the Dead, added to the former Craft, that of bringing sudden News into *Exchange-Alley*, calculated to the Wagers he had to lay, or to any he had to hedge off, and by this gain'd immense Sums of Money, (were he living I should give it an harder Name.) Why should it be thought so strange, that my Lord *Marr* and his Broker should trump up a Story from *Italy*, send a Sett of Post-Chaises with Gentlemen in Disguise,

Epilogue

THE STOCK MARKET is many things to many people. To some it is a means to prove themselves, to some it is a means to good income (as well as a little of the first), to others a way to make it big without too much effort. To the informed minority it represents another way to redistribute wealth from the middle and upper-middle classes and the scions of the rich to themselves. The first three provide easy prey to the informed minority because of their lack of understanding of money and business. Thus it was that a former executive of the DuPont chemical company told me of the standard joke around the place every Monday when, in an allegorical sense, three or four guys used to gather at the front entrance to choose which of the DuPont sons they would "take" that week.

And though the Rockefeller name still carries with it the aura of wealth and perspicacity, perhaps less of the latter should be emphasized. And there is the junior Loeb, who took on the Holly Sugar Company, and the White son, who commanded, coincidentally, Great Western United (formerly Great Western Sugar), neither of which did much subsequently.

The real smart money are better represented by the Tex Thorntons and Roy Ashes of Litton, the Leon Hesses of Amerada Hess, and some lesser-known ones, such as Thomas D. Neelands, Jr.

Neelands had built up and sold, in informed minority fashion, many companies, including Capital Airlines, Consolidated Instrument, and the predecessor to Beech Aircraft, resulting in his becoming a millionaire many times over. I had come in late, when he was still guiding Proctor-Silex, later sold out to SCM. My function had been to find Mr. Neelands another vehicle, and though I did so, at that particular time he was otherwise involved.

One story about him is perhaps indicative of informed minority thinking, though it may perhaps disturb art devotees:

It was early 1969, and Tom Neelands had sold out much of his stock in anticipation of a market collapse (he was right, as usual). Now he wondered what to do with his money. Being somewhat of an art collector, he hit on the idea of going to England and attending art auctions such as Sotheby's and possibly using some paintings for investment.

It did not take him long to wonder at the high prices going on at the time. So he flew back to the States, picked up some of his paintings, and returned to England to sell.

Perhaps this provides a lesson for investors. But I also miss Tom Neelands, the free spirit. In his sixties he zipped around Mexico on a motorcycle or raced his Ferrari around the winter-abandoned roads around Jones Beach, New York. I shall miss him. (Tom Neelands died on January 27, 1972.)

Suggested Reading

I WISH THAT THERE were a vast body of informed writing on what the stock market is really all about, but alas there is not. As suggested in the Epilogue, most of those people who do best in the market (other than the informed minority) seek no publicity, and if they seek it, they do not have the P.R. flair of some of the phonies. I specifically refer to the better ones, such as Tony R., whom I consider to be the world's greatest chartist, and who, when he puts his mind to it, makes around 50 percent a year in the market. But he does not put his mind to it very often—only doing so to indulge his real love, flying.

Then there is Sal A., who labors away at a lesser-known brokerage house and who has evolved a timing method somewhat better than that employed by the mutual funds—who, as a group, find themselves fully invested at the tops of markets and sold out at the bottom, when they are most bearish (see Chapter Three).

There are others, of course, some of whom are brokers. But these are in the tiny minority of people who for the most part enter the business as a way of avoiding work. If you doubt me, take a look at ten brokerage offices at five o'clock any weekday. If two have half their desks occupied, I'll refund the price of this book. And I have never known any of the informed minority who did not put in seventy or eighty hours a week.

Nevertheless, it is customary to suggest sources of edification, so try these: *The Battle for Investment Survival*, by Gerald L. Loeb. Not bad. Stands out in a weak field. *A Strategy of Day to Day Stock*

Market Timing, by Joseph Granville. Ignore the title and read the book.

That's all? I would consign the rest of the market literature to the same scrap garbage heap as the *Protocoles of the Elders of Zion.* Of course, there may be some I haven't read. But the reader will get a better understanding of the market by steeping himself in the study of our culture. Any text in sociology will do for a start.

There Is Another

Oh, yes. There is another book you may wish to read giving the background of the New York Central Railroad and its colorful Robert R. Young era: *Robert R. Young: The Populist of Wall Street* by Joseph Borkin. It describes the abilities of Alfred Perlman, who really was a top-flight executive. The following is taken from the book for its relevance to our thesis. It was part of the testimony on May 25, 1933, of George Whitney, a partner in J. P. Morgan & Company, before the U. S. Senate Banking and Currency Committee:

"We [J. P. Morgan] have never [sold common stock] for very many reasons. The chief, perhaps, is that our reputation in connection with the security business has been on sound investments. We do not think common stock ought to be sold publicly, or by us, at least, for the reason that we think they get into the hands of people who do not know what they are buying. We think, secondly, that if you have an offering of common stock, or perhaps if we did, that that might carry with it some implication of speculations which we would not want to be a party to. Now, I am afraid I have talked a little more than I meant to."

Times do change—and so do the money-making efforts of the informed minority.